TEACHER'S MANUAL
AND ACHIEVEMENT TESTS

NORTHSTAR 5
LISTENING AND SPEAKING
THIRD EDITION

AUTHOR
Sherry Preiss

SERIES EDITORS
Frances Boyd
Carol Numrich

PEARSON
Longman

NorthStar: Listening and Speaking Level 5, Third Edition
Teacher's Manual and Achievement Tests

Pearson Education, 10 Bank Street, White Plains, NY 10606

Teacher's Manual by Dorothy Zemach. Activities for secondary schools by Ann Hilborn.

Achievement Tests developed by: Dr. Joan Jamieson and Dr. Carol Chapelle.

Achievement Tests by Elizabeth Henly.

Staff credits: The people who made up the *NorthStar: Listening and Speaking Level 5, Third Edition Teacher's Manual* team, representing editorial, production, design, and manufacturing, are Nan Clarke, Dave Dickey, Christine Edmonds, Ann France, Gosia Jaros-White, Dana Klinek, Melissa Leyva, Sherry Preiss, Robert Ruvo, Debbie Sistino, Kathleen Smith, Jennifer Stem, and Paula Van Ells.

Listening selections and text credits: **T-2** "Time to Do Everything Except Think" from *Newsweek on Air,* April 30, 2001 © Newsweek Inc. and the Associated Press. All rights reserved. Used with permission; **T-8** excerpts from *The Infinite Mind,* "Lies, Lies, Lies" broadcast on May 1, 2007, copyright © 2007 Lichtenstein Creative Media, Inc. Used with permission; **T-15** © NPR. The text and audio of the news report by NPR's Alex Chadwick was originally broadcast in 1995 and are used with permission of NPR. Any unauthorized duplication is strictly prohibited; **T-21** "Tipping Points in Fighting Crime" interview with Malcolm Gladwell by Todd Mundt. © 2001. Reprinted by permission by Michigan Radio; **T-27** "Feng Shui in the Newsroom" interview with Kirsten Lagatree and Steve Scher on KUOW Public Radio on February 6, 1996. Reprinted by permission of KUOW Public Radio; **T-33** The text and audio of the news report by NPR's Duncan Moon was originally broadcast on NPR's All Things Considered® on December 14, 2001 and are used with permission of NPR. Any unauthorized duplication is strictly prohibited; **T-45** "Michael Ignatieff's Views on War" on *Fresh Air* with Terry Gross on March 31, 1997. Reprinted by permission of WHYY in Philadelphia, PA, USA; **T-52** The text and audio of the news report by NPR's Michelle Trudeau was originally broadcast on NPR's All Things Considered® on May 22, 1996 and are used with permission of NPR. Any unauthorized duplication is strictly prohibited; **T-58** "Microfinance" interview with Alex Counts, Raj Shah, and Matt Flannery by Ross Reynolds on KUOW Public Radio on July 17, 2006 on *Weekday.* Reprinted by permission of KUOW Public Radio.

Cover Art: Silvia Rojas/Getty Images
Text composition: ElectraGraphics, Inc.
Text font: 11.5/13 Minion

ISBN-10: 0-13-233642-1
ISBN-13: 978-0-13-233642-0

PEARSON LONGMAN ON THE WEB

Pearsonlongman.com offers online resources for teachers and students. Access our Companion Websites, our online catalog, and our local offices around the world.

Visit us at **www.pearsonlongman.com**.

Printed in the United States of America
1 2 3 4 5 6 7 8 9 10—HAM—13 12 11 10 09 08

CONTENTS

WELCOME TO NORTHSTAR

THIRD EDITION

NorthStar, now in its third edition, motivates students to succeed in their **academic** as well as **personal** language goals.

For each of the five levels, the two strands—*Reading and Writing* and *Listening and Speaking*—provide a fully integrated approach for students and teachers.

WHAT IS SPECIAL ABOUT THE THIRD EDITION?

NEW THEMES

New themes and **updated content**—presented in a **variety of genres**, including literature and lectures, and in **authentic reading and listening selections**—challenge students intellectually.

ACADEMIC SKILLS

More purposeful **integration of critical thinking** and an enhanced focus on **academic skills** such as inferencing, synthesizing, note taking, and test taking help students develop strategies for **success** in the **classroom** and on **standardized tests**. A **culminating productive task** galvanizes content, language, and **critical thinking skills**.

➤ In the *Listening and Speaking* strand, a **structured approach** gives students opportunities for **more extended and creative oral practice**, for example, presentations, simulations, debates, case studies, and public service announcements.

➤ In the *Reading and Writing* strand, a new, **fully integrated writing section** leads students through the **writing process** with engaging writing assignments focusing on various rhetorical modes.

NEW DESIGN

Full **color pages** with more **photos, illustrations, and graphic organizers** foster student engagement and make the content and activities come alive.

MyNorthStarLab

MyNorthStarLab, an easy-to-use **online learning and assessment program**, offers:

➤ Unlimited access to reading and listening selections and DVD segments.

➤ Focused test preparation to help students succeed on international exams such as TOEFL® and IELTS®. Pre- and post-unit assessments improve results by providing individualized instruction, instant feedback, and personalized study plans.

➤ Original activities that support and extend the *NorthStar* program. These include pronunciation practice using voice recording tools, and activities to build note taking skills and academic vocabulary.

➤ Tools that save time. These include a flexible gradebook and authoring features that give teachers control of content and help them track student progress.

THE NORTHSTAR APPROACH

The *NorthStar* series is based on **current research in language acquisition** and on the **experiences of teachers and curriculum designers**. Five principles guide the *NorthStar* approach.

PRINCIPLES

1 The more profoundly students are stimulated intellectually and emotionally, the more language they will use and retain.

The thematic organization of *NorthStar* promotes intellectual and emotional stimulation. The 50 sophisticated themes in *NorthStar* present intriguing topics such as recycled fashion, restorative justice, personal carbon footprints, and microfinance. The authentic content engages students, links them to language use outside of the classroom, and encourages personal expression and critical thinking.

2 Students can learn both the form and content of the language.

Grammar, vocabulary, and culture are inextricably woven into the units, providing students with systematic and multiple exposures to language forms in a variety of contexts. As the theme is developed, students can express complex thoughts using a higher level of language.

3 Successful students are active learners.

Tasks are designed to be creative, active, and varied. Topics are interesting and up-to-date. Together these tasks and topics (1) allow teachers to bring the outside world into the classroom and (2) motivate students to apply their classroom learning in the outside world.

4 Students need feedback.

This feedback comes naturally when students work together practicing language and participating in open-ended opinion and inference tasks. Whole class activities invite teachers' feedback on the spot or via audio/video recordings or notes. The innovative new MyNorthStarLab gives students immediate feedback as they complete computer-graded language activities online; it also gives students the opportunity to submit writing or speaking assignments electronically to their instructor for feedback later.

5 The quality of relationships in the language classroom is important because students are asked to express themselves on issues and ideas.

The information and activities in *NorthStar* promote genuine interaction, acceptance of differences, and authentic communication. By building skills and exploring ideas, the exercises help students participate in discussions and write essays of an increasingly complex and sophisticated nature.

THE NORTHSTAR UNIT

① FOCUS ON THE TOPIC

This section introduces students to the unifying theme
of the listening selections.

> **PREDICT** and **SHARE INFORMATION** foster interest in the unit topic and help
> students develop a personal connection to it.
>
> **BACKGROUND** AND **VOCABULARY** activities provide students with tools for
> understanding the first listening selection. Later in the unit, students review
> this vocabulary and learn related idioms, collocations, and word forms. This
> helps them explore content and expand their written and spoken language.

UNIT 7

Workplace Privacy

① FOCUS ON THE TOPIC

Ⓐ PREDICT

1. Look at the cartoon. It shows employees arriving at their offices. The man says he is willing to give up civil liberties in order to gain security. However, he is worried that doing so might mean there will be few civil liberties left. Can you guess what he means by "civil liberties" and "security"?

2. What do you think of when you hear the word *privacy*? What does it mean to you? Brainstorm topics or words that may come up when discussing this issue, such as *snooping*, *confidential*, and *wiretapping*.

147

Ⓑ SHARE INFORMATION

In a small group, discuss your answers to the questions.

1. Our ability to enjoy privacy often depends on the physical nature of the space we inhabit. Think about the home you grew up in and the home you are living in now. How does your sense of privacy compare in the two places? What factors make it easy or difficult to find privacy?

2. Think of different cultures you are familiar with. Comment on how the sense of privacy may differ. Think of home, school, and workplace. How much privacy do people expect? How is privacy protected?

3. When do you feel your privacy is being invaded? For example, would you feel your privacy was being invaded if _____?
   a. an employer opened and read your office mail or e-mail
   b. a colleague looked through your files, either on paper or on a computer
   c. someone you just met asked your age, marital status, or salary

Ⓒ BACKGROUND AND VOCABULARY

To keep up-to-date on workplace privacy and other important issues, many professionals write and read blogs (web logs) on the Internet. The following blog is a composite of information and opinion based on real blogs. On the blog, interested people bring up various aspects of workplace privacy, answering and raising questions. Readers then add their responses in order to conduct a public discussion.

🎧 *Read and listen to the blog and then match the boldfaced vocabulary with the definitions and synonyms that follow.*

148   UNIT 7

② FOCUS ON LISTENING

This section focuses on understanding two contrasting listening selections.

LISTENING ONE is a radio report, interview, lecture, or other genre that addresses the unit topic. In levels 1 to 3, listenings are based on authentic materials. In levels 4 and 5, all the listenings are authentic.

LISTEN FOR MAIN IDEAS and **LISTEN FOR DETAILS** are comprehension activities that lead students to an understanding and appreciation of the first selection.

The **MAKE INFERENCES** activity prompts students to "listen between the lines," move beyond the literal meaning, exercise critical thinking skills, and understand the listening on a more academic level. Students follow up with pair or group work to discuss topics in the **EXPRESS OPINIONS** section.

---

② FOCUS ON LISTENING

Ⓐ LISTENING ONE: Interview with an Internet Addiction Counselor

Because so many students overuse the Internet, some university health services offer help with the problem. Dr. Jonathan Kandell, a psychologist from the University of Maryland in the United States, was interviewed by Ira Flatow, host of *Science Friday* from NPR® (National Public Radio). Dr. Kandell discusses his approach to students with symptoms of Internet addiction.

🎧 *Work with a partner. Listen to the first 35 seconds of the interview. Write down three questions that you think Ira Flatow might ask Dr. Kandell, the counselor.*

1. _____
2. _____
3. _____

◖ LISTEN FOR MAIN IDEAS

🎧 *Look at the chart. Listen to the interview and take notes on the main ideas. Use a separate piece of paper if necessary. (You will note details later.) Work with a partner to compare and revise your notes.*

MAIN IDEAS	DETAILS
Focus of interview *unusual or "other" addictions*	Examples of addictions *gambling, . . .*
Kandell's view of Internet addiction	Evidence for this view
Chief symptoms/warning signs of Internet addiction	Other symptoms/warning signs
Possible treatment	Reasons this treatment is helpful

◖ LISTEN FOR DETAILS

🎧 *Read the chart again. Fill in as many details as possible to support the main ideas. Then listen to the interview again to check your work. Work with a partner to compare and revise your notes.*

◖ MAKE INFERENCES

When you are listening, making inferences means understanding something that is not literally stated, but which you believe is true based on the intention, attitude, voice, pausing, and choice of words of the speakers.

Read the questions. Then listen to each excerpt from the interview. Write your answers and then discuss them with a partner. Give reasons for your choices. Each question has more than one possible answer.

🎧 **Excerpt One**

A *groupie* usually refers to someone, especially a young woman, who likes a musician, movie star, or sports star and follows this person around hoping to meet the star. Why does Ira Flatow, the host, use the word *groupie* when he advises the radio audience to listen carefully? What does the word *groupie* imply in this context?

_____
_____

🎧 **Excerpt Two**

Dr. Kandell doesn't answer Flatow's question directly. What expressions show his hesitation? Why doesn't he answer Flatow directly?

_____
_____

🎧 **Excerpt Three**

How does Flatow feel about this topic at this point in the interview? How do you know? What words and tone of voice does he use to indicate his attitude?

_____
_____

◖ EXPRESS OPINIONS

Discuss the questions with the class. Give your opinions and give reasons for them.

1. Do you know people who overuse the Internet? Do you overuse it? What are the warning signs? What treatment would you recommend for Internet addicts?

2. Dr. Kandell runs a support group for Internet addicts at his university. Do you think that universities should have this service? How helpful can such a support group be? Explain. What other support groups do you know of? Would you ever join one? Why or why not?

3. Anne Lamott, author of a book of essays called *Bird by Bird*, writes, "Getting all of one's addictions under control is a little like putting an octopus to bed." What does she mean? How do you feel about her analogy? Explain.

LISTENING TWO offers another perspective on the topic and is usually another genre. Again, in levels 1 to 3, the listenings are based on authentic materials and in levels 4 and 5, they are authentic. This second listening is followed by an activity that challenges students to question ideas they formed about the first listening, and to use appropriate language skills to analyze and explain their ideas.

INTEGRATE LISTENINGS ONE AND TWO presents culminating activities. Students are challenged to take what they have learned, organize the information, and synthesize it in a meaningful way. Students practice skills that are essential for success in authentic academic settings and on standardized tests.

B **LISTENING TWO: Interview with a Microfinance Director**

Listen to a microfinance expert, Will Bullard, tell the story of a woman in a village in Honduras, Central America. This real story illustrates how a local lending organization, or "assembly," works—the benefits and pitfalls.

Part One: Maria Jose's Story

Check (✓) the true statements. Correct the false statements.

_____ 1. Maria Jose Perona had nine children, all of whom were malnourished.

_____ 2. The women in the assembly decide who gets the loan.

_____ 3. The women did not vote to grant Maria Jose Perona the loan because they thought she would spend the loan on food, not on the business.

_____ 4. The women finally agreed and gave her a loan of 25 dollars.

_____ 5. Maria Jose Perona had to take a test to get the 25 dollars.

_____ 6. Maria Jose Perona bought flour and cooking supplies with her loan.

_____ 7. She created a small meat pie business in front of the school.

_____ 8. Although she paid her friend back, she was not allowed into the assembly.

_____ 9. She finally became successful and was then allowed into the assembly.

_____ 10. She built a concrete house and became president of the assembly.

Part Two: Non-Monetary Benefits of Microfinance

Check (✓) the non-monetary benefits (other benefits not related to money) that the speaker mentions or implies.

_____ 11. sales and marketing skills

_____ 12. education

_____ 13. confidence

_____ 14. risk-taking ability

Part Three: Business Training

Check (✓) the phrases that complete the statement accurately.

The speaker believes that business training is important because the women _____.

_____ 15. find the loans too small

_____ 16. don't know how to manage their money carefully

_____ 17. sell very similar things

_____ 18. should sell things that bring them more money

Microfinance: Changing Lives $50 at a Time **235**

C **INTEGRATE LISTENINGS ONE AND TWO**

STEP 1: Organize

Review Listenings One and Two. In each listening, speakers refer to three major benefits of microfinance. Work with a partner. Complete the chart by identifying specific examples of these benefits from each listening.

BENEFITS OF MICROFINANCE	EXAMPLES: LISTENING ONE	EXAMPLES: LISTENING TWO
Financial changes		
Non-monetary changes		
Sustainability		

STEP 2: Synthesize

Work in groups of three. Each person will choose one of the benefits listed in the chart above. Review the related examples from Listening One and Listening Two. After two minutes, close your book and present a one-minute summary to the group. Use examples.

3 **FOCUS ON SPEAKING**

A **VOCABULARY**

REVIEW

A journalist for *Economic Daily*, Pedro Martinez, broadcast an "audio postcard" about his recent trip to La Ceiba, Honduras.

236 UNIT 10

---

③ FOCUS ON SPEAKING

This section emphasizes development of productive skills for speaking. It includes sections on vocabulary, grammar, pronunciation, functional language, and an extended speaking task.

The **VOCABULARY** section leads students from reviewing the unit vocabulary, to practicing and expanding their use of it, and then working with it—using it creatively in both this section and in the final speaking task.

Students learn useful structures for speaking in the **GRAMMAR** section, which offers a concise presentation and targeted practice. Vocabulary items are recycled here, providing multiple exposures leading to mastery. For additional practice with the grammar presented, students and teachers can consult the GRAMMAR BOOK REFERENCES at the end of the book for corresponding material in the *Focus on Grammar* and Azar series.

---

1 Read the transcript of Martinez's report. Fill in the blanks with the appropriate word or expression from the list. Use the phrases under the blanks to help you.

anecdote	had faith in	panacea	took a hit
compelling	hit a ceiling	pitfalls	wiped out
diminish	kicker	sustainable	the world over
elaborate	malnourished		

Greetings from La Ceiba, Honduras. First, I must tell you that this little speck on Earth is just unbelievably gorgeous—beautiful, lush, with breathtaking cloud formations hugging spectacular green mountains.

Still, on the drive from the airport to my lodge I witnessed the pervasive poverty we see _____:
1. (in every area of the world)
skinny, _____ children standing next
2. (sick or weak due to lack of food)
to houses and shops still not rebuilt since Hurricane Mitch _____ much of the country in 1988. Already the
3. (destroyed)
second poorest country in Latin America, Honduras _____ and never recovered. To research
4. (was negatively affected)
my article, I set out to visit microfinance institutions as well as meet the microcredit client to whom I had lent money from my laptop in Mexico City, where I live.

Kiva.org is a nonprofit microcredit organization that allows individuals with access to the Internet to fight global poverty in a _____ way by making a
5. (able to continue long-term)
direct personal loan to poor entrepreneurs anywhere in the world. On the Kiva website I came across the _____ photo and story of Julia
6. (so interesting or exciting that you have to pay attention)
Marta Mendez, a fascinating Honduran widow in her late thirties with six children, to whom I

Microfinance: Changing Lives $50 at a Time **237**

B **GRAMMAR: Count and Non-Count Nouns and Their Quantifiers**

1 Work with a partner. Examine the statements, and discuss the questions that follow.

- <u>Very few</u> spiritual **journeys** can compare to visiting the monasteries on Mt. Athos.
- With 20 monasteries and a limit of four days, it took Claassen <u>quite a bit</u> of **effort** to see more than six monasteries on one trip.
- Some monks are concerned about <u>the growing number of</u> **pilgrimages** to Mt. Athos these days.
- It takes <u>a great deal of</u> **discipline** to fast for a month.

1. Categorize the boldfaced nouns into count and non-count nouns.
2. What do the underlined expressions of quantity tell us?

COUNT AND NON-COUNT NOUNS

All nouns in English can be divided into two groups: count nouns and non-count nouns. **Count nouns** are those that can be counted and made plural (*monasteries, monks*). In contrast, **non-count nouns** can be considered as a mass and cannot be made plural (*spirituality, air*). Non-count nouns may refer to categories made up of different things (*money, furniture*), phenomena that occur in nature (*darkness, weather*), or abstractions (*violence, greed, honesty*).

Certain expressions of quantity, called **quantifiers**, state the amount of the noun. Some quantifiers are used with count nouns, and others are used with non-count nouns.

Quantifiers before Count Nouns	Quantifiers before Non-Count Nouns
a lot of	a lot of
many / a great many	a great deal of
quite a few	quite a bit of
a bunch of	a large amount of
a (large) number of	
certain	
not many	not much
very few (just a few / only a few)	very little (just a little / only a little)
a few / few	a little / little
fewer	less

GRAMMAR TIP: Notice the change in meaning when the indefinite article *a* is placed before *few* and *little*.

Few / Little	A few / A little
• negative meaning	• positive meaning
• similar to *not much* and *not many*	• similar to *some* (when talking about a small quantity)

Compare:
- *Few people can fast more than three days in a row.*
- *A few people from our group decided to return to the monastery for another visit.*

136 UNIT 6

Welcome to **NorthStar** ix

The **PRONUNCIATION** section presents both controlled and freer, communicative practice of the sounds and patterns of English. Models from the listening selections reinforce content and vocabulary. This is followed by the **FUNCTION** section where students are exposed to functional language that prepares them to express ideas on a higher level. Examples have been chosen based on frequency, variety, and usefulness for the final speaking task.

The **PRODUCTION** section gives students an opportunity to integrate the ideas, vocabulary, grammar, pronunciation, and function presented in the unit. This final speaking task is the culminating activity of the unit and gets students to exchange ideas and express opinions in sustained speaking contexts. Activities are presented in a sequence that builds confidence and fluency, and allows for more than one "try" at expression. When appropriate, students practice some presentation skills: audience analysis, organization, eye contact, or use of visuals.

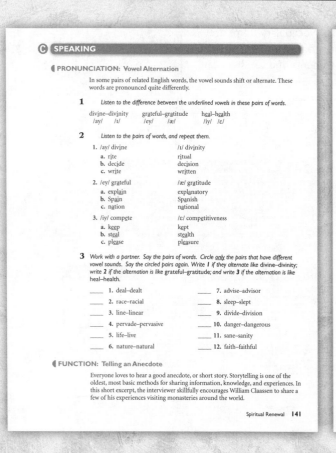

C SPEAKING

PRONUNCIATION: Vowel Alternation

In some pairs of related English words, the vowel sounds shift or alternate. These words are pronounced quite differently.

1 Listen to the difference between the underlined vowels in these pairs of words.

divine–divinity   grateful–gratitude   heal–health
/ay/   /ɪ/   /ey/   /æ/   /iy/   /ɛ/

2 Listen to the pairs of words, and repeat them.

1. /ay/ divine   /ɪ/ divinity
   a. rite   ritual
   b. decide   decision
   c. write   written

2. /ey/ grateful   /æ/ gratitude
   a. explain   explanatory
   b. Spain   Spanish
   c. nation   national

3. /iy/ compete   /ɛ/ competitiveness
   a. keep   kept
   b. steal   stealth
   c. please   pleasure

3 Work with a partner. Say the pairs of words. Circle only the pairs that have different vowel sounds. Say the circled pairs again. Write **1** if they alternate like divine–divinity; write **2** if the alternation is like grateful–gratitude; and write **3** if the alternation is like heal–health.

_____ 1. deal–dealt   _____ 7. advise–advisor

_____ 2. race–racial   _____ 8. sleep–slept

_____ 3. line–linear   _____ 9. divide–division

_____ 4. pervade–pervasive   _____ 10. danger–dangerous

_____ 5. life–live   _____ 11. sane–sanity

_____ 6. nature–natural   _____ 12. faith–faithful

FUNCTION: Telling an Anecdote

Everyone loves to hear a good anecdote, or short story. Storytelling is one of the oldest, most basic methods for sharing information, knowledge, and experiences. In this short excerpt, the interviewer skillfully encourages William Claassen to share a few of his experiences visiting monasteries around the world.

Spiritual Renewal **141**

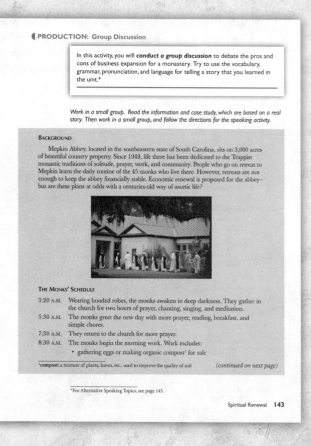

PRODUCTION: Group Discussion

In this activity, you will **conduct a group discussion** to debate the pros and cons of business expansion for a monastery. Try to use the vocabulary, grammar, pronunciation, and language for telling a story that you learned in the unit.*

Work in a small group. Read the information and case study, which are based on a real story. Then work in a small group, and follow the directions for the speaking activity.

BACKGROUND

Mepkin Abbey, located in the southeastern state of South Carolina, sits on 3,000 acres of beautiful country property. Since 1949, life there has been dedicated to the Trappist monastic traditions of solitude, prayer, work, and community. People who go on retreat to Mepkin learn the daily routine of the 45 monks who live there. However, retreats are not enough to keep the abbey financially stable. Economic renewal is proposed for the abbey—but are these plans at odds with a centuries-old way of ascetic life?

THE MONKS' SCHEDULE

3:20 A.M.   Wearing hooded robes, the monks awaken in deep darkness. They gather in the church for two hours of prayer, chanting, singing, and meditation.

5:30 A.M.   The monks greet the new day with more prayer, reading, breakfast, and simple chores.

7:30 A.M.   They return to the church for more prayer.

8:30 A.M.   The monks begin the morning work. Work includes:
   • gathering eggs or making organic compost[1] for sale

[1]**compost:** a mixture of plants, leaves, etc., used to improve the quality of soil   *(continued on next page)*

*For Alternative Speaking Topics, see page 145.

Spiritual Renewal **143**

ALTERNATIVE SPEAKING TOPICS are provided at the end of the unit. They can be used as *alternatives* to the final speaking task, or as *additional* assignments. RESEARCH TOPICS tied to the theme of the unit are organized in a special section at the back of the book.

MyNorthStarLab

MyNorthStarLab supports students with **individualized instruction**, **feedback**, and **extra help**. A wide array of resources, including a flexible **gradebook**, helps teachers manage student progress.

The MyNorthStarLab **WELCOME** page **organizes assignments and grades**, and **facilitates communication** between students and teachers.

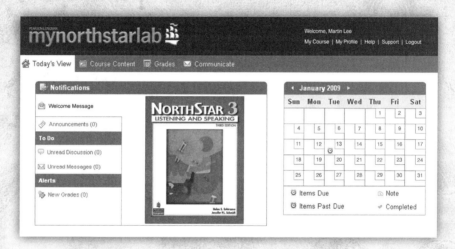

For each unit, MyNorthStarLab provides a **READINESS CHECK**.

➤ Activities **assess** student knowledge **before** beginning the unit and **follow up** with individualized instruction.

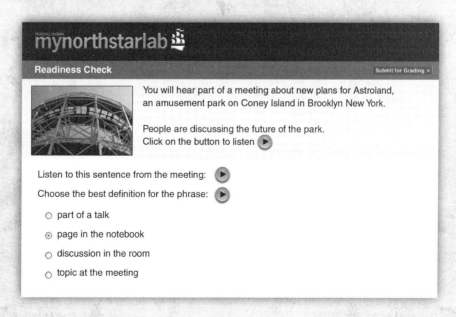

Student book material and **new** practice activities are available to students online.

➤ Students benefit from virtually unlimited **practice anywhere, anytime**.

Interaction with **Internet** and **video** materials will:

➤ Expand students' knowledge of the topic.

➤ Help students practice new vocabulary and grammar.

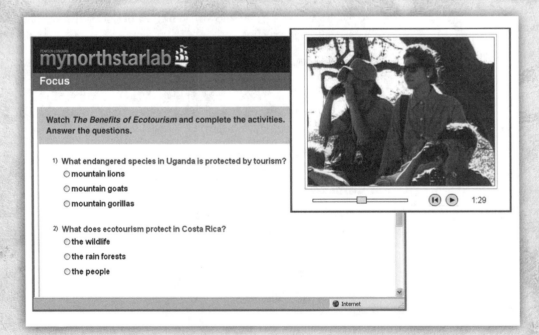

INTEGRATED SKILL ACTIVITIES in MyNorthStarLab challenge students to bring together the **language skills** and **critical thinking skills** that they have practiced throughout the unit.

The MyNorthStarLab **ASSESSMENT** tools allow instructors to customize and deliver achievement tests online.

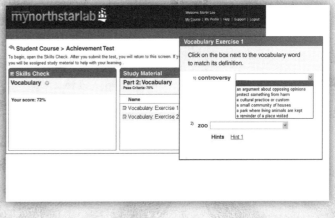

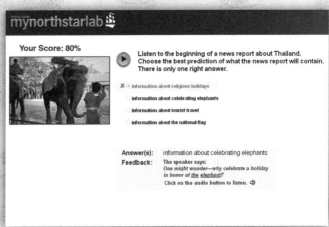

OVERVIEW OF THE TEACHER'S MANUAL AND ACHIEVEMENT TESTS

The *NorthStar Teacher's Manual* includes:

➤ Specific suggestions for teaching each unit

➤ Student Book Answer Key

➤ An alphabetized-by-unit word list of the key vocabulary items practiced in each unit

➤ Reproducible Achievement Tests with Answer Keys—including the test audioscript and test audio CD

UNIT-BY-UNIT TEACHING SUGGESTIONS

Unit-by-unit overview (scope and sequence), list of skills practiced in each section of the student book, suggested teaching times, teaching suggestions, suggestions on how to use *NorthStar* in secondary classes, Expansion/Homework activities, cross-references to the companion strand, techniques and instructions for using MyNorthStarLab

---

UNIT 2 Honesty Is the Best Policy

OVERVIEW

Theme: Lying
This unit deals with the concepts of truth, honesty, and deception, and whether there are ever justifications for lying. Students consider why people keep secrets and if secrets are a type of lie. The unit also addresses academic plagiarism and modern methods for detecting it.

Listening One: *Interview with a Psychiatrist* is a radio interview with a psychiatrist about what lies are, the many reasons that people lie, and some consequences of lying.

Listening Two: *Family Secrets* is an interview with a filmmaker who uncovered a secret from her father's past.

Critical Thinking

Clarify values relating to truth and lying
Infer word meaning from context
Consider the effects of mistrust

Investigate motivations for keeping secrets and exposing the lies of others
Investigate multiple sides to an ethical issue

Listening

Make predictions
Listen for main ideas
Listen for details
Make inferences based on tone, pace, and vocabulary

Relate listenings to personal experiences and values
Organize ands synthesize information from the listenings

Speaking

Express and solicit opinions and values
Relate personal experiences
Express agreement and disagreement

Role-play a scripted conversation
Introduce, defend, and express the different sides of an issue

Vocabulary

Use context clues to determine sequence
Identify and use word forms

Grammar

Modals—degrees of certainty

Pronunciation

Reduction of the auxiliary *have*

📁 **MyNorthStarLab**
Readiness Check, Background and Vocabulary, Listenings One and Two, Notetaking and Academic Skills Practice, Vocabulary and Grammar, Achievement Test

NorthStar: Reading and Writing 5
Unit 2 deals with liars and the lies they tell and the nature of truth.

14

ᵒᵒᵒ Ⓐ **LISTENING ONE: Interview with a Psychiatrist**

📁 Go to www.mynorthstarlab.com to listen to *Interview with a Psychiatrist*.

Suggested Time: 5 minutes

Listening One is a radio interview with a psychiatrist who gives a profile of someone who lies. He talks about the reasons people lie, the definition of a lie, and some consequences of lying.

1. Read the introductory paragraph aloud or have students read it silently. Give students time to write down their predictions.

2. Have students share their predictions with a partner or with the whole class. Write each prediction on the board. After students have finished listening for main ideas and details, check to see which ideas the class was able to predict and what they predicted that was not mentioned.

LISTENING STRATEGY: Anticipation/Reaction Guide

Provide five statements about lying that are discussed in the interview and have students mark the statements *Agree/Disagree*. Then ask them to explain their answers. After listening to the interview, students should revisit the statements and respond a second time, again explaining their answers. The second explanation will be specific to what they learned from the report.

ᵒᵒᵒ **LISTEN FOR MAIN IDEAS**　　　　**Suggested Time: 10 minutes**

1. Give students time to read the topics.

2. Play the interview and have students write down the main ideas. They can write notes instead of complete sentences. Let students discuss their responses and then go over answers with the whole class.

REACHING ALL STUDENTS: Listen for Main Ideas

• **Less Proficient:** Tell students in advance that they are going to hear nine reasons people lie. Have them listen specifically for those reasons. Then have them work in small groups to complete any they missed.

• **More Proficient:** Tell students to write specific examples from their own experience for each reason to lie. Then have them compare their responses in small groups.

Honesty Is the Best Policy　**17**

USING *NORTHSTAR* IN SECONDARY CLASSES

Each unit of the *Teacher's Manual* offers a set of strategies that provide opportunities for greater differentiation in a typical mixed classroom to meet the needs of multi-level secondary students. These strategies are equally beneficial in academic and adult classes. The scaffolded instruction enables teachers to facilitate student mastery of complex skills and ideas. Repeated exposure to concepts helps accelerate English language learning.

Reading/Listening Strategies give teachers additional support to guide students who have limited experience with basic reading/listening skills as they learn to explore and understand academic content. Suggestions are given to help students understand how to predict, determine main idea and supporting details, navigate and comprehend a text, monitor their understanding, and organize information.

Reaching All Students are activity suggestions for two levels of language proficiency, intended to assist less proficient students and challenge students with higher proficiencies. These are generally included in the Reading/Listening section to help teachers to modify reading/listening activities.

Critical Thinking suggestions focus on a hierarchy of questions using Bloom's taxonomy. These are designed specifically to scaffold questions to move students from knowledge-based questions to higher order thinking.

Vocabulary Expansion builds upon vocabulary introduced in each unit to help students further integrate vocabulary. The expansion activities are offered as word analyses or as vocabulary strategies to reinforce vocabulary skills and provide opportunities for review.

COURSE PLANNERS

Each unit contains approximately eight hours of classroom material, plus expansion, homework, and support material, including MyNorthStarLab. Teachers can customize the units by assigning some exercises for homework and/or eliminating others. To help teachers customize the units for their specific teaching situation, the unit-by-unit teaching suggestions in the *Teacher's Manual* include 1, 2, or 3 stars to indicate the relative importance of each section or exercise as follows:

✪✪✪ **Essential:** Predict, Background and Vocabulary, Listening One, Listen for Main Ideas, Listen for Details, Make Inferences, Express Opinions, Listening Two, Integrate Listenings One and Two, Production

✪✪ **Recommended:** Share Information, Expand, Grammar, Pronunciation, Function

✪ **Optional:** Review, Create, Speaking Topics, Research Topics

Class time available per unit	Sections to complete
8 hours or more	Essential (✪✪✪), Recommended (✪✪), Optional (✪)
6 hours	Essential (✪✪✪), Recommended (✪✪)
4 hours	Essential (✪✪✪) only

For more detailed, downloadable unit-by-unit course planners, visit www.mynorthstarlab.com or www.longman.com/northstar.

ACHIEVEMENT TESTS

The reproducible Achievement Tests allow teachers to evaluate students' progress and to identify areas where the students might have problems developing their listening and speaking skills. The Achievement Tests should be given upon completion of the corresponding unit.

Description

There are four parts for every test:

Parts 1 and **2** test students' receptive skills. Part 1 assesses students' mastery of listening comprehension. Part 2 assesses the knowledge of the vocabulary introduced in the unit. **Parts 3** and **4** test students' productive skills. Part 3 assesses students' knowledge of the grammar, pronunciation, and functions introduced in the unit. Part 4 is a speaking test related to the content of the unit.

Administration

All parts of each test should be taken in class and students should not be allowed access to any *NorthStar* materials or to their dictionaries. Students should be able to complete Parts 1–3 within 40 minutes and Part 4 within 10 minutes.

Teachers can decide how to incorporate Part 4 (the speaking task) into their testing situations. Some teachers will assign each speaking task immediately after students complete Parts 1–3; others may decide to set aside another time to complete it.

Scoring the Parts

Parts 1–3: Individual test items are worth one point, for a maximum total of 30 points per test. A student's raw score can be obtained by adding together the number of correct items, or by subtracting the total number of incorrect items from 30. To convert the raw score to a percentage score, multiply it by 3.33.

Part 4: The speaking tasks are evaluated based on speaking skills and function. There are two shorter test items in this part, each worth one point. These should be scored according to the suggestions provided in the answer key for each test. The extended speaking tasks are evaluated holistically using scoring rubrics. The scale ranges from 0–4 and includes information from the listening and fluency/pronunciation, connectedness, structures and vocabulary from the unit, and errors.

Combining scores from Parts 1–3 and Part 4: To get a total Achievement Test score, multiply the extended speaking task score by 2. Add the score for the shorter speaking items to this score for the extended speaking task. Then, add the score in Parts 1–3. Multiply this new score by 2.5 to get a percentage score.

Example 1	**Example 2**
Score on Test Parts 1–3 = 30	Score on Parts 1–3 = 25
Score on Part 4 (extended task) = 4	Score on Part 4 (extended task) = 2
Multiply 4 x 2	Multiply 2 x 2
Score on Part 4 (shorter items) = 2	Score on Part 4 (shorter items) = 1
Add 10 to 30	Add 5 to 25
Multiply 40 x 2.5	Multiply 30 by 2.5
Total score = 100%	Total score = 72.5%

Using the Scoring Rubrics

The *NorthStar Listening and Speaking* rubrics are adapted from the integrated speaking rubric of TOEFL iBT. Whereas the TOEFL iBT scoring rubric is intended to distinguish levels of English proficiency among candidates to colleges and universities, the *NorthStar* scoring rubrics are intended to show progress in students' speaking at each of the five *NorthStar* levels. Therefore, *NorthStar* scoring bands make finer distinctions than TOEFL iBT's scoring band. In this way, students at each level will be able to both see improvement in their scores and receive high marks. The detailed scoring rubric is included in the Achievement Tests Answer Key.

Relationship between TOEFL iBT Rubric and *NorthStar 5* Integrated Speaking Rubric		
TOEFL iBT	⟷	*NorthStar 5*
4	⟷	4
4	⟷	3
3	⟷	2
2–3	⟷	1
1–2	⟷	0
0	⟷	

OTHER NorthStar COMPONENTS

EXAMVIEW

NorthStar ExamView is a stand-alone CD-ROM that allows teachers to **create and customize** their own *NorthStar* tests.

DVD

The *NorthStar* DVD has **engaging, authentic video clips**, including animation, documentaries, interviews, and biographies, that correspond to the themes in *NorthStar*. Each theme contains a three- to five-minute segment that can be used with either the *Reading and Writing* strand or the *Listening and Speaking* strand. The video clips can also be viewed in MyNorthStarLab.

COMPANION WEBSITE

The companion website, www.longman.com/northstar, includes resources for teachers, such as the scope and sequence, correlations to other Longman products and to state standards, and podcasts from the *NorthStar* authors and series editors.

UNIT 1

The Internet and Other Addictions

OVERVIEW

Theme: Addiction

This unit deals with Internet addiction and whether it can be considered a true addiction. Other modern addictions are also discussed. Students discuss the topic and participate in a group discussion in which they play the roles of psychologists attending a conference about addictions.

Listening One: *Interview with an Internet Addiction Counselor* is a radio interview with a psychologist who discusses problems with Internet addiction among college students.

Listening Two: *Time to Do Everything Except Think* is a radio commentary in which a writer argues that people today are bombarded by communication and don't have time to reflect and develop their creativity.

Critical Thinking

Infer word meaning from context

Recognize personal assumptions about technology

Infer information not explicit in the interviews

Compare and contrast differing viewpoints

Support opinions with information from the interviews

Hypothesize another's point of view

Listening

Make predictions

Listen for main ideas

Listen for details

Make inferences

Relate listenings to personal experiences and values

Organize and synthesize information from the listenings

Speaking

Express and solicit opinions

Relate personal experiences

Role-play a scripted conversation

Express wishes

Add information and opinions to others' ideas

Participate in and summarize a discussion

Vocabulary

Use context clues to infer meaning

Identify and use word forms

Identify synonyms and idiomatic expressions

Grammar

Wish statements—expressing unreality

Pronunciation

Stressing important words

 MyNorthStarLab
Readiness Check, Background and Vocabulary, Listenings One and Two, Notetaking and Academic Skills Practice, Vocabulary and Grammar, Achievement Test

 NorthStar: Reading and Writing 5
Unit I deals with the life story of a baseball player, Mickey Mantle, who suffered from alcoholism, a destructive and pervasive addiction.

1 FOCUS ON THE TOPIC

◀ SKILLS

Predict content; use prior knowledge; preview vocabulary; infer the meaning of new vocabulary from context.

✪✪✪ A PREDICT

Suggested Time: 5–10 minutes

1. Ask students to look at the title of the unit. Make sure students know the definition of *addiction* (the condition of being unable to stop a certain behavior).

2. Have students read the cartoon and pair up with a classmate to discuss their responses. Circulate while students are discussing. Make sure that students understand what the cartoon shows: a support group of people who share a common problem. If necessary, point out that in such support groups, people commonly do not give their last names (to protect their privacy) and that admitting they have a problem is considered to be a crucial step in overcoming that problem. Then have pairs report their ideas to the class.

✪✪ B SHARE INFORMATION

Suggested Time: 15 minutes

Have students work alone to complete the survey and then share and discuss their responses with a partner. Then follow up with the class by reading the statements from the survey aloud and having students raise their hands if they agree or disagree. Let volunteers explain their positions to the class.

Expansion/Homework
Have students complete the survey with friends, family, and acquaintances and report their answers back to the class. Write the tally of A and D responses on the board. Discuss which views are the most common and which are the most controversial.

❖❖❖ C BACKGROUND AND VOCABULARY

 Go to www.mynorthstarlab.com for *Background and Vocabulary*.

Suggested Time: 20 minutes

1. Point out that the bold words and expressions are target vocabulary for the unit and the upcoming listening tasks. Point out the footnoted words and their definitions. Then ask students to follow along in their books while they listen to the article.

2. To check comprehension, ask: *What is an addiction, according to the article? How has the definition changed in recent times? What do some psychologists recommend for people with an Internet addiction? What are some symptoms and consequences of excessive computer use?*

3. Have students work with a partner to complete the vocabulary exercise or work alone and then compare answers with a partner. Remind students to reread the context sentence in the article, as well as the previous and subsequent sentences, for clues.

4. Go over the answers as a class. Make sure students know how to pronounce each word.

Expansion/Homework

(**1**) Have students work alone or with a partner to write new sentences with each of the vocabulary words. Call on volunteers to write their sentences on the board, or put two pairs together to read their new sentences aloud, without including the vocabulary word (they can say *blank* instead). The other pair guesses which vocabulary word completes the sentence. (**2**) Have students discuss in groups or with the whole class which activities mentioned in the article they also do (for example, downloading music, using Google®, blogging) and what other online activities they do. Which online activities are most popular among the class? What is the average amount of time spent on the most popular activities? (**3**) Students could also read the background and complete the vocabulary exercise as homework. However, if time permits, have students listen to the article in class afterwards. (**4**) As an alternate presentation, before students read and listen to the article, write the sentences from the box in the article on the board, but with the percentages missing. Tell students that 2,513 U.S. adults were surveyed about their Internet usage. Have students work in pairs to guess what the percentages are that complete each blank. Then have students read and/or listen to find the correct answers. Were any of the answers surprising? Would a poll of adults in their own countries yield similar answers?

 Link to *NorthStar: Reading and Writing 5*
If students are also using the companion text, have them work in groups to use the target vocabulary to summarize Mickey Mantle's story.

 Go to www.mynorthstarlab.com for additional *Background and Vocabulary* practice.

# ②FOCUS ON LISTENING

❮ SKILLS

Predict content; understand main ideas and details; make inferences; express opinions.

✪✪✪ Ⓐ **LISTENING ONE:** Interview with an Internet Addiction Counselor

📁 Go to www.mynorthstarlab.com to listen to *Interview with an Internet Addiction Counselor.*

Suggested Time: 5 minutes

Listening One is a radio interview with a university counselor from the University of Maryland. He talks about Internet addiction and how to recognize and cope with it. He also discusses how to tell when Internet usage has become a problem and the role of support groups in treating this kind of addiction.

1. Read the introductory paragraph aloud or have students read it silently. Check to see if they know where the University of Maryland is (Maryland is a small state in the United States near Washington, D.C.).

2. After you play the first part of the interview and partners predict what questions they might hear, have a few volunteers share their predictions.

Expansion/Homework
Call on volunteers to share some of their questions, and write them on the board. As a wrap-up to Listening One, come back and check (✔) the questions on the board that were asked and answered in the interview. Ask the class to guess how Dr. Kandell might have answered any of the questions that were not addressed in the interview.

LISTENING STRATEGY: Quick Write

Quick Write is a good strategy to activate prior knowledge. Give students this beginning: *The Internet is* . . . and ask them to write for a few minutes without stopping. Tell them to write anything that comes to mind, even if it seems off topic. If students say they can't think of anything to write, have them write the word *Internet* repeatedly until an idea comes. Keeping their pens on the paper and moving facilitates the flow of ideas. Repeat the process with the phrase *Addiction is* . . . Then ask students to share which Quick Write was easier for them.

✪✪✪ LISTEN FOR MAIN IDEAS

Suggested Time: 15 minutes

1. Give students time to read the main ideas column in the chart. Have students work in pairs to try to guess some of the information they might hear.

2. Play the interview and have students take notes in the main ideas column.

3. Have students compare answers with a partner's. Let students discuss different responses and revise their notes if they want to.

4. Go over the answers with the whole class, or wait to check answers until students have filled out the details column. Answers might vary in terms of which information students designate as main ideas or details. If all the information is written first, it is easier to sift through it and identify main concepts and details.

REACHING ALL STUDENTS: Listen for Main Ideas

- **Less Proficient:** Have students listen to the introduction several times, if necessary, so they have a clear idea of the focus of this interview. Then have them write the main idea of the interview in a single sentence before they listen to the rest of the report.

- **More Proficient:** Have students write the main idea of the report and then write phrases from the questions to identify the supporting ideas for the piece.

✪✪✪ LISTEN FOR DETAILS

Suggested Time: 10 minutes

1. Give students time to read the details column in the chart. Have them fill in any information they remember. Play the interview again for students to check their answers and write in any missing information. Remind students that they can write notes instead of complete sentences.

2. Have students compare answers with a partner's. If there are any disagreements, play the interview again.

Expansion/Homework
Have students reread the list of vocabulary on page 3. Play the interview again, and have students raise their hands when they hear the vocabulary.

✪✪✪ MAKE INFERENCES

Suggested Time: 10 minutes

1. Explain that *making inferences* involves drawing conclusions about what we hear from indirect information—for example, vocabulary choice, hesitations, and tone of voice. In this section, then, the answers will not be given directly in the listening passages; rather, students must use context clues to figure out what the speakers mean.

2. Have students read the questions before you play the excerpts. Play each excerpt and have students discuss their answers after each one. Encourage them to explain how they made their choices.

3. Go over the answers with the whole class. Replay the excerpts if necessary.

✹✹✹ **EXPRESS OPINIONS**   Suggested Time: 15 minutes

Have students work in groups of three or four to read the questions and express their opinions. For students new to group discussions, write some phrases on the board that will support participation, such as *What do you think? Do you agree? How about you? Can you explain what you mean? Can you give an example?* Circulate to answer questions and keep discussions on track. If time allows, invite one student from each group to summarize the group's opinions on one question.

Expansion/Homework
Ask students what an analogy is (a comparison between two things that are similar in some respects). Draw a picture of an octopus on the board. Point out how the eight long wiggling arms of a slippery octopus would be difficult to control. In groups, pairs, or individually, have students create their own analogy for dealing with one or more addictions, either in class or as homework. Then have students share their new analogies with the class. Encourage (but do not require) students to illustrate their analogies with a simple drawing.

CRITICAL THINKING

Give students the following questions for discussion in small groups before discussing as a whole class:

1. What is the purpose of this interview?

   Answers will vary, but students should recognize that it is informative, so their responses might include teaching or informing people about Internet addiction.

2. According to the article, how do people learn that they're addicted to the Internet?

   Answer: It shows up through other problems such as relationships, grades, work.

3. What can you conclude from the information in Question/Answer 2?

   Answers will vary, but students might conclude that people don't recognize their addiction to the Internet; that Internet addiction causes other problems.

4. How can you use the information in this report in your own life?

   Answers will vary, but students should support their ideas with information from the text and from their own experience.

✹✹✹ **B** **LISTENING TWO: Time to Do Everything Except Think**

Go to www.mynorthstarlab.com to listen to *Time to Do Everything Except Think.*

Suggested Time: 15 minutes

In Listening Two, a journalist discusses some dangers from the overuse of modern technology and gadgets, especially on one's creativity.

1. Ask students to raise their hands if they own and use a laptop, a wireless handheld device, or a cell phone. You can also ask about MP3 players, although they are not mentioned in the interview.

2. Give students time to read the categories in the main ideas column in the chart; then work in pairs to predict what they might hear.

3. Play the interview, have students take notes individually, and compare answers with a partner's.

4. Go over the answers for the main ideas before students listen for details. Because the details directly support the main ideas, they will need to know what the main ideas are before they listen for details. Explain what Brooks means by *playful noodling* (brainstorming; having creative, spontaneous thoughts) and *hooked* (connected).

5. Have students fill in any details they remember before they listen. Then play the interview one or two more times for students to complete the chart. Have them compare answers with a partner's before you go over the answers with the whole class.

Expansion/Homework
Have students listen to the interview again, writing down any positive aspects of technology and modern communication that the interviewers and Brooks mention (*brings us information; multitasking may make our brains work better; there has been a worldwide increase in IQ points; skills are enhanced, such as the ability to make fast decisions, answer many e-mails quickly, and answer standardized tests*). In groups, have students brainstorm additional advantages. You could have students use their notes to write up a summary of the interview.

Link to *NorthStar: Reading and Writing 5*
(**1**) If students are also using the companion text, ask them to read their notes about the symptoms and warning signs of addiction and think about what happened to Mickey Mantle's social skills as he became addicted to alcohol. Ask students, *How does the example of Mickey Mantle's alcoholism compare in severity to the damage of Internet addiction?* (**2**) Have students work in groups to analyze whether Internet addiction and/or dependence on other modern devices would qualify as "addiction" according to the psychology text in Reading Two. Which of the influential factors that are discussed in the reading are most likely to apply to people who are addicted to the Internet and other electronic devices?

✱✱✱ C INTEGRATE LISTENINGS ONE AND TWO

◖ SKILLS

Organize and compare information from two audio segments; synthesize and apply the information to a cartoon about computer addiction.

STEP 1: Organize

Suggested Time: 10 minutes

Have students work alone, with a partner, or with a small group to complete the chart. Students might find it helpful to look back at the notes they took on the two listenings to refresh their memories. Go over the answers with the entire class.

STEP 2: Synthesize

Suggested Time: 15 minutes

1. Have students work with a partner to discuss the questions about the cartoon. Remind the class to use the information they categorized in Step 1.

2. Circulate and provide help where necessary. Make sure students know that *junkie* is a slang term for a drug addict.

3. Call on volunteers to share some of their answers to questions #2 and #4 with the class.

Expansion/Homework
Either write the vocabulary from page 5 on the board while students are talking, or have one student in each pair keep a book open to page 5. Ask students to try to use the words and expressions as they talk.

Link to *NorthStar: Reading and Writing 5*
If students are using the companion text, you may also want to include vocabulary from that unit's section 1C on the board. Alternatively, you could create a list integrating the vocabulary from both the *Listening and Speaking* and *Reading and Writing* strands. See the Word List for each unit at the end of the *Teacher's Manual.* Have students check (✔) each word and expression as they use it.

 Go to www.mynorthstarlab.com for *Notetaking* and *Academic Skills Practice.*

③ FOCUS ON SPEAKING

Ⓐ VOCABULARY

❮ SKILLS

Review vocabulary from Listenings One and Two; identify and use different word forms; use vocabulary in free discussions.

Go to www.mynorthstarlab.com for *Review Exercise 1*.

1. Focus the class' attention on the word forms chart. Elicit from the class some common word endings for nouns (*-ion, -ness, -ment, -y*), for verbs (*-ize*), and adjectives (*-ed, -ous, -ive, -ing, -ic*). Remind students that not all nouns, verbs, and adjectives use these endings, but are one more clue that students can use to help determine the part of speech of an unfamiliar word.

2. Have students work with a partner to complete the chart. Let students use dictionaries if available.

3. Go over the answers with the class, checking pronunciation and spelling. Where there are two different noun or adjective forms for one word, make sure students know what the difference between the two terms is (e.g., an *addict* is a person; an *addiction* is a condition).

Expansion/Homework

(1) You may want to assign the exercise as homework and then use class time to check answers and correct pronunciation. Point out the word ending *-aholism* and *-aholic* that come originally from the terms *alcoholism/alcoholic* (for addiction to alcohol) but are now used informally to create new words to describe addictions. These endings can even be used humorously, as in *chocoholic* for someone "addicted" to chocolate. (2) Divide the class into groups of three. If necessary, have one group of four, with two students sharing a role, or a group of two, with one student reading both B and C. (3) Tell students to skim the entire conversation before filling in the vocabulary because they will need the context to help them choose the appropriate words. Then have the groups work together to fill in the blanks. (4) Check answers with the whole class. Check comprehension of the entire conversation by asking volunteers to explain *shop 'til you drop* (shop for a long time), *that little piece of plastic* (a credit card), *a few hundred bucks* (two to three hundred dollars), *kick the habit* (give up an addiction or behavior), and *a private shrink* (a psychiatrist who treats patients individually). (5) Have students read the conversation aloud in their groups. Encourage them to read with expression. If time permits, have students read through two or three roles. (6) Have groups rehearse their role plays until they feel comfortable, and then call on groups to perform for the class or another group. (7) In pairs or small groups, have students create a script for a support group with a different kind of addiction. Students can write out the entire script or just make notes to speak from. Remind them to use vocabulary from the unit.

○○ **EXPAND** **Suggested Time: 10 minutes**

1. As a class, practice pronouncing the boldfaced words and expressions.

2. Have students work individually and then compare answers with a partner's, or work with a partner and then compare answers with another pair's. Remind students to use context clues in the sentence to help them guess the meaning of the boldfaced words and expressions. Then check the answers as a class.

Expansion/Homework

(**1**)This exercise can also be assigned as homework. Then use class time to check answers and correct pronunciation. (**2**) Students can work in pairs or individually in class or for homework to write new sentences or a short dialogue about addictions using some of the new vocabulary. Students using *Northstar: Reading and Writing 5* could write a dialogue with Mickey Mantle. Have students share their sentences or read their dialogues to the class.

VOCABULARY EXPANSION: Specialized Terms

Tell students that most professions and organizations have terms that are used frequently by those groups. Have students create a section in their Personal Dictionary particularly for those specialized terms that are used by various groups (e.g., medical, technology, education). Provide these words from Unit I and have students list them according to the general area or profession they are associated with: *addiction counselor, present with, therapy, support groups* (medical/psychology), *blog/blogger, surf the net, google* (technology/Internet). Ask if they know of other terms that are specific to particular groups or professions.

✪ CREATE

Suggested Time: 15 minutes

1. Call on two volunteers to read the example aloud. Point out that there is no "correct" way to answer the question, and that the point of the exercise is to use the vocabulary words to talk about the unit topic. Students do not need to worry about giving true information, but rather can give imaginative answers.

2. Have students work in pairs. Tell students to take some time to think of ideas and plan their answers before they begin speaking. Encourage students to make eye contact with each other as they speak. If time permits, have students change partners and repeat the exercise, switching roles.

Go to www.mynorthstarlab.com for additional *Vocabulary* practice.

✪✪ B GRAMMAR: Wish Statements—Expressing Unreality

Go to www.mynorthstarlab.com for *Grammar Chart* and *Exercise 1*.

◀ SKILLS

Understand and practice the use of wish statements to express thoughts about unreal conditions.

Suggested Time: 25 minutes

1. Call on pairs of volunteers to read the sample dialogues aloud. Make sure students understand that the information in brackets is not read aloud, but is written in the book for clarification of the grammar point. Point out how *wish* and *would* are both stressed in short-answer responses.

2. Have students work in pairs to practice the conversations and discuss the questions. Then go over the answers with the whole class.

3. Study the grammar chart with the class by reading the information aloud or having the class read the information silently. Point out that the final modal in a short answer can contract with *not*, but not with the pronoun (so, *I wish I hadn't*, but not **I wish I'd*).

4. Have students do **Exercise 2** in pairs. Less proficient students can fill out the answers before practicing the conversations. If time permits, have students change partners and repeat the exercise, switching roles.

Expansion/Homework
(**1**) If students have trouble with Exercise 2, read the prompts yourself and have the class give the answer in chorus. Repeat until they can respond fluently. (**2**) For further practice, offer exercises from *Focus on Grammar 5,* 3rd Edition or Azar's *Understanding and Using English Grammar,* 3rd Edition. See the Grammar Book References on page 267 of the student book for specific units and chapters.

 Go to www.mynorthstarlab.com for additional *Grammar* practice.

ⓒ SPEAKING

◖ SKILLS

Raise pitch; lengthen vowel sounds and use volume to add emphasis to the important words in a sentence; use expressions to build on others' ideas; integrate the concepts, vocabulary, grammar, pronunciation, and function from the unit to conduct a group discussion.

☉☉ PRONUNCIATION: Stressing Important Words

Suggested Time: 20 minutes

1. Read the explanation to the class. Point out that a common misconception is that English speakers add emphasis to words only through volume, but that pitch and length are important ways to add emphasis as well.

2. Play the audio for the two example sentences. If necessary, repeat it a few times. The class might listen with their eyes closed so they can focus just on the pronunciation.

3. Have the class repeat the example sentences, mimicking the intonation they heard and raising their hands when they speak the words with the high pitch. Point out that when learning a new pronunciation or intonation pattern in another language, exaggerating helps. They may feel that they are over-doing the intonation, but it will probably sound natural to a native speaker.

4. Play the audio for **Exercise 1**. You might stop after each sentence and have the class repeat. Then replay the audio and go over answers with the whole class.

5. In pairs, have students practice saying the sentences. Remind them to raise their hands when saying the emphasized word and that a little exaggeration will often result in the most natural intonation.

6. Have students switch roles and repeat the exercise, so that each person has a chance to say all of the sentences.

7. For **Exercise 2**, have students work in pairs to read the dialogue and guess which words are stressed (there can be more than one correct interpretation). Then play the audio for students to check their guesses.

8. Have students work in pairs to read the dialogue, taking turns and practicing each role. If time permits, call on a few volunteer pairs to perform the dialogue for the class.

✪✪ FUNCTION: Expressions for Building on Others' Ideas

Suggested Time: 20 minutes

1. Go over the expressions in the chart with the whole class. Point out what follows each expression: *To add to your idea*, + a complete sentence; *Not only that, but I would also say that* + a complete sentence; *Your point makes me think of* + a noun phrase + an explanation; *Another thing I'd like to bring up is* + a noun clause; *You speak of* + a noun (gerund) phrase; *then, can I also assume that* + a complete sentence, or in this case, a question. Point out that most of the phrases imply an agreement with the previous speaker, but if you wish to disagree, you could first state an opposing opinion and then add to it.

2. Have volunteers read the example dialogue aloud. Have the class brainstorm additional sentences that B could say, or that A could say in response. Ask how B could use one of the Function phrases if B disagreed with A (by saying two sentences, such as *Well, I think people will become used to handling so much information.* **Not only that, but I would also say that** *more information will help people lead better lives*).

3. If time permits after partners have completed the exercise, have students change partners, switch roles, and repeat the exercise.

✪✪✪ PRODUCTION: A Group Discussion

Suggested Time: 40 minutes

If you wish to assign a different speaking task than the one in this section, see page 21 of the student book. The alternative topics relate to the theme of the unit, but may not target the same grammar, pronunciation, or function taught in the unit.

1. Read the introductory box aloud to the class. Read the situation to the class before they break into groups.

2. Divide the class into three groups. Assign each group one of the sessions. Make sure each group has selected a leader, a note-taker, and someone who will summarize the group's discussion for the class.

3. Give students a few minutes to check back through the unit for vocabulary, grammar, pronunciation, and functions.

4. Give students a time limit of 15–20 minutes for their discussion. Circulate while students are discussing to monitor and help out. Then call on groups to report their summaries to the class.

✪ ALTERNATIVE SPEAKING TOPICS

These topics give students an alternative opportunity to explore and discuss issues related to the unit theme.

✪ RESEARCH TOPICS

Suggested Time: 30 minutes in class

1. Have students turn to pages 259–260. For Step 1, have students take the quiz by themselves, or work in pairs and ask the questions to a partner. Then have students score the quiz according to the scale and read the comments about their scores.

2. Have students discuss in small groups or with the whole class whether they think the scores are accurate. Encourage them to support their answers with specific reasons and examples.

3. For Step 2, have students work with a partner to create a similar quiz. You may wish to limit the number of pairs who write quizzes for the same topic. If students will not be doing Step 3 together with their partners, make sure that each student makes a copy of the pair's quiz.

4. For Step 3, students can interview people outside the class or can give the quiz to classmates. Students can also give the quiz to more than one person, so that they can compare results.

5. For Step 4, have students summarize and share the results from their quizzes. Ask them, *Do you think your quiz was accurate? Were there any other questions you wish you had asked?*

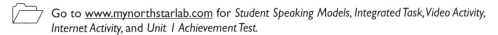 Go to www.mynorthstarlab.com for *Student Speaking Models, Integrated Task, Video Activity, Internet Activity*, and *Unit 1 Achievement Test.*

UNIT 2

Honesty Is the Best Policy

OVERVIEW

Theme: Lying
This unit deals with the concepts of truth, honesty, and deception, and whether there are ever justifications for lying. Students consider why people keep secrets and if secrets are a type of lie. The unit also addresses academic plagiarism and modern methods for detecting it.

Listening One: *Interview with a Psychiatrist* is a radio interview with a psychiatrist about what lies are, the many reasons that people lie, and some consequences of lying.

Listening Two: *Family Secrets* is an interview with a filmmaker who uncovered a secret from her father's past.

Critical Thinking

Clarify values relating to truth and lying
Infer word meaning from context
Consider the effects of mistrust

Investigate motivations for keeping secrets and exposing the lies of others
Investigate multiple sides to an ethical issue

Listening

Make predictions
Listen for main ideas
Listen for details
Make inferences based on tone, pace, and vocabulary

Relate listenings to personal experiences and values
Organize ands synthesize information from the listenings

Speaking

Express and solicit opinions and values
Relate personal experiences
Express agreement and disagreement

Role-play a scripted conversation
Introduce, defend, and express the different sides of an issue

---

Vocabulary	Grammar
Use context clues to determine sequence Identify and use word forms	Modals—degrees of certainty
	Pronunciation
	Reduction of the auxiliary *have*

 MyNorthStarLab
Readiness Check, Background and Vocabulary, Listenings One and Two, Notetaking and Academic Skills Practice, Vocabulary and Grammar, Achievement Test

 NorthStar: Reading and Writing 5
Unit 2 deals with liars and the lies they tell and the nature of truth.

---

1 FOCUS ON THE TOPIC

◖ SKILLS

Predict content; use prior knowledge; preview vocabulary; infer the meaning of new vocabulary from context.

✪✪✪ A PREDICT

Suggested Time: 5 minutes

1. Tell the class that "Honesty is the best policy" is a common expression in English. Have students read the cartoon and then discuss the questions with a partner, small group, or the whole class. As a follow-up, ask students what kinds of things people might lie about on a resumé. You could also ask them what they believe the consequences should be if someone is discovered to have lied on a resumé while applying for a job/after being offered a job.

2. Have students continue to work with the same partners or groups to discuss the other questions. Then call on pairs to report some of their ideas back to the whole class.

✪✪ B SHARE INFORMATION

Suggested Time: 15 minutes

1. Have students fill out the survey individually and then compare their responses with a partner, or talk with a partner as they complete the survey. Then put two pairs together to share their responses.

2. If time permits, survey the class by reading each item aloud and having students raise their hands to indicate if they checked *Never, Sometimes, Often,* or *Always.* Let students explain their choices. Students may need to use the expression *It depends on. . . .*

Expansion/Homework
(1) Have students collect answers to the survey from friends, family, and acquaintances and report their answers back to the class. Write the tally of responses on the board. As a class, discuss which views are most commonly held. (2) Alone or in pairs, have students write some scenarios to use as a similar survey. In class, have them exchange surveys with another student or pair, complete the surveys, and then discuss their responses with the person or pair who created the survey.

Go to www.mynorthstarlab.com for *Background and Vocabulary*.

Suggested Time: 20 minutes

1. Read the introductory paragraph about plagiarism. Before students read and listen to the article, ask students to share their ideas on how plagiarism can be detected.

2. Ask students to follow along in their books while they listen to the letters. Point out that the bold words and expressions are target words for the unit and the upcoming listening tasks. Make sure students notice the footnoted words and their definitions.

3. Check students' comprehension by asking after the first letter: *How do professors at Midlake University check students' papers for plagiarism? What reason does Dean Miller give for why some students plagiarize?* After the second letter: *What examples of non-academic plagiarism does the writer give? Whom does the writer think should be responsible for stopping academic plagiarism? How does he suggest this be done?* After the third letter: *Why is the student upset with university administrators? What "solution" does she propose for plagiarism?*

4. Have students work with a partner to complete the vocabulary exercise, or have students work alone and then compare answers with a partner's. Remind students to reread the context sentence in the letters, as well as the previous and subsequent sentences, for clues. Then go over the answers as a class. Make sure students know how to pronounce each word.

Expansion/Homework

(**1**) As homework, have students individually or with a partner research famous cases of plagiarism on the Internet and write a short summary of the case, using as much of the target vocabulary as they can. Then have them read their summaries to the class. (**2**) For homework, have students research the plagiarism policies of the institution where they are currently studying. If possible, have them interview an administrator or instructor from another class about how common a problem it is. Have students report their findings back to the class. (**3**) Students could also read the background and complete the vocabulary exercise as homework. However, if time permits, have students listen to the letters in class afterwards.

Go to www.mynorthstarlab.com for additional *Background and Vocabulary* practice.

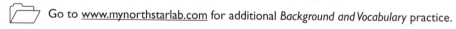

②FOCUS ON LISTENING

◀ SKILLS

Predict; understand main ideas and details; make inferences; express opinions.

✪✪✪ A LISTENING ONE: Interview with a Psychiatrist

📁 Go to www.mynorthstarlab.com to listen to *Interview with a Psychiatrist.*

Suggested Time: 5 minutes

Listening One is a radio interview with a psychiatrist who gives a profile of someone who lies. He talks about the reasons people lie, the definition of a lie, and some consequences of lying.

1. Read the introductory paragraph aloud or have students read it silently. Give students time to write down their predictions.

2. Have students share their predictions with a partner or with the whole class. Write each prediction on the board. After students have finished listening for main ideas and details, check to see which ideas the class was able to predict and what they predicted that was not mentioned.

LISTENING STRATEGY: Anticipation/Reaction Guide

Provide five statements about lying that are discussed in the interview and have students mark the statements *Agree/Disagree.* Then ask them to explain their answers. After listening to the interview, students should revisit the statements and respond a second time, again explaining their answers. The second explanation will be specific to what they learned from the report.

✪✪✪ LISTEN FOR MAIN IDEAS   **Suggested Time: 10 minutes**

1. Give students time to read the topics.

2. Play the interview and have students write down the main ideas. They can write notes instead of complete the sentences. Let students discuss their responses and then go over the answers with the whole class.

REACHING ALL STUDENTS: Listen for Main Ideas

• **Less Proficient:** Tell students in advance that they are going to hear nine reasons people lie. Have them listen specifically for those reasons. Then have them work in small groups to complete any they missed.
• **More Proficient:** Tell students to write specific examples from their own experience for each reason to lie. Then have them compare their responses in small groups.

✿✿✿ LISTEN FOR DETAILS

Suggested Time: 10 minutes

1. Give students time to read the details column in the chart. Answer any questions about the information already filled in. Have students fill in any information they remember.

2. Play the interview again for students to check their answers and write in the missing information. Tell students they can write notes instead of complete sentences. Then have students compare their answers with a partner's. If there are any disagreements, play the interview again.

Expansion/Homework

Have students reread the boldfaced vocabulary on pages 26–27. Play the interview again, and have students raise their hands when they hear the vocabulary.

 Link to *NorthStar: Reading and Writing 5*

If students are also using the companion text, they can add the appropriate details from *Looking for the Lie* to support the main ideas in the chart. Ask them to notice which details are similar to the ones in Listening One and which are different.

✿✿✿ MAKE INFERENCES

Suggested Time: 10 minutes

1. Read the paragraph about making inferences to the class. Make sure they understand what is meant by *tone of voice, attitude,* and *choice of words.* Brainstorm with the class words they can use to describe tone (*high, low, deep,* etc.) and pace (*fast, rapid, slow, deliberate, uneven, measured,* etc.). Give examples if necessary.

2. Give students time to read the questions before you play the excerpts. Because the excerpts are not linked, you can check answers after each one.

3. Play each excerpt and have students discuss their answers. Repeat the excerpts a few times if necessary.

4. Go over the answers with the whole class. Replay the excerpts if necessary.

✿✿✿ EXPRESS OPINIONS

Suggested Time: 15 minutes

1. Before students form groups and begin to discuss the questions, tell them that they do not need to agree with one another. However, whether they agree or disagree, they should be able to support their answers.

2. Call on volunteers to share with the class why they agree with the first statement, and elicit reasons from students who disagree. Repeat the procedure with the second statement.

Expansion/Homework

Have students choose one of the excerpts from Make Inferences and follow along with the audioscript while you play that section again. Have them practice reading the lines with the same intonation. Repeat the excerpts a few times, and then have students read their chosen excerpts aloud to a group or the whole class.

CRITICAL THINKING

Give students the following questions for discussion in small groups before discussing as a whole class:

1. According to Dr. Eckman, what are the nine different reasons people lie?

   Answer: To avoid punishment, to get a reward, to protect another person or self, to win admiration, to get out of a social situation, to avoid embarrassment, to get power, or to maintain privacy.

2. Are any of these acceptable reasons for you, personally, to lie? Explain.

   Answers will vary, but students should be prepared to explain the circumstance (for example, to protect my family).

3. If you knew a student was cheating on a test, which is a form of lying, what would you do?

   Answers will vary, but students should be prepared to defend their answers.

4. Why does Dr. Eckman say that you should ask yourself if you want a future relationship with someone when you're thinking about lying to him/her? Is that the best reason to lie or not to lie?

   Answer: He believes that lying erodes trust, and if the other person should find out, it would damage the relationship. The answer to the second part will vary. Students must support their answers from the interview and/or from their own experience.

✪✪✪ B LISTENING TWO: Family Secrets

 Go to www.mynorthstarlab.com to listen to *Family Secrets*.

Suggested Time: 15 minutes

Listening Two is an interview with a filmmaker who talks about how she discovered a secret her father kept from the family, the secret, and her opinions about it.

1. Read the opening paragraph aloud to the class. For **Exercise 1**, have partners write their predictions and call on students to share predictions with the class. If you like, write the different predictions on the board and check them as the class listens to each section. After the class listens to each section, call on a volunteer to give the correct answers.

2. For **Exercise 2**, students can compare their guesses with another pair by telling the story in order: *First, Rapaport's father dies. Then, . . .*

3. After the small group discussions in **Exercise 3**, bring the class together and call on volunteers from each group to share some of their ideas with the whole class.

SKILLS

Organize, compare, and synthesize information from two audio segments; apply the information and ideas to other areas.

STEP 1: Organize
Suggested Time: 15 minutes

Have students work alone or with a partner to complete the chart, using the notes they took on the two listenings. Then go over the answers with the entire class. Where answers vary, have students explain their reasoning.

STEP 2: Synthesize
Suggested Time: 15 minutes

1. If they wish, pairs can brainstorm ideas for each role together. Point out that the student role-playing Pola can use information from the left column and the student role-playing Dr. Eckman can use information from the right column.

2. Call on volunteers to perform their role plays for the class.

Expansion/Homework
Have students work in pairs to role-play another situation where someone confronts a person who has kept a secret. The situation can be real or imaginary. Give students a few ideas to get them going: A manager confronts an employee who didn't turn in a co-worker who has been stealing; a teacher asks a student to explain why he/she plagiarized a term paper; a parent confronts a child who has lied about doing his/her chores.

 Go to www.mynorthstarlab.com for *Notetaking* and *Academic Skills Practice*.

③ FOCUS ON SPEAKING

A VOCABULARY

SKILLS

Review vocabulary from Listenings One and Two; infer the meaning of words and expressions from context; use vocabulary in free discussions.

✪ REVIEW

 Go to www.mynorthstarlab.com for *Review*.

1. Direct the class to review the definitions of the vocabulary on page 27. If necessary they can also reread the context sentences. Call on volunteers to give the class an example sentence for each of the words and expressions.

2. Have students work with a partner to complete the article. Circulate while students are working to answer questions about additional new vocabulary in the paragraphs.

3. Check answers by calling on volunteers to read a paragraph or several sentences aloud. Give students who are listening time to correct their answers if necessary. If a map of the world is available, point out to students or call on volunteers to point out where Chile, Argentina, Moldova, and Botswana are.

Expansion/Homework

You may want to assign the exercise as homework and then use class time to check answers and correct pronunciation.

✪✪ EXPAND

Suggested Time: 10 minutes

1. Read the introductory paragraph aloud to the class.

2. You can stop and check answers after each part, or check answers after students have completed parts One and Two. However, check answers before having students practice the conversation on their own.

3. Check answers by calling on pairs of students to read one remark and one response. Go over pronunciation of the new words and idioms if necessary. Point out that *fess* in *fess up* is a shortened form of the word *confess*. *Confess* is never used with *up*, however.

4. Before students complete conversations in pairs, encourage them to read with expression.

Expansion/Homework

(1) This exercise can also be assigned as homework. Then use class time to check answers, correct pronunciation, and have students practice the conversation in pairs. (2) Students can work in pairs or individually in class or for homework to write a dialogue between Dr. Sanborn and Martin. Encourage them to use vocabulary from both Review and Expand. Then call on pairs to role-play their conversations for the class.

VOCABULARY EXPANSION: Class Thesaurus

Since many of the words are synonymous with lying, suggest that students use this to begin a class thesaurus. Provide a large binder or larger scrapbook and have students contribute synonyms and meanings as they encounter new words.

✪ CREATE
Suggested Time: 15 minutes

1. Read the instructions to the class, and then call on two volunteers to read the example aloud. Tell students that their answers can be more than one sentence long, and that, of course, they can use additional vocabulary from the unit in their responses.

2. Have partners take some time to think of ideas and plan their answers before they begin speaking. Encourage students to speak expressively and to make eye contact with each other as they speak.

3. If time permits, have students change partners and repeat the exercise, switching roles.

📁 Go to www.mynorthstarlab.com for additional *Vocabulary* practice.

✪✪ B GRAMMAR: Modals—Degrees of Certainty

📁 Go to www.mynorthstarlab.com for *Grammar Chart* and *Exercise 1*.

◀ SKILLS

Understand and practice the use of modals to express different degrees of certainty about past, present, and future situations.

Suggested Time: 35 minutes

1. As an alternative to having students work in pairs in **Exercise 1**, call on volunteers to read the statements aloud to the class. (Make sure they understand that the modals are boldfaced because they are focus words for the grammar point of the unit and not because they should be stressed when speaking.) Then discuss the questions as a whole class. If students discussed the questions in pairs, go over the answers with the whole class.

2. Study the grammar chart with the class. Read the example sentences aloud or call on volunteers to read them. Then ask for volunteers to paraphrase the sentences with modals to show the same meaning but without using a modal. For example, *Clearly, one of them must be lying* could be paraphrased as *I am sure that one of them is lying*. If necessary, have the class repeat in chorus the reduced forms of modal + *have*.

3. Have students do **Exercise 2** in pairs. Less proficient students can fill out the answers before practicing the conversations. Students can work with the same partner for **Exercise 3** or choose a new one.

4. Check answers to Exercises 2 and 3 by calling on pairs to read a question/response aloud to the class.

Expansion/Homework
(1) If students have trouble with Exercises 2 and 3, read the prompts yourself and have the class give the answer in chorus. Repeat until they can respond fluently.
(2) For further practice, offer exercises from *Focus on Grammar 5*, 3rd Edition or

Azar's *Understanding and Using English Grammar*, 3rd Edition. See the Grammar Book References on page 267 of the student book for specific units and chapters.

 Go to www.mynorthstarlab.com for additional *Grammar* practice.

C SPEAKING

◀ SKILLS

Use reductions; use phrases that express different sides of an issue; integrate the concepts, vocabulary, grammar, pronunciation, and function from the unit to conduct a group discussion.

✪ PRONUNCIATION: Reductions with the Auxiliary *Have*

Suggested Time: 20 minutes

1. Remind students that working on pronunciation will help both listening comprehension and speaking. Play the audio while students follow along in their books. If necessary, repeat it a few times. It might help to have the class listen with their eyes closed so they can focus just on the pronunciation.

2. Read the explanation to the class. Then play the audio for **Exercise 1**.

3. For **Exercises 2** and **3**, have pairs of students (from different language backgrounds) practice the dialogues. Call on volunteers to read the exchanges aloud for the class. Correct pronunciation as necessary.

✪ FUNCTION: Seeing Multiple Sides to an Issue

Suggested Time: 20 minutes

1. Read the introductory paragraph aloud to the class. Ask the class to brainstorm reasons why it is important to consider several angles to an issue.

2. Read the expressions in the chart aloud and have the class repeat, or call on volunteers to read the expressions aloud.

3. If necessary, teach the class how to flip a coin before beginning the exercise. If coins are not available, students can play *Rock-Paper-Scissors* instead. The "winner" defends the action, and the "loser" presents an additional, alternative, or opposing view. The person who defends the action should also introduce the dilemma with a phrase, such as *I think it's fine to (take office supplies), I don't have any problem with (taking office supplies), I don't think it's unethical to (take office supplies),* etc. Have the class brainstorm a few such openings and write them on the board for students to refer to as they do the exercise.

Link to *Northstar: Reading and Writing 5*

If students are also using the companion text, have them discuss the issues raised in *There Is Such a Thing as Truth* and/or *Truth and History* using the expressions for seeing multiple sides.

✪✪✪ PRODUCTION: A Group Discussion

Suggested Time: 45 minutes

If you wish to assign a different speaking task than the one in this section, see page 44. The alternative topics relate to the theme of the unit, but may not target the same grammar, pronunciation, or function taught in the unit.

1. Read the introductory box aloud to the class. If you wish, read the explanation to the class before they break into groups.

2. Divide the class into groups of four. If your class doesn't divide evenly, have one or two groups of three.

3. Give students a few minutes to check back through the unit for vocabulary, grammar, pronunciation, and function.

4. Make sure each group has chosen a dilemma for each member before they begin. Circulate while students are reading about their dilemmas to answer any questions.

5. Continue to circulate as students take turns presenting their dilemmas, take notes, and then discuss the situations. Give students a time limit of 15 minutes for their discussion.

6. Call on groups to report their discussion of one dilemma to the class. One person can present the group's views, or each member can share some of the group's opinions.

✪ ALTERNATIVE SPEAKING TOPICS

These topics give students an alternative opportunity to explore and discuss issues related to the unit theme.

✪ RESEARCH TOPICS

Suggested Time: 30 minutes in class

1. Have students turn to page 260. Decide whether the whole class will do the same research project or choose different ones.

2. For Topic 1, either choose one of the movies to watch as a whole class, or have students choose one to watch alone, with a partner, or with a small group. In class, have students summarize the movie plot and theme to the whole class. Discuss what the movie showed about truthfulness and lying.

3. For Topic 2, have students work individually or in pairs to research one of the items listed. If you like, let the class brainstorm additional relevant topics to choose from. Have students give a short oral presentation about their topic to the class. Encourage the audience to ask questions.

4. For Topic 3, have students work individually to conduct their interviews. Then have students share the stories they heard in small groups or with the whole class. Have them also discuss any similarities and differences among the stories that they collected.

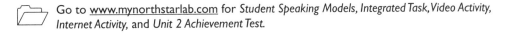 Go to www.mynorthstarlab.com for *Student Speaking Models, Integrated Task, Video Activity, Internet Activity,* and *Unit 2 Achievement Test.*

UNIT 3 The Bold and the Bashful

OVERVIEW

Theme: Personality
This unit deals with a cross-cultural view of shyness and other personality traits. It explores the traits of optimism and pessimism.

Listening One: *Americans Are Getting Shyer* is a radio interview with a professor who talks about shyness in Americans and what problems it causes them.

Listening Two: *The Pollyanna Syndrome* is a humorous radio commentary about how optimism is not always the best response to a frustrating or disappointing situation.

Critical Thinking

Infer word meaning from context
Analyze the impact of shyness on one's life
Infer information not explicit in the interviews
Categorize and apply descriptive vocabulary

Support opinions with information from the interviews
Draw conclusions about personality types and roles

Listening

Listen for main ideas
Listen for details
Make inferences based on tone, pace, and vocabulary

Relate listenings to personal experiences and values
Organize and synthesize information from the listenings

Speaking

Describe personality
Express opinions
Express and defend preferences

Begin and maintain conversations
Role-play discussion in a personality consulting company

Vocabulary

Use context clues to infer meaning
Use colloquial language
Identify and use synonyms and idiomatic expressions
Categorize descriptive language

Grammar

Adjective clauses—identifying and nonidentifying

Pronunciation

Grouping words together

 MyNorthStarLab
Readiness Check, Background and Vocabulary, Listenings One and Two, Notetaking and Academic Skills Practice, Vocabulary and Grammar, Achievement Test

 NorthStar: Reading and Writing 5
Unit 3 deals with the impact of optimism, determination, and self-confidence on the pursuit of success.

FOCUS ON THE TOPIC

◀ SKILLS

Predict content; use prior knowledge; preview vocabulary and concepts; infer the meaning of new vocabulary from context.

✪✪✪ A PREDICT

Suggested Time: 5 minutes

1. Ask students to look at the title of the unit. Make sure students know the meaning of the words *bold* and *bashful*.

2. Have students read the cartoon, pair up with a neighboring classmate to discuss their responses, and then report their ideas to the class.

Expansion/Homework

(1) As follow-up questions, ask the class, *Do you think it's possible to advise people on how to overcome a problem that you still have? Why or why not?* If students say it is possible, have them give specific examples. (2) Have students work with a partner or a small group to make a list of behaviors of shy people. Then call on pairs or groups to share their lists with the class. Does everyone agree that the behaviors listed mean that someone is shy?

✪✪ B SHARE INFORMATION

Suggested Time: 15 minutes

1. After students complete the survey and score their responses, have them work in small groups to discuss the questions.

2. Ask a few volunteers to share the range of scores their group members had on the shyness quiz and some of their responses to the discussion questions.

Expansion/Homework

(1) To explore how students feel when speaking English, ask them to take the quiz twice: the first time thinking only about their native-language context, and the second time thinking only about an English-speaking context. Have them identify differences between the scores and discuss with the class any reaction they may have. (2) You may want to have students evaluate the quiz, thinking critically about its validity for them personally and across cultures. (3) Have students work in pairs to create a similar boldness quiz. Ask them to write items that describe specific bold behaviors (rather than simply writing statements that are opposites of the ones in

the shyness quiz). Then have them give and respond to the quizzes orally with another pair.

✳✳✳ Ⓒ BACKGROUND AND VOCABULARY

📁 Go to www.mynorthstarlab.com for *Background and Vocabulary*.

Suggested Time: 20 minutes

1. Ask students to follow along in their books while they listen to the sentences in **Exercise 1**. Point out that the boldfaced words are target vocabulary for the unit and the upcoming listening tasks. Encourage students to use context clues instead of a dictionary to guess the meaning of the words.

2. Check comprehension of the sentences by asking students to paraphrase each one with a partner. If the pair cannot paraphrase a sentence, have them ask another pair or you for help.

3. Have students work with a partner to complete **Exercise 2**, or have students work alone and then compare answers with a partner's. Remind students to reread sentences for clues.

4. Go over the answers as a class. Make sure students know how to pronounce each word.

Expansion/Homework

(1) If students are having trouble, you may want to do the exercise together as a class. Point out what parts of the sentence give clues to the meaning of the bold word: explanations set off by commas or dashes; contrasts; examples, etc. (2) Students could also read the background and complete the vocabulary exercise as homework. However, if time permits, have students listen to the sentences in class afterwards. (3) If you have students from the cultures mentioned in the sentences, ask them if they think the generalizations are true for their country in general and them in particular. Do students from other countries feel their cultures are naturally shy or naturally bold?

📁 Go to www.mynorthstarlab.com for additional *Background and Vocabulary* practice.

②FOCUS ON LISTENING

❰ SKILLS

Predict; understand main ideas and details; make inferences; express opinions.

📁 Go to www.mynorthstarlab.com to listen to *Americans Are Getting Shyer*.

Suggested Time: 5 minutes

Listening One is a radio interview with a psychology professor from Stanford University who shares his research on the extent of shyness in the American population.

Read the introductory paragraph aloud or have students read it silently. Check to see if they know where Stanford University is (in Palo Alto, California, in the San Francisco Bay area).

Expansion/Homework
(1) Call on volunteers to share some of their predictions, and write them on the board. As a wrap-up to Listening One, come back and check (✔) the predictions on the board that were accurate. (2) Before you begin the listening, you may want to discuss the distinction between cultural and social factors. Cultural factors focus on the values of a society; social factors focus on the social communication and the structure of social units in a society.

LISTENING STRATEGY: Imagine

To prepare students to listen, tell them to imagine what it would be like to be at a party where they didn't know anyone. Suggest that students first imagine they are extroverts who meet people easily, and then have them imagine that they are shy and uncomfortable meeting new people. Then have them discuss each scenario with a partner, including how they would feel and what they would do.

✸✸✸ LISTEN FOR MAIN IDEAS   **Suggested Time: 10 minutes**

1. After students compare answers with a partner's, give them time to revise or add to their notes if they want to.

2. Go over the answers with the whole class, or wait to check answers until students have completed the Listen for Details section.

✸✸✸ LISTEN FOR DETAILS   **Suggested Time: 10 minutes**

After students have read the questions and answered the ones they already know, play the interview again, letting students compare answers after each part. If disagreements arise, replay the segment rather than giving the answer.

Expansion/Homework
As a way to either predict or check answers, have pairs of students quiz each other, reading the questions aloud. Student A reads the questions in Part One to Student B. In Part Two, they switch roles. To help them express predictions, you may want to write phrases for expressing uncertainty on the board (*I guess . . . / Perhaps . . . /I suppose . . .*).

• **Less Proficient:** Have students make two columns or boxes: Problem-Solution. Then have them listen once for the problems expressed in the interview, and then listen again for the solutions.	• **More Proficient:** Have students complete the Problem-Solution chart and then write a few paragraphs on the subject of shyness. They should introduce the problem in the first paragraph and the solutions in the next paragraph(s).

✪✪✪ MAKE INFERENCES   Suggested Time: 15 minutes

1. Remind students that making inferences involves drawing conclusions about what we hear from indirect information—for example, vocabulary choice, hesitations, and tone of voice. In this section, then, the answers will not be given directly in the listening passages; rather, students must use context clues to figure out what the speakers intend.

2. Give students time to read the questions before you play the excerpts. Because the excerpts are not linked, you can check answers after each one.

3. Play each excerpt and have students discuss their answers with a partner. Because these passages are especially challenging, you may want to play each excerpt twice.

4. Go over the answers with the whole class. Replay the excerpts if necessary. Students can also follow along with the audio script in the back of their books.

✪✪✪ EXPRESS OPINIONS   Suggested Time: 20 minutes

1. Read the questions in **Exercise 1** aloud. Make sure students understand the phrases *to come out of (one's) shell* (which refers to an animal such as a turtle, snail, or hermit crab) and *shrinking violet* (which refers to a small, delicate flower).

2. For **Exercise 2**, have students work with the same partner to rate the factors that may contribute to shyness. Then have pairs share their ratings with another pair or the whole class, explaining their choices.

3. After pairs have discussed the cartoon in **Exercise 3**, bring the class back together and have pairs share their ideas about what causes low self-esteem and what advice they would give to someone with low self-esteem.

Expansion/Homework
(**1**) Have students think of a particularly shy person they know (or have heard or read about—the person could even be fictional from a popular book, movie, or TV show) and prepare and deliver a short presentation to the class that explains how this person's shyness is demonstrated and what factors might have contributed to the person being shy. (**2**) Some people complain that in the United States, members of "Generation Y" (people born in the 1970's and 1980's) in fact have *too much* self-esteem, and therefore feel entitled to respect and admiration that they have not

earned. In addition, they are not able to cope with setbacks and disappointments. Ask students if they feel there is a similar trend in their own cultures.

CRITICAL THINKING

Give students the following questions for discussion in small groups before discussing as a whole class:

1. According to the article, what are people's opinions about shyness?

   Answer: People say that shyness is undesirable, that shy people are less popular, have fewer friends, lower self-esteem, make less money, their life is more boring, less intimate; they have fewer leadership skills, less social support, and they're more likely to be depressed.

2. Do you agree or disagree with this assessment?

   Answers will vary, and students can analyze the list on a case-by-case basis, providing reasons and examples to support their opinions.

3. Do you think people are accurate when they say that they are shy, or do you believe they expect too much of themselves?

   Answers will vary, but students should support their opinions with information from the text and their own experience.

4. How would you advise someone who wants to overcome shyness? Explain.

   Answers will vary, but students can use information from the text and from their own experience in formulating this advice. They should be encouraged to elaborate, rather than to give short answers.

✪✪✪ B LISTENING TWO: The Pollyanna Syndrome

Go to www.mynorthstarlab.com to listen to *The Pollyanna Syndrome*.

Suggested Time: 10 minutes

Listening Two is a radio commentary by Julie Danis who explains why she thinks that *not* looking at the bright side all the time might be a suitable approach to life.

1. Read the introductory paragraph aloud to the class. Make sure students understand the meaning of "make lemonade out of lemons," a shortening of the adage "When life hands you lemons, make lemonade," meaning to try to find something positive in a bad situation. Have students describe any Pollyannas that they know. Encourage them to describe both the benefits of having a positive attitude and how a persistent optimism can seem annoying to others. Explain that even though many people have not read the original book, the term "Pollyanna" is familiar to most North American English speakers.

2. The ideas in this commentary are made through tone of voice as well as word choice. The first time that students listen, have them close their books. You may also ask students to close their eyes.

3. After they have listened once, have students read the exercise and match any items that they remember. Then play the audio again.

4. Check answers with the whole class.

Expansion/Homework

(**1**) After listening to the passages, ask students: What is Julie Danis' resolution? Why does she plan to suck on some lemons? (**2**) This listening is quite challenging. As a final wrap up, you may want students to listen to the commentary as they read along. Stop the audio frequently to allow students to ask questions. Get students to focus on irony and tone as a key to comprehension. (**3**) For homework, have students research the plot line of the original novel *Pollyanna* online and note examples of "lemon" incidents that Pollyanna turned into "lemonade." As a class, discuss Pollyanna's reactions: Were they realistic? Admirable? Something else? (**4**) If time permits, show some or all of the 1960 film version of *Pollyanna*.

 Link to *NorthStar: Reading and Writing 5*
Students using the companion text can discuss the ways in which the main character in Reading One, *Gotta Dance*, was optimistic.

✸✸✸ⓒ INTEGRATE LISTENINGS ONE AND TWO

◖ SKILLS

Organize, compare, and synthesize information from two audio segments; apply the information and ideas to other areas.

STEP I: Organize   Suggested Time: 10 minutes

1. Have students work alone or with a partner to complete the chart. Students might find it helpful to look back at the exercises from the two listenings to refresh their memories.

2. Go over answers with the entire class. You may wish to copy the chart onto the board and fill in the squares with students' ideas as you elicit them.

STEP 2: Synthesize   Suggested Time: 15 minutes

1. You can have each pair do both role plays or just choose one. Encourage them to exaggerate the personalities of their roles to bring out the contrasts and add humor.

2. Allow students to make notes for their conversations if they wish, but have them practice enough times that they can eventually speak without checking their notes. Call on pairs to act out their conversations for the class.

 Go to www.mynorthstarlab.com for *Notetaking* and *Academic Skills Practice*.

3 FOCUS ON SPEAKING

A VOCABULARY

◀ SKILLS

Review vocabulary from Listenings One and Two; use colloquial expressions; use vocabulary in free discussions; apply concepts from the listenings to the theory of the affect of birth order on personality.

✪ REVIEW   Suggested Time: 10–15 minutes

 Go to www.mynorthstarlab.com for *Review*.

1. Read the introduction aloud to the class. Ask students to show by raising their hands how many of them are an only child, the first born, a middle child, and the youngest child.

2. Have students work with a partner (of a different language background, if possible) to complete the exercise. Remind them that they can use parts of speech as clues.

3. Check answers with the class by calling on volunteers to read the letters aloud.

Expansion/Homework
(1) If class time is limited, you may want to assign this exercise as homework, and then use class time to check answers and work on pronunciation. (2) You may want to have students choose one letter and write down three vocabulary words from that letter. In pairs of their choosing, students can then conduct *Star Daily* interviews on birth order. Students can take on the character of the person in the letter and try to use the three words they have chosen as they answer the reporter's questions. (3) As a follow-up, have students work in groups or as a whole class to discuss the information and ideas in the letters. Have them summarize what the assumptions are about the personalities of first-born children, only children, and youngest children. Do the people who wrote the letters agree with the assumptions? Does your class? Have students describe the personalities of people they know who are a first-born, a middle child, a youngest child, or an only child. Are there any common traits? (4) Have students write a brief statement of their birth order and how they think it has affected their personality, perhaps using the first, second, and fourth letters in Exercise 1 as models. Encourage them to use as much of the unit vocabulary as they can. This written assignment can be submitted directly to you or read aloud in class in small groups or to the whole class.

✪✪ EXPAND

1. As a class, practice pronouncing the words and expressions.

2. As students write the words from **Exercise 1** into the correct column, have them also note the part of speech. You might want to have students write an article before the nouns (***the** life of the party*, ***a** Pollyanna, **a** shrinking violet*). Note that although *Pollyanna* is a proper noun and a person's name, it is used in this unit as a more general label and therefore does require an article before it.

3. Check the answers as a class.

4. Encourage them to give specific examples of behavior or attitudes to justify the labels they use to describe themselves.

Expansion/Homework

(**1**) Exercise 1 can also be assigned as homework. Then use class time to check answers, correct pronunciation, and do **Exercise 2**. (**2**) You could also have students write or give an oral description of a close friend or family member using as many of these words as possible. Have students bring in a photograph to show while they read or give their descriptions aloud in small groups.

VOCABULARY EXPANSION: Roots and Affixes

Ask students to look up the roots and affixes for these words: *chronic, phobia, extrovert, misattribute, syndrome, condescending*. Then have them construct other words using the root or affix and add these to their personal dictionary in a section reserved for roots and affixes.

✪ CREATE

1. Read the instructions aloud to the class. If necessary, give some examples of a "devil's advocate" (for example, if a person complains that the rain has canceled a planned picnic, a devil's advocate might say, "Yes, but the rain is good for farmers." A devil's advocate could either make lemonade out of lemons, or suck lemons instead of making lemonade).

2. As students work in small groups, have at least one student in each group keep the textbook open to page 57 so the group can see the target vocabulary. Encourage groups to defend each position, if necessary by having at least one student deliberately play the devil's advocate.

3. Bring the class back together and have students show by raising their hands which person they would choose in each situation (here, students should give their true opinion). Call on volunteers to explain their choices.

Go to www.mynorthstarlab.com for additional *Vocabulary* practice.

✪✪ B GRAMMAR: Adjective Clauses—Identifying and Nonidentifying

Go to www.mynorthstarlab.com for *Grammar Chart* and *Exercise 1*.

◖ SKILLS

Understand and practice the use of identifying and nonidentifying adjective clauses to add more information and sophistication to spoken sentences.

Suggested Time: 25–30 minutes

1. Read the sentences in **Exercise 1** aloud to the class. Slightly exaggerate the pause at the commas in the first and fourth sentences. Have students work in pairs to study the sentences and answer the questions. Then go over the answers with the whole class.

2. Study the grammar chart with the class by reading the information aloud or by letting the class read the information silently. Students who have studied grammar before may have learned the terms *restrictive* and *nonrestrictive* for the clauses.

3. Point out that nonidentifying clauses are set off in writing by commas and in speech by intonation. Identifying clauses are not marked by commas or pauses. Read the example sentences aloud.

4. Have students work individually to underline the adjective clauses in **Exercise 2** and identify the nouns they describe. Go over the answers with the whole class. Then have students practice reading the paragraph to a partner, pausing where there are commas.

5. Model the first exchange in **Exercise 3** so that students understand that Student A presents the question and that Student B must cover Column A and only read the prompt in Column B. Remind students to switch roles when they finish the first part.

Expansion/Homework

(**1**) Exercise 2 works well for homework. Students can complete the exercise at home and then go over the answers in class. (**2**) For further practice, offer exercises from *Focus on Grammar 5,* 3rd Edition or Azar's *Understanding and Using English Grammar,* 3rd Edition. See the Grammar Book References on page 267 of the student book for specific units and chapters.

Go to www.mynorthstarlab.com for additional *Grammar* practice.

◀ **SKILLS**

Recognize and use thought groups; use language to break the ice and maintain a conversation; integrate the concepts, vocabulary, grammar, pronunciation, and function from the unit to discuss a case study.

✪✪ PRONUNCIATION: Grouping Words Together

Suggested Time: 15 minutes

1. Remind students that working on pronunciation will help both listening comprehension and speaking. Read the explanation to the class. Point out that even very fluent speakers make short breaks in sentences when they are speaking. These breaks add emphasis and help the listener follow the ideas. Read the example sentence aloud. Exaggerate the thought groups. Then read the sentence again with less exaggeration.

2. After students have listened to the sentences and underlined the thought groups in **Exercise 1**, have students (of different language backgrounds, if possible) work in pairs to practice pronouncing these sentences. Encourage students to exaggerate the intonation that shows thought groups. Often what feels "over the top" to a non-native speaker will sound quite natural to a native speaker.

3. For **Exercise 2**, have students read the sentences before listening. You could even have them underline the thought groups in each sentence before listening. Point out that both sentences are grammatically correct, but they have different meanings. Go over the differences before playing the audio.

4. Play the audio and have students identify the correct sentences. If disagreements arise, replay the segment rather than giving the answer. Then have students practice saying the sentences with a partner.

✪✪ FUNCTION: Breaking the Ice and Maintaining a Conversation

Suggested Time: 15–20 minutes

1. Read the first paragraph aloud. Explain that "Zorba the Greek" is a character from a novel that was made into a film. Zorba is an extrovert who loves life. Point out that "breaking the ice" is a cultural phenomenon used to introduce yourself to strangers, and that it is more common in the West than in Asia. Even though many Americans are shy, the ability to strike up a conversation at a party is regarded as a desirable skill. Similarly, maintaining a conversation is different in different cultures. Americans appreciate an active participant who asks and answers questions, makes comments when information is presented, and answers questions with more than one sentence.

2. Read the information in the chart and call on volunteers to read the example sentences aloud. This is a good time to point out that English speakers rarely

ask a stranger for his/her name, but rather introduce themselves first. This is a cue to the listener that the speaker would like to know his/her name.

3. Students can choose one or two of the situations, or, if time permits, try them all. Make sure that each student has a chance to be the one to start a conversation.

Expansion/Homework

(1) For each of the situations, ask the class if a) they would begin a conversation in such a situation; b) how they would react if someone else began a conversation with them in such a situation; and c) whether people from their cultures would typically begin a conversation in such a situation. (2) Have students record their exchanges and then listen to hear their own performance. You can listen for pronunciation and usage errors, which you can write down and have them correct. (3) As an alternative presentation or an extension, have the class imagine that they are at a large reception or party where they do not know anyone. Give students a few minutes to invent a personality and role for themselves, including a new name, occupation, and hobby or interest. Then have students stand up and mingle, striking up a conversation with a "new" person. Call "Time!" after three minutes and have students move on to a new partner. Continue in the same way until you feel that students have improved their fluency.

✪✪✪ PRODUCTION: A Case Study

If you wish to assign a different speaking task than the one in this section, see page 67. The alternative speaking topics relate to the theme of the unit, but may not target the same grammar, pronunciation, or function taught in the unit.

Suggested Time: 40–45 minutes

1. Read the introductory box aloud to the class. If you wish, read the background and the client profiles to the class before they break into groups.

2. After groups of three or four are set up, make sure students understand that they should choose one of the clients to work for, not all three. Circulate while groups are choosing their clients to answer questions.

3. Before they begin their discussion, make sure each group has selected a leader, a note-taker who will write the group's ideas in the chart, and at least one person who will present the group's ideas to the class.

4. If you wish, give students a few minutes to check back through the unit for vocabulary, grammar, pronunciation, and functions.

5. Give students a time limit of 15 minutes for their discussion. Circulate while students are discussing to monitor and help out.

6. Call on groups to make their presentations to the class.

Expansion/Homework

Groups could also work on their presentations outside of class and then deliver them during class. Have each group design a poster or other visual presentation aid to use during their presentation.

⊙ ALTERNATIVE SPEAKING TOPICS

These topics give students an alternative opportunity to explore and discuss issues related to the unit theme.

⊙ RESEARCH TOPICS

Suggested Time: 30 minutes in class

1. Have students turn to pages 260–261. For Step 1, have students work individually or with a partner to choose a phobia from the list or to find a different one (they may wish to visit a website that gives a long list of phobias).

2. For Step 2, have students conduct their research. Remind them to paraphrase or quote and credit information, and not just to copy and paste information from other sources.

3. Have students give their presentations in small groups or to the whole class. Encourage the audience to ask questions. If you like, videotape the presentations and play them back so that students can assess their own performance.

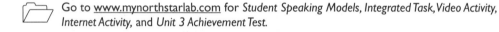 Go to www.mynorthstarlab.com for *Student Speaking Models, Integrated Task, Video Activity, Internet Activity,* and *Unit 3 Achievement Test.*

UNIT 4 The Tipping Point

Theme: Trends

This unit explores a social behavior theory put forth by Malcolm Gladwell in his book *The Tipping Point: How Little Things Can Make a Big Difference.* The general theory is explained and then applied to the incidence of crime in New York City.

Listening One: *The Tipping Point* is a radio interview with Malcolm Gladwell about three types of people who spread information.

Listening Two: *Tipping Points in Fighting Crime* is a radio interview with Malcolm Gladwell about how the city of New York made some small simple changes that lowered the crime rate.

Critical Thinking

Interpret graphs

Analyze book reviews

Infer word meaning from context

Analyze different opinions

Investigate reasons for trends and changes

Understand metaphorical language

Listening

Predict content

Listen for main ideas

Listen for details

Make inferences based on tone, pace, and vocabulary

Relate information to others' viewpoints

Organize and synthesize information from the listenings

Speaking

Identify and use different forms of the same root word

Understand and use metaphorical expressions

Role-play a scripted conversation

Discuss trends and viral marketing

Add to others' ideas

Create and present a public service announcement

Vocabulary

Use context clues to find meaning

Identify and use word forms

Identify and use synonyms and metaphorical expressions

Grammar

Adverb clauses of result

Pronunciation

Stress changing suffixes

 MyNorthStarLab
Readiness Check, Background and Vocabulary, Listenings One and Two, Notetaking and Academic Skills Practice, Vocabulary and Grammar, Achievement Test

 NorthStar: Reading and Writing 5
Unit 4 explores how the book *Silent Spring* by Rachel Carson galvanized the popular environmental movement.

Go to www.mynorthstarlab.com for the MyNorthStarLab *Readiness Check*.

FOCUS ON THE TOPIC

◖ SKILLS

Analyze graphs and trends; predict content; preview vocabulary; infer the meaning of new vocabulary from context.

✪✪✪ A PREDICT

Suggested Time: 10 minutes

1. Ask students to read the title and look at the graphs. To check graph comprehension, ask: *How many murders were there in New York City in 1992? How about in 1997? How many cell phone subscribers were there in Asia in the year 2000? How many were there in the Middle East and Africa in 2005? How many subscribers were there in Latin America in 2007?*

2. Have students work in groups to continue verbalizing what they see in the graphs and to discuss the questions. You may need to explain that "tipping" here is used in the sense of something "tipping over," or suddenly shifting from one state to another. This less common use of the word might not be in students' dictionaries.

3. Have volunteers from different groups report their ideas to the class.

✪✪ B SHARE INFORMATION

Suggested Time: 15–20 minutes

1. After students have surveyed their partners and recorded the answers in **Exercise 1**, have them discuss the questions in **Exercise 2** with another pair.

2. Follow up with the class by reading the questions of the survey and having the class show by raising their hands how many of them chose each answer. You could also write the tally of answers on the board. Are there any class trends that stand out?

Expansion/Homework
Have students survey friends, family, and acquaintances and report their answers back to the class. Tally the responses on the board. Were the results of the broader survey similar to or different from the results of the class survey?

📁 Go to www.mynorthstarlab.com for *Background and Vocabulary*.

Suggested Time: 25 minutes

1. Set the context by asking students to quickly skim the passages. Then ask, *Where do you usually see reviews like this? Why do people read this kind of review? Why do people write this kind of review? Were the reviews positive or negative?*

2. Ask students to follow along in their books while they listen to the reviews. Point out that the boldfaced words and expressions are target vocabulary for the unit and the upcoming listening tasks.

3. Before partners begin the vocabulary exercise, remind students to reread the context sentence in the article, as well as the previous and subsequent sentences, for clues.

4. Go over the answers as a class. Make sure students know how to pronounce each word.

5. Check comprehension of the passages by calling on volunteers to paraphrase the main idea of each review (review 1: Word-of-mouth advertising can make a product suddenly popular; review 2: Psychologists helped TV producers discover a winning format for a children's television program; review 3: The "rule of 150" states that organizations with fewer than 150 members operate the most efficiently).

Expansion/Homework

(**1**) Students could also read the reviews and complete the vocabulary exercise as homework. Then use class time to check answers and pronunciation. If time permits, have students listen to the reviews in class afterwards. (**2**) Have students work alone or with a partner to write new sentences with each of the vocabulary words. Call on volunteers to write their sentences on the board. Alternatively, put two pairs together to read their new sentences aloud, though without including the vocabulary word (they can say *blank* instead). The other pair guesses which vocabulary word completes the sentence. (**3**) To help students memorize vocabulary, have them work in pairs to quiz each other on the definitions in Exercise 2: one is the teacher; the other is the student. Then they switch roles.

📁 Go to www.mynorthstarlab.com for additional *Background and Vocabulary* practice.

FOCUS ON LISTENING

◀ SKILLS

Predict; understand main ideas and details; make inferences; express opinions.

✪✪✪ Ⓐ LISTENING ONE: *The Tipping Point*

📁 Go to www.mynorthstarlab.com to listen to *The Tipping Point*.

Suggested Time: 5–10 minutes

Listening One is a radio interview with Malcom Gladwell who explains some of the ideas in his book *The Tipping Point: How Little Things Can Make a Big Difference.* He talks about how people he labels connectors, mavens, and salesmen spread ideas and start trends.

1. Read the introductory paragraph and the instructions for the exercise aloud or have students read them silently. Then have students work in pairs to write their predictions. Remind them that it's OK if their predictions are not correct, but that they should try to think of reasonable descriptions. If you like, call on volunteers to share their predictions and write them on the board.

2. Play the first part of the interview and have students check their predictions.

LISTENING STRATEGY: Set a Purpose for Listening

Remind students that setting a purpose for listening will help them to understand the information they are hearing. Have students offer reasons for listening (to understand, to evaluate, to be able to recall information or answer questions, to be entertained, to learn a process). Have them work in a small group to determine what actions they can take in order to be able to understand based upon their reason for listening. Have students share their ideas with the whole group, and ask each student to select one method to use for this interview. After listening, have student pairs share their results as to the effectiveness of the process they chose.

✪✪✪ LISTEN FOR MAIN IDEAS   **Suggested Time: 10 minutes**

1. Read or give students time to read the instructions and exercise. Ask students why *salespeople* is a more commonly accepted term than *salesmen* (because many salespeople are women).

2. Play the interview and have students write their definitions. Then have students compare their ideas with a partner's. If disagreements arise, play the interview as many times as needed for students to write satisfactory definitions.

Expansion/Homework

You may want to explicitly connect the notion of a "tipping point" with the discussion of important communicators, such as connectors, mavens, and salesmen. Ask students, *How do connectors, mavens, and salesmen influence people's behavior? How do these special people create new trends?*

✪✪✪ LISTEN FOR DETAILS   Suggested Time: 15 minutes

1. First have students read the statements, writing in answers they already know.

2. Play the interview again. Have students complete their responses and then compare their answers with a neighboring classmate. If disagreements arise, replay the interview rather than giving the answer.

Expansion/Homework

(1) Have students correct the false statements to make them true. Play the interview again if necessary. Then have students share their corrections with a partner, a group, or the whole class. (2) Have students reread the list of vocabulary on page 74. Play the interview again, and have students raise their hands when they hear the vocabulary. (3) You could ask each student to write an additional true or false statement to present to the class.

REACHING ALL STUDENTS: Listen for Details	
• **Less Proficient:** To help students recall information, ask them to create a web for each type of person mentioned in the interview. Then have them compare their webs with a partner to fill in the gaps.	• **More Proficient:** Suggest that students create a web for each type mentioned and then select the type that they would most like to be. Have them write a paragraph explaining the type and why they would like to be this kind of person.

✪✪✪ MAKE INFERENCES   Suggested Time: 15 minutes

1. Explain that *making inferences* involves drawing conclusions about what we hear from indirect information—for example, vocabulary choice, hesitations, and tone of voice. In this section, then, the answers will not be given directly in the listening passages; rather, students must use context clues to figure out what the speakers intend. Give students time to read the exercise before you play the excerpts. Because the excerpts are not linked, you can check answers after each one.

2. Play each excerpt and have students discuss their answers. Encourage them to explain how they made their choices.

3. Go over the answers with the whole class. Replay the excerpts if necessary. For excerpts 2, 3, and 4, you could demonstrate or ask students to demonstrate how the tone of voice would have been different if the speaker had been showing one of the other feelings. Use facial expressions and gestures to add emphasis.

✪✪✪ EXPRESS OPINIONS

1. Read the introductory paragraph aloud to the class. Then call on volunteers to read the statements from the different people aloud. Encourage them to read with expression.

2. Tell students that as they work in groups, it is not necessary for them to reach a consensus about whether they agree or disagree with the opinions. However, even when they agree, group members should support their opinions with reasons.

Expansion/Homework

Have each group tally and report to the class the number of people who agreed and disagreed with the statements.

CRITICAL THINKING

Give students the following questions for discussion in small groups before discussing as a whole class:

1. What are the characteristics of the three groups of people Gladwell talks about?

   Answer: Mavens have specialized knowledge; connectors know a lot of people; and salesmen are very persuasive.

2. Imagine that you are going to open a new retail store. What is the advantage of knowing these three types of people? Be specific as to the advantage for each type.

   There will be some variation in answers, but generally: connectors will spread the word because they are socially connected; mavens' specialized knowledge (for example, where to shop) will send people to you, and salesmen can persuade people to come to your shop.

3. Imagine that you are going to run for office at school. Which of these people would be of greatest benefit to you?

   Answers will vary, but students should be able to defend their choices with convincing reasons.

✪✪✪ Ⓑ LISTENING TWO: Tipping Points in Fighting Crime

📁 Go to www.mynorthstarlab.com to listen to *Tipping Points in Fighting Crime*.

Suggested Time: 15 minutes

Listening Two is another radio interview with Malcom Gladwell in which he relates how small changes in the management of the New York City subway in the 1990's resulted in a decrease in subway crime.

1. Read the introduction aloud to the class. Ask students, *What do you think the city of New York did that reduced crime?* If you like, write the guesses on the board, and check them again after the class has listened to the interview.

2. Give students time to read **Exercise 1**. Then play the interview and have students choose the correct answers.

3. Have students check answers with a partner, and replay the audio if necessary to resolve differences of opinion. Then go over the answers with the class.

4. Before students begin to work in groups for **Exercise 2**, encourage them to think of specific places that could be affected by measures such as those taken in the New York City subway.

5. Call on volunteers to summarize their group's ideas.

Expansion/Homework
Have students work in groups to choose a problem that could be affected by the "broken window" approach and propose workable solutions. Each group prepares a presentation to the class that includes a visual aid such as a poster or PowerPoint slides. Presentations should explain the problem, propose solutions, and end with a call to action. This activity could also be done following the Synthesize exercise in C.

✪✪✪ C INTEGRATE LISTENINGS ONE AND TWO

◀ SKILLS

Organize, compare, and synthesize information from two audio segments; apply the information and ideas to other areas.

STEP 1: Organize   Suggested Time: 10–15 minutes

1. Read or give students time to read the introductory summary. Then have students work alone or with a partner to organize the ideas into the flowchart.

2. Go over the answers with the entire class.

STEP 2: Synthesize   Suggested Time: 20 minutes

1. Read the instructions aloud to the class, and set a time limit (15 or 20 minutes) for small group discussions.

2. Circulate while students are working to help out and keep groups on task. Remind students that it is OK to anticipate reactions to their proposed solutions.

3. As groups present their ideas to the class, let other class members ask questions about the problem and solutions.

Expansion/Homework
(**1**) Have groups add specific suggestions for using mavens, connectors, and salespeople in their plans. (**2**) Either write the vocabulary from page 74 on the board while students are talking, or have one student in each pair keep a book open to page 74. Ask students to try to use the words and expressions as they talk. If students are using the companion text, *NorthStar: Reading and Writing 5*, you may also want

to include vocabulary from that unit's section 1C on the board. Alternatively, you could create a list integrating the vocabulary from both the *Listening and Speaking* and *Reading and Writing* strands. See the Word List for each unit at the end of the *Teacher's Manual*. Have students check (✔) each word and expression as they use it. (**3**) After their presentations, students could incorporate the feedback they receive from the class and write up a final "clean up" plan to record in their audio journal. (**4**) Encourage your students to follow this topic in the news or online. Have them bring to class any articles in which they find mention of "tipping points."

 Go to www.mynorthstarlab.com for *Notetaking* and *Academic Skills Practice*.

Link to *NorthStar: Reading and Writing 5*
Students using the companion text can create a flowchart of the increase in public awareness of the dangers of DDT.

③ FOCUS ON SPEAKING

A VOCABULARY

◀ SKILLS

Review vocabulary from Listenings One and Two; identify and use different word forms; use vocabulary in free discussions.

✪ REVIEW   Suggested Time: 10–15 minutes

 Go to www.mynorthstarlab.com for *Review*.

1. Focus the class' attention on the word forms chart. Elicit from the class some common word endings for nouns (*-ion, -ness, -ment, -y*), for verbs (*-ize*), and adjectives (*-ed, -ous, -ive, -ing, -ic*). Remind students that, of course, not all nouns, verbs, and adjectives use these endings, but they are one more cue that students can use to help determine the part of speech of an unfamiliar word.

2. Let students use dictionaries, if available, as they work with a partner to complete the chart.

3. Go over the answers with the class, checking pronunciation and spelling. Where there are two different noun or adjective forms for one word, make sure students know what the difference between the two terms is (e.g., an *immunization* is a vaccination or inoculation; *immunity* is the body's ability to resist a disease).

Expansion/Homework

(**1**) You may want to assign the exercise as homework and then use class time to check answers and correct pronunciation. (**2**) Have students work in pairs to write example sentences that use the different word forms, if possible keeping the same context for each word family. Check pairs' sentences as they are working. Then put two pairs together to quiz each other. A student from each pair takes turns reading the sentences aloud but letting a student from the other pair supply the missing word.

✪✪ EXPAND

Suggested Time: 15 minutes

1. Read the introduction and example aloud to the class. Explain that metaphorical expressions are sometimes cultural, although there are often surprising cultural similarities. As the class works with the expressions in Expand, encourage them to note any cultural similarities to or differences with other languages they know.

2. As a class, practice pronouncing the words and expressions in the box.

3. Let students use dictionaries if available as they work in groups for **Exercise 1**. At this point, it's OK if students use literal meanings of the words or expressions to place them in the chart. Check the answers as a class.

4. After students have completed **Exercise 2**, call on volunteers to read their definitions to the class. You may want to have several volunteers read definitions for each expression.

Expansion/Homework

Have students work alone or with a partner to write new sentences that use the words in a metaphorical sense. You may wish to give them a few examples, such as *a viral video, a viral fashion trend, a contagious attitude,* etc. Have students check their sentences with you to make sure the usage is correct, and then share them with the class.

VOCABULARY EXPANSION: Drawing Vocabulary Clues

To review the vocabulary for the first four units, have students play a game similar to *Pictionary.* Have students compete in teams of five; a student will take a word from a bowl or paper bag and attempt to draw clues to that word on the chalkboard or dry erase board. After the team guesses the word, they should use it in a sentence. Teams win points based on the amount of time required to complete the process (1–3 minutes/points).

✪ CREATE

Suggested Time: 15–20 minutes

1. Read the instructions to the class, and then have students complete the dialogue.

2. Check answers by calling on volunteers to read the sentences aloud. Then have students practice the conversation in pairs. Encourage them to read with expression.

3. If time permits, have students change partners and repeat the exercise, switching roles.

📁 Go to www.mynorthstarlab.com for additional *Vocabulary* practice.

✪✪ B GRAMMAR: Adverb Clauses of Result

📁 Go to www.mynorthstarlab.com for *Grammar Chart* and *Exercise 2*.

◖ SKILLS

Understand and practice the use of adverb clauses of result to add information and examples to sentences.

Suggested Time: 35–40 minutes

1. Have students work with a partner to read the sentences, or call on volunteers to read them aloud to the class. After students have worked in pairs to discuss the questions in **Exercise 1**, go over the answers with the whole class.

2. Read or give students time to read the grammar chart.

3. Have students do **Exercise 2** in pairs. They can either fill in the answers individually and then check with a partner, or do each item together.

4. Check comprehension of the story by asking: *Who was Paul Revere? Who was William Dawes? Why was Paul Revere's ride so successful?*

5. Read the instructions for **Exercise 3** aloud. Have two volunteers model number 1. Then have students work in pairs to complete the exercise. If time permits, have them switch roles and repeat the exercise with a new partner. They can repeat the exercise until Student B's answers are comfortable and fluent.

Expansion/Homework

(**1**) For additional practice with placing *So* or *Such* at the beginning of a sentence, have students rewrite the example sentences in Exercise 1 and the chart with this emphatic order (*Such an extraordinary salesman is Tom Gau that . . . ; So effective were the solutions that . . . ; So sensitive to subtle environmental changes were New York City criminals that . . . ; Such a mess were the subways that . . .* etc.). (**2**) Students can complete Exercise 2 as homework then go over the answers in class to work on pronunciation and discuss the story. (**3**) Have students relate the story of Paul Revere and William Dawes without checking the book, using adverb clauses of result where they can. (**4**) For further practice, offer exercises from *Focus on Grammar 5*, 3rd Edition or Azar's *Understanding and Using English Grammar,* 3rd Edition. See the Grammar Book References on page 267 of the student book for specific units and chapters.

📁 Go to www.mynorthstarlab.com for additional *Grammar* practice.

C SPEAKING

❰ SKILLS

Identify the shift in stress patterns when suffixes are added to root words; use metaphors to make a point; integrate the concepts, vocabulary, grammar, pronunciation, and function from the unit to prepare and present a public service announcement.

✪✪ PRONUNCIATION: Stress Changing Suffixes

Suggested Time: 20–25 minutes

1. Remind students that working on pronunciation will help both listening comprehension and speaking. Read the explanation to the class. Read the words slowly so that students can focus on the stress in each word.

2. Play the audio for **Exercise 1** and have students listen and repeat the words using the same stress pattern they heard. Give them time to mark the stress on the words. Go over answers with the class. Repeat this procedure for the next set of words in **Exercise 2**, but have students work with a partner (from a different language background, if possible).

3. For **Exercise 3**, let students use a dictionary if necessary as they work with a partner to add the suffixes. Circulate while students are working to help with spelling. Check answers with the whole class by calling on volunteers to spell and pronounce the new words. If necessary, have the class repeat the words in chorus.

Expansion/Homework

(**1**) You could have students mark the stress on the words before they listen, and then listen to the audio to check their answers. (**2**) If you wish to check pronunciation, call on students individually to read the words aloud. If any student makes a mistake, have the class repeat the word in chorus. (**3**) Encourage students to raise their hand or tap their desk when they say the syllable that should be stressed. Have the class do this in unison so students don't feel embarrassed at first.

✪✪ FUNCTION: Making a Point with Metaphors

Suggested Time: 20 minutes

1. Read or ask students to read (silently or aloud) the introductory information, before having students complete **Exercise 1**. After students have completed the exercise, go over their answers as a class.

2. Read the directions and list of expressions in **Exercise 2**. Model the example with another student.

3. Pair up students of similar fluency levels to complete the exercise. You may want to write the expressions on the board so that students don't refer to their books. Be sure that students switch roles after number 2. Encourage students to

make eye contact while speaking. Circulate among the pairs, listening in and correcting.

Expansion/Homework
(1) If possible, have students record these exchanges and then listen to hear their own performances. They can listen for pronunciation and usage errors, which they may then correct. (2) For a written assignment, students can restate all four prompts using appropriate metaphors.

✪✪✪ PRODUCTION: A Public Service Announcement

Suggested Time: 40–45 minutes

If you wish to assign a different speaking task than the one in this section, see page 97. The alternative speaking topics relate to the theme of the unit, but may not target the same grammar, pronunciation, or function taught in the unit.

1. Read or have students read the introductory information about "sticky" messages and PSAs.

2. Have students close their eyes as they listen to the PSA for the first time.

3. Have students read the questions in **Exercise 1**, and play the PSA again. Have students answer the questions with a partner. Call on volunteers to share some of their answers.

4. Give students time to read **Exercise 2**, and play the PSA again. Have students complete the outline and check their answers with a partner. If necessary, replay the PSA.

5. Divide the class into small groups for **Exercise 3**. If you wish, give students a few minutes to check back through the unit for vocabulary, grammar, pronunciation, and functions.

6. Give students a time limit of 15 or 20 minutes to create the PSA. Circulate while students are discussing to monitor and help out. Have students record their PSA if possible. If not, they will present it orally to the class. After they play or present their PSA, have the rest of the class answer the questions about it.

Extension/Homework
(1) For intensive listening practice, have the class complete the outline in Exercise 2 for one or more of the PSAs that groups present. (2) As students present their PSAs, note pronunciation and usage errors. Concentrate on the target language from this unit (you may also wish to include language points from previous units). At the end of the presentations, present your notes—either for the class or for each group— and have students correct the errors. Help students work on pronunciation.

Link to *Northstar: Reading and Writing 5*
Students could also develop a PSA with one of the messages in Rachel Carson's book, *Silent Spring* or on a similar environmental topic.

⊙ ALTERNATIVE SPEAKING TOPICS

These topics give students an alternative opportunity to explore and discuss issues related to the unit theme.

⊙ RESEARCH TOPICS

Suggested Time: 30 minutes in class

1. Have students turn to pages 261–262. Decide whether the whole class will do the same research project or choose different ones.

2. For Topic 1, have students work in a small group to choose a trend to instigate. Approve all trends for appropriacy before letting students develop a strategy.

3. Have each group write up a strategy plan. Encourage them to be as specific as possible. If your situation permits, allow groups to try out some of their ideas.

4. Have students present their strategies to the class. Make sure that all group members contribute to the presentation in some way, even if only some of them actually speak.

5. For Topic 2, have the class brainstorm companies that could be contacted. (Alternatively, students could brainstorm successful products, and research them online.) Then have students work individually or in pairs to conduct their interviews. Make sure each student or pair thinks of at least two companies to contact, in case they have trouble finding someone to interview.

6. Have students present their reports to the whole class. Encourage the class to notice similarities and differences among the different marketing approaches.

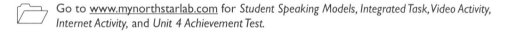 Go to www.mynorthstarlab.com for *Student Speaking Models, Integrated Task, Video Activity, Internet Activity,* and *Unit 4 Achievement Test.*

UNIT 5 Feng Shui: Ancient Wisdom Travels West

OVERVIEW

Theme: Cross-cultural insights

This unit deals with the Western approach to feng shui, the ancient Asian practice of designing architectural spaces to create physical and psychological comfort.

Listening One: *Interview with a Feng Shui Expert* is a radio interview with a feng shui practitioner about feng shui's purpose and effects.

Listening Two: *Feng Shui in the Newsroom* is a radio interview in which a feng shui expert gives advice about rearranging the furniture in an office to maximize positive feng shui.

Critical Thinking

Consider the impact of a philosophy on daily life
Infer word meaning from context
Infer information not explicit in the interviews
Compare and contrast differing viewpoints

Support opinions with information from the interviews
Choose information in a passage to mark and highlight

Listening

Make predictions
Listen for main ideas
Listen for details
Make inferences based on vocabulary choices and tone of voice

Relate listenings to personal experiences
Organize and synthesize information from both listenings

Speaking

Express and solicit opinions
Relate personal experiences and knowledge
Role-play a scripted conversation
Use target vocabulary in free responses

Emphasize a point
Express and solicit opinions
Present an argument based on a written article

Vocabulary

Use context clues to infer meaning
Identify and use word forms
Identify and use idiomatic expressions

Grammar

Spoken discourse connectors

Pronunciation

Intonation on sentence introducers

 MyNorthStarLab
Readiness Check, Background and Vocabulary, Listenings One and Two, Notetaking and Academic Skills Practice, Vocabulary and Grammar, Achievement Test

 NorthStar: Reading and Writing 5
Unit 5 explores the impact of immigration on families.

①FOCUS ON THE TOPIC

◀ SKILLS

Predict content; use prior knowledge; preview vocabulary; infer the meaning of new vocabulary from context; summarize.

✿✿✿ A PREDICT

Suggested Time: 5 minutes

1. Ask students to look at the title of the unit. Ask them to guess where feng shui is traveling from (the East).

2. Have students read the cartoon and then pair up with a neighboring classmate to discuss their responses. Circulate while students are discussing. Make sure that students understand the use of *heavy* here (expensive).

3. Have pairs report their guesses to the class. If you wish, you can write the guesses on the board for students to check as they do the rest of the Focus on the Topic exercises, which will explain feng shui.

✿✿ B SHARE INFORMATION

Suggested Time: 15 minutes

1. For **Exercise 1**, make sure that students understand *achieve harmony* (reach a feeling of peace and completion) in the directions, and *cemetery* (a place where dead people are buried), *dead-end street* (the end of a street that doesn't connect to any other streets) and *bats* (the flying animal, not a piece of sports equipment). Have students work with a partner to discuss the items in the chart and check (✔) their guesses and write their reasons. They may write short notes in the "reason" section instead of complete sentences.

2. Before students check their answers, have them share their guesses and reasons with another pair or the whole class. Then have students check their answers.

3. Have students discuss their answers to the discussion question in **Exercise 2**. Call on volunteers to share their thoughts with the class.

Expansion/Homework
(1) Have students think about a room, apartment, house, or other interior that they know well and describe it to a partner or small group. Ask, *Which of the aspects in the chart are present in that space? Overall, does the space seem to have good or poor*

feng shui? (**2**) Ask students to analyze their own classroom environment: *How does this classroom enhance or detract from your learning experience? How do the seating arrangement, lighting, noise level, and size of the room affect how you work together and learn in this room?* (**3**) Encourage students to follow this topic in the news or online. Have them bring to class any articles in which they find mention of feng shui.

✦✦✦ C BACKGROUND AND VOCABULARY

📁 Go to www.mynorthstarlab.com for *Background and Vocabulary.*

Suggested Time: 25–30 minutes

1. Ask students to follow along in their books while they listen to the passage. Point out that the boldfaced words and expressions are target vocabulary for the unit and the upcoming listening tasks.

2. You may want to have students work alone and then compare answers with a partner. Remind students to reread the context sentence in the passage, as well as the previous and subsequent sentences, for clues.

3. Go over the answers to **Exercise 1** as a class. Make sure students know how to pronounce each word.

4. Divide the class into groups of five for **Exercise 2**. If your class does not divide evenly, ask a stronger student to be responsible for two paragraphs. Circulate while students are reading and taking notes to help out as needed. Have students practice giving their summaries from their notes aloud or silently at least once before they summarize to their groups.

Expansion/Homework
(**1**) Play the audio again and have students listen with their eyes closed. Ask them to focus on the meaning and the use and pronunciation of the new vocabulary.
(**2**) Have students work alone or with a partner to write new sentences with each of the vocabulary words. Call on volunteers to write their sentences on the board. Alternatively, put two pairs together to read their new sentences aloud, though without including the vocabulary word (they can say *blank* instead). The other pair guesses which vocabulary word completes the sentence. (**3**) Students could also read the background and complete the vocabulary exercise as homework. However, if time permits, have students listen to the article in class afterwards.

📁 Go to www.mynorthstarlab.com for additional *Background and Vocabulary* practice.

FOCUS ON LISTENING

SKILLS

Predict; understand main ideas and details; make inferences; express opinions.

LISTENING ONE: Interview with a Feng Shui Expert

Go to www.mynorthstarlab.com to listen to *Interview with a Feng Shui Expert.*

Suggested Time: 5–10 minutes

Listening One is a radio interview with Kirsten Lagatree, author of the book *Feng Shui: Arranging Your Home to Change Your Life.* In the interview she defines feng shui, gives some examples, and talks about its purpose.

1. To encourage use of the vocabulary learned in Section 1C, write the words on the board for students' reference before they make their predictions.

2. Have students listen to the excerpt and compare that list with their own. Ask students to share any reactions with the class.

Expansion/Homework

Call on volunteers to share some of their predictions, and write them on the board. As a wrap-up to Listening One, come back and check (✔) the predictions that were correct. Talk about the other predictions. Does the class think that Lagatree would agree with them as well? Why?

LISTENING STRATEGY: Check for Understanding

Remind students that good listeners, like good readers, constantly check for understanding. They make and confirm predictions, make inferences, reflect on how the information affects their lives, and adjust their listening as needed. Select a portion of the interview and do a think-aloud for students to demonstrate questioning, predicting, inferring, reflecting, and adjusting. Put resulting notes on the overhead or chalkboard so students can see the outcome of this ongoing listening process.

LISTEN FOR MAIN IDEAS   **Suggested Time: 10 minutes**

1. Give students time to read the main ideas column in the chart. If you like, have students work in pairs to try to guess some of the information they might hear. If necessary, explain who Donald Trump is (a wealthy American real estate developer, businessman, and TV personality; he lives in New York City).

2. Play the interview as students write their notes. They do not need to write complete sentences. You might need to play the interview more than once for students to grasp all the key points.

3. Have students compare their notes with a partner's. Let students discuss different responses and revise their notes if they want to.

4. Go over the answers with the whole class.

✪✪✪ LISTEN FOR DETAILS   Suggested Time: 15 minutes

1. Give students time to read the questions and fill in any answers they remember.

2. Play the interview again for students to check their answers and write in any missing information. Let them compare answers with a partner after each part. If there are any disagreements, play the interview again.

3. Go over the answers with the whole class.

Expansion/Homework
(1) Have students reread the vocabulary on pages 101–102 or write it on the board. Play the interview again and have students raise their hands when they hear the vocabulary. (2) You could have pairs of students quiz each other by reading the questions aloud. Student A reads the questions in Part One to Student B, and then for Part Two, they switch roles. You may want to write some phrases for expressing uncertainty on the board: *I guess . . . /Perhaps . . . /I have no idea./Beats me* (informal).

✪✪✪ MAKE INFERENCES   Suggested Time: 10 minutes

1. Explain that making inferences involves drawing conclusions about what we hear from indirect information—for example, vocabulary choice, hesitations, and tone of voice. In this section, then, the answers will not be given directly in the listening passages; rather, students must use context clues to figure out what the speakers intend. Give students time to read the questions before you play the excerpts. Because the excerpts are not linked, you can check answers after each one.

2. Play each excerpt and have students discuss their answers. Encourage them to explain how they made their choices.

3. Go over the answers with the whole class. Replay the excerpts if necessary.

Expansion/Homework
(1) To teach students to infer meaning and look for a range of answers, you may want to do one excerpt as a class before playing the others. Encourage a range of responses by writing all students' ideas on the board. Emphasize that it is possible for students to have varying inferences as long as their reasoning is sound. (2) Have students follow along with the audioscript in the back of their books as you replay the excerpts. Then have students repeat the lines, trying to use the same intonation.

- **Less Proficient:** To help students pay attention to the language used in inference questions, have pairs underline the words that indicate an inference/conclusion question.

- **More Proficient:** Have student pairs note the language of the questions and write two inference questions similar to those given.

✪✪✪ EXPRESS OPINIONS

Suggested Time: 15–20 minutes

1. Have students work in groups of three or four, reading the questions and expressing their opinions. Remind them that they can draw on information from the Background and Vocabulary section as well as Listening One. Circulate while groups are talking to answer questions and make sure discussions stay on track.

2. If time allows, invite one representative from each group to summarize the group's opinions on one of the questions.

Expansion/Homework

Ask groups to make a quick list of other Eastern practices that have become popular in the West (karate, tae kwon do, karaoke) and Western practices that have become popular in the East (ballroom dancing, jazz music, rap and hip-hop, baseball). Ask, *In what ways do Western practices change when they become Easternized? These days, do you think there are still practices that are more Eastern or Western, or have they become truly global?*

Link to *NorthStar: Reading and Writing 5*

In the companion unit, Eva Hoffman and Elizabeth Wong describe feeling "lost in translation" as they adapted to their new cultures. Ask: *Do ideas and trends, as well as people, get lost in translation as they are adapted to new cultures? If so, how?* Encourage students to illustrate their points with concrete examples from their own cultures.

CRITICAL THINKING

Give students the following questions for discussion in small groups before discussing as a whole class:

1. According to the interview, how does the average person know if a room or house has good feng shui?

   Answer: The way you feel is a good indicator.

2. What are some of the principles of feng shui?

   Answer: Arranging furniture so your back isn't to a door, mirrors in all rooms except bedrooms.

(continued on next page)

3. Would you use feng shui in your house?

Answers will vary, but students should support their responses with clear reasons.

4. What does she mean by the "common sense and the transcendent explanation"?

Answer: There is an explanation that is common to our experience (common sense) like not wanting to be startled by someone coming from behind us and a spiritual or non-physical explanation like allowing the energy in a room to move more freely or reflecting the energy with mirrors to increase abundance.

 B LISTENING TWO: Feng Shui in the Newsroom

Go to www.mynorthstarlab.com to listen to *Feng Shui in the Newsroom*.

Suggested Time: 10–15 minutes

Listening Two is another radio interview with Kirsten Lagatree in which she applies her knowledge of feng shui to a radio newsroom.

1. Have students look at the chart on page 107 carefully before listening to the audio. Have them discuss with a partner the types of items that they will be listening for (areas of life, elements, seasons, animals, colors, and numbers).

2. Have students listen once with their books closed, focusing on understanding the interview.

3. Play the interview again and have students complete the chart and draw arrows to show where Lagatree suggests moving the furniture. (Some information on the audio is not addressed in the chart.)

4. Have students compare answers with a partner's. Play the interview again if necessary. Then go over the answers with the whole class.

Expansion/Homework
Have students write down extra information from the interview that is not represented in the chart on a separate piece of paper to compare with a classmate or small group.

C INTEGRATE LISTENINGS ONE AND TWO

❨ SKILLS

Organize, compare, and synthesize information from two audio segments; apply information and ideas to other areas.

STEP 1: Organize   **Suggested Time: 15 minutes**

1. Have students work individually to analyze and redecorate a space using feng shui. Have one student in each pair take notes on the problems and the other

student be responsible for taking notes about the solutions. Remind students to also think about the goals of the people using that space—do they want to earn more money? feel more peaceful? be more creative?

2. Have students look back through the unit for information on feng shui. Encourage them to think creatively about how they could apply feng shui to the space (for example, if it is impossible to add an aquarium, they could use a small table top fountain or even a poster of a waterfall or lake or a photograph of some fish).

STEP 2: Synthesize   Suggested Time: 15 minutes

1. When presenting their ideas, have students use a large sheet of paper divided into two sections: one for the current layout, and one for the new layout with favorable feng shui.

2. Have students give their presentations to the whole class or to a large group. Give each pair a time limit of 5–7 minutes, depending on your class size. Encourage audience members to ask questions and give additional suggestions.

Expansion/Homework

(1) If practical, let students work in groups to develop new layouts for the classroom or your office. Have each group present its ideas with the guidelines mentioned above. The class can then vote on which layout would bring the most favorable feng shui. If possible, try rearranging the classroom according to the best layout, and, after a few weeks, ask students to comment on whether it has influenced them and how. (2) As students present their plans, note pronunciation and usage errors. At the end of the presentations, present your notes—either for the class or for each group—and have students correct the errors. Help students work on pronunciation. (3) Either write the vocabulary from pages 101–102 on the board while students are discussing the questions in Step 1, or have one student in each pair keep a book open to pages 101–102. Ask students to try to use the words and expressions as they talk. If students are using the companion text, *NorthStar: Reading and Writing 5*, you may also want to include vocabulary from that unit's section 1C on the board. Alternatively, you could create a list integrating the vocabulary from both the *Listening and Speaking* and *Reading and Writing* strands. See the Word List for each unit at the end of the *Teacher's Manual*. Have students check (✔) each word and expression as they use it.

 Go to www.mynorthstarlab.com for *Notetaking* and *Academic Skills Practice*.

3 FOCUS ON SPEAKING

A VOCABULARY

◀ SKILLS

Review vocabulary from Listenings One and Two; identify and use different word forms; use vocabulary in free discussions.

✪ REVIEW
Suggested Time: 15 minutes

 Go to www.mynorthstarlab.com for *Review*.

1. Focus the class' attention on the word forms chart. Elicit from the class some common word endings for nouns (*-ance, -ion, -ness, -ment, -y*), for verbs (*-ize*), and adjectives (*-ant/-ent, -ed, -ive, -able, -al, -ic*). Alternatively, write the word endings on the board first and ask students to say what part of speech they signal. If students guess incorrectly, write one or two examples from the chart on the board and help them self-correct. Remind students that of course not all nouns, verbs, and adjectives use these endings, but they are one more clue that students can use to help determine the part of speech of an unfamiliar word.

2. Have students work with a partner to complete the chart. Let students use dictionaries if available.

3. Go over the answers with the class, checking pronunciation and spelling. Where there are two different noun or adjective forms for one word, make sure students know what the difference between the two terms is (e.g., *government* is a system; *governance* is a method).

✪✪ EXPAND
Suggested Time: 15 minutes

1. As a class, read through the list of vocabulary. Correct pronunciation as necessary. Go over the meanings of the expressions before students work on completing the interview. Point out that some of the expressions (*peppy, scare the heck out of*) are informal, and that some are used in a metaphorical sense (*sharp = intelligent; clean = simple; huge = popular*).

2. Before students begin completing the interview, remind them to change verbs to agree with person and time as necessary.

3. Go over the answers with the class, making sure each student has the correct answer written down.

4. Have students practice the conversation in pairs. If time permits, have both students practice each role.

Expansion/Homework

(1) This exercise can also be assigned as homework. Then use class time to check answers and correct pronunciation. (2) Videotape or record pairs of students reading the conversation. Then play the audio back to them so that they can monitor their own pronunciation and intonation. Let students re-record the interview if they are not satisfied the first time. (3) Using the pronunciation skills they learned in Unit 3, students could silently read through the completed conversation and mark the thought groups before they read their roles aloud. (4) To give further practice of the vocabulary in this unit, assign students to write a paragraph using as many of the expressions as possible. For fun, they could imagine a letter to Lagatree or Trump, and write it in groups or as a class.

VOCABULARY EXPANSION: Words in Context

Remind students that some words can be figured out in the context of the interview. Provide these words: *anecdote, off guard, transcendent, sense*. Then provide the audioscript or the portions of the script where these words are used. Have students work with a partner to locate the words, sentences, or paragraph that give them the clues to help them understand the word.

✪ CREATE
Suggested Time: 15 minutes

1. Call on two volunteers to read the example aloud. Point out that there is no "correct" way to answer the question, and that the point of the exercise is to use the vocabulary words to talk about the unit topic. Therefore students do not need to worry about giving true information, but rather can use their imaginations to answer.

2. Tell students to take some time to think of ideas and plan their answers before they begin speaking. Encourage students to make eye contact with each other as they speak.

3. If time permits, have students change partners and repeat the exercise, switching roles.

Expansion/Homework

Less proficient students could work together to plan Student B's answers before they practice asking and answering the questions. Have them repeat each question and answer a few times until they feel comfortable and fluent.

Go to www.mynorthstarlab.com for additional *Vocabulary* practice.

Go to www.mynorthstarlab.com for *Grammar Chart* and *Exercise 2.*

❨ SKILLS

Understand and practice the use of connectors in spoken discourse to provide cohesion.

Suggested Time: 25–30 minutes

1. Have students read the title of the section. Explain that *discourse* here means a longer spoken passage. *Connectors* are words or phrases that link ideas. In writing, they are sometimes called *transitions.*

2. For **Exercise 1**, have students work in pairs to examine the excerpt and answer the questions. Encourage pairs to take turns reading the excerpt aloud.

3. Go over the answers with the whole class.

4. Study the grammar chart with the class.

5. Have students work alone or with a partner to fill in the story in **Exercise 2**. Circulate while students are working to answer questions and check their work. Then have students take turns reading the story aloud. Point out that the discourse markers are often emphasized in spoken English—that is, they are said more slowly, louder, and at a higher pitch. To promote the conversational tone of this exercise, remind students to make lots of eye contact and to only speak when looking up at their partner.

6. Have students change partners to practice the statements in **Exercise 3**. Remind them to emphasize the discourse markers. Less proficient students might wish to write out their additional statements.

Expansion/Homework
(1) Have students work in a small group to briefly recap the presentations they gave in Step 2: Synthesize. Have them use at least three discourse markers in their summaries. As the class listens, have them write down the connectors they hear. (2) For further practice, offer exercises from *Focus on Grammar 5,* 3rd Edition or Azar's *Understanding and Using English Grammar,* 3rd Edition. See the Grammar Book References on page 267 of the student book for specific units and chapters.

 Link to *NorthStar: Reading and Writing 5*
If students are also using the companion text, have them take turns telling Alinka's story, using discourse connectors. They can tell her story in first or third person. Have students use at least three connectors in their talks. As the class listens, have them write down the connectors they hear.

Go to www.mynorthstarlab.com for additional *Grammar* practice.

◀ **SKILLS**

Use appropriate intonation in sentence introducers; use language to emphasize a point; integrate the concepts, vocabulary, grammar, pronunciation, and function from the unit to present an argument.

✪✪ PRONUNCIATION: Intonation on Sentence Introducers

Suggested Time: 25 minutes

1. Read aloud or ask students to read the introductory passage.

2. Play the audio while students follow along in their books. If you wish, play the examples a second time and pause after each sentence. Have the class repeat the sentence in chorus, imitating the intonation and expression. If necessary, have them mark the words in each sentence that receive the greatest stress.

3. Go over the information after the examples on page 114. Ask the class if they know who Bruce Lee was (a famous Chinese martial arts practitioner and actor).

4. If you like, have students work in pairs to read the story and try to guess what verbs will be used in the story. However, do not have students write anything yet. You can list guesses on the board if you wish.

5. Play the audio while students listen with their books closed. Then repeat the audio and have students fill in the blanks as they listen.

6. Go over the answers with the whole class. Then play the audio a final time, and ask students to pay special attention to the intonation of the sentence introducers.

7. For **Exercise 3**, tell students that they might want to practice each exchange a few times to work on fluency. In lower-level classes, Student B could look at Student A's questions and think of what to say in advance, or even write out a response before practicing the exchanges.

8. If time permits, have students change partners, switch roles, and repeat the exercise.

Expansion/Homework
(**1**) If possible, have students record the exchanges in Exercise 3, and then listen to their own performances. They can listen for pronunciation and usage errors, which they can write down and then correct. (**2**) If recording is not possible, circulate around the room, listening in as students speak. Note any errors using a divided page: Usage/Pronunciation. As a class, have students correct the usage errors and mark the pronunciation words with stress marks over the stressed syllables.

✪✪ FUNCTION: Emphasizing a Point

Suggested Time: 20–25 minutes

1. Read aloud or ask students to read the introductory passage. Then have them complete **Exercise 1**.

2. Go over the chart on page 117 before students begin **Exercise 2**.

3. If time permits, have students change partners, switch roles, and repeat the exercise.

✪✪✪ PRODUCTION: Present an Argument

Suggested Time: 40–45 minutes

If you wish to assign a different speaking task than the one in this section, see page 120. The alternative speaking topics relate to the theme of the unit, but might not target the same grammar, pronunciation, or function taught in this unit.

1. Read the introductory box aloud to the class. If you wish, read the situation to the class before they break into groups.

2. Call on volunteers to read the article aloud, read it aloud yourself, or give students time to read it silently to themselves. Check comprehension by asking, *What are some unpleasant features of the university? What were some problems that professors and students had? Who is Luis Miguel Sanchez? What does he hope to do? How do the students feel about his plan? How do the professors feel? How does the government feel?*

3. If you wish, give students a few minutes to check back through the unit for vocabulary, grammar, pronunciation, and functions.

4. Divide the class into two groups. Have each group read the directions and outline its arguments, referring back to the transcripts and notes for any supporting information. Give students a time limit of 10 minutes. Circulate while students are discussing to monitor and help out.

5. You can be the meeting chairperson. Invite each group to present its position and then let them discuss the strengths and weaknesses of each other's arguments. Work toward a solution.

Expansion/Homework

(**1**) Have students write their personal opinions in a paragraph that they can submit to you for evaluation. (**2**) During the meeting, take note of the most salient usage and pronunciation errors, and comment on the content and delivery of ideas. You can then distribute these notes to the individual students. Have them return the papers to you with the usage errors corrected and the pronunciation words marked with stress marks over the stressed syllables. As a class, review the pronunciation of the most frequent errors.

✪ ALTERNATIVE SPEAKING TOPICS

These topics give students an alternative opportunity to explore and discuss issues related to the unit theme.

✪ RESEARCH TOPICS

Suggested Time: 30 minutes in class

1. Have students turn to pages 262–263. Decide whether the whole class will do the same research project or choose different ones.

2. For Topic 1, go over the list of traditional Eastern practices with the class. If you like, have students brainstorm as a class other Eastern practices that are now popular or trendy in the West. Then have students choose, either individually or with a partner, a practice they'd like to explore. Ask them to work to find a practitioner to interview. Encourage students to find contact information for more than one practitioner if possible, in case their first choice is not available.

3. Have students brainstorm and then write down their questions. Encourage them to think of follow-up questions and discussion topics, too.

4. Have students conduct the interview. They can take notes, or they can record the interview, as long as they have the permission of the person being interviewed.

5. Have students present their reports to the whole class. Encourage the class to notice similarities and differences among the different practices. What are the similarities to and differences from feng shui?

6. For Topic 2, if possible, bring copies or examples of advertising for feng shui cosmetics to class to help students visualize the topic. Explain that students can search for any kind of application of feng shui that seems interesting or unusual, and that they need not limit themselves to cosmetics. Then have students do their research. If necessary, help them brainstorm search terms and key words in advance. Have them take notes—not directly copy information—about what they find. Encourage them to bring pictures to class for their presentations if possible.

7. Have students present their reports to the whole class. Encourage the class to notice similarities and differences among the different products and marketing approaches. If you like, have the class vote on the most/least useful and unusual products, or rate each product from 1–5 for usefulness or innovation.

Go to www.mynorthstarlab.com for *Student Speaking Models, Integrated Task, Video Activity, Internet Activity,* and *Unit 5 Achievement Test.*

UNIT
6
Spiritual Renewal

OVERVIEW

Theme: Religion
This unit explores the appeal and work of monasteries in contemporary society and examines methods of spiritual renewal and fulfillment from different religions.

Listening One: *The Religious Tradition of Fasting* is a radio interview with four professors who talk about the role and purpose of fasting in different world religions.

Listening Two: *Describing Monastic Life* is a radio interview with William Claassen about his experiences exploring monasteries around the world.

Critical Thinking

Separate fact from myth
Infer word meaning from context
Analyze and discuss different opinions

Recognize similarities and differences among various religions
Understand the importance and value of religious rituals

Listening

Make predictions
Listen for main ideas
Listen for details

Make inferences about a speaker's intention
Organize and synthesize information from the listenings

Speaking

Discuss background knowledge and personal beliefs
Role-play scripted and semi-scripted conversations

Tell and encourage others to tell an anecdote
Role-play a group discussion

Vocabulary	Grammar
Use context clues to infer meaning Identify and use word forms Identify and use idiomatic expressions	Count and non-count nouns and their quantifiers
	Pronunciation
	Vowel alternation

 MyNorthStarLab
Readiness Check, Background and Vocabulary, Listenings One and Two, Notetaking and Academic Skills Practice, Vocabulary and Grammar, Achievement Test

 NorthStar: Reading and Writing 5
Unit 6 deals with the role of faith and a definition of religion.

 ①FOCUS ON THE TOPIC

❮ SKILLS

Separate truth from myth; predict content; preview vocabulary; infer the meaning of new vocabulary from context.

✪✪✪ A PREDICT

Suggested Time: 5 minutes

1. Ask students to read the title of the unit. Ask, *What does spiritual mean?* Elicit or explain that it can refer both to religious practices and to non-religious ways of examining profound issues such as the meaning of life, death, and love. Make sure students understand *renewal* as it is used here (refreshing or giving new life to something or someone that is tired or worn out).

2. Have students work in groups or as a whole class to look at the photo and discuss the questions. If necessary, give a brief definition of what a monastery is (a special residence for members of a particular religion). However, students will learn more about monasteries in Section B.

3. If students worked in groups, have them report their ideas to the class. At this point, do not say whether information they have guessed about monasteries is correct or not.

Expansion/Homework

Write students' guesses about monasteries on the board. After the class finishes checking their guesses to the *Fact or Myth?* quiz in Section B, check back to see if students identified any of the same facts or myths.

✪✪ B SHARE INFORMATION

Suggested Time: 15–20 minutes

1. Read or call on a volunteer to read the introductory information. Answer any vocabulary questions.

2. Have students complete the quiz on their own, and then compare answers with a classmate's. Give pairs time to discuss their answers before having the class check the answers.

3. Follow up with the class by asking students to show by raising their hands how many facts and myths they were able to correctly identify. Then ask, *Did any information surprise you?*

Expansion/Homework

(1) For lower-proficiency students, pre-teach or assign for homework some of the vocabulary used in the introduction and quiz: *ritual, retreat, withdraw, mainstream, transcend, hermit, harmony, communal, introverted, devote*. (2) You can convert this into a listening/speaking exercise. Read the statements orally. Have the class discuss whether they are fact or myth. If students are unable to decide, read aloud the information on pages 257–258 of the student book (omitting the answer) and have them decide.

✸✸✸ C BACKGROUND AND VOCABULARY

📁 Go to www.mynorthstarlab.com for *Background and Vocabulary.*

Suggested Time: 25 minutes

1. Have students read the blog entries and match the boldfaced words with their definitions on page 126. Remind them to use context and parts of speech as clues.

2. Go over the answers as a class, with students reading them aloud so you can correct pronunciation.

Expansion/Homework

(1) Students could also read the blog and complete the vocabulary exercise as homework. Then use class time to check answers and pronunciation. If time permits, have students listen to the text in class afterwards. (2) To help students memorize vocabulary, have them work in pairs to quiz each other on the definitions: one is the teacher; the other is the student. Then they switch roles. (3) To check comprehension, have students work in pairs. Student A closes the book. Student B makes statements about information in the book, and Student A says whether they are true or false. After every three statements, they switch roles.

📁 Go to www.mynorthstarlab.com for additional *Background and Vocabulary* practice.

FOCUS ON LISTENING

SKILLS

Predict; understand main ideas and details; make inferences; express opinions.

✪✪✪ Ⓐ LISTENING ONE: The Religious Tradition of Fasting

📁 Go to www.mynorthstarlab.com to listen to *The Religious Tradition of Fasting.*

Suggested Time: 10 minutes

Listening One is a radio interview with four professors who talk about the religious practice of fasting.

1. Read the introduction aloud or have students read it silently. Then have students work in pairs to write their predictions. If you like, call on volunteers to share their predictions and write them on the board.

2. Play the first part of the interview and have students check their predictions.

LISTENING STRATEGY: Creating Questions

Remind students that creating questions is a good listening or reading strategy which they can use successfully in all of their classes. Have students use the title, *The Religious Tradition of Fasting,* to develop questions to guide their listening. Students might begin with *wh-* questions and add others as they think of them. Have them think of opposites like good/bad, positive/negative, easy/difficult, advantages/ disadvantages as they create questions (for example, *What is fasting? Is fasting good/bad? Is fasting easy? Is it difficult? Are there advantages to fasting?*). Suggest that students list questions in a two-column chart leaving the right column to write answers as they listen.

✪✪✪ LISTEN FOR MAIN IDEAS   Suggested Time: 10 minutes

Read or give students time to read the instructions and exercise. Explain any unfamiliar vocabulary or let students check their dictionaries. If necessary, explain that Episcopalians and Mormons are Christian. Play the interview while students complete the exercise. Review students' answers as a class. If there is disagreement, have students listen to the interview again.

Expansion/Homework
If necessary, explain the different word forms to talk about the religions: *Name of the religion*: Christianity, Islam, Judaism, Mormonism, the Episcopal Church; *Name of someone who follows the religion*: Christian, Muslim, Jew, Mormon, Episcopalian; *Adjective:* Christian, Islamic, Jewish, Mormon, Episcopalian or Episcopal.

- **Less Proficient:** To help students identify the various ideas on the subject, have them listen once to identify each speaker and his/her name in a chart with horizontal or vertical columns. Students can add speaker's information during a second or third listening.

- **More Proficient:** As students listen to identify the speakers, ask them also to write one or two words that will help them to connect the ideas and the speaker. They can expand on this in a second listening.

✪✪✪ LISTEN FOR DETAILS   Suggested Time: 10 minutes

1. First have students read the statements, writing in answers they already know.

2. Play the interview again. If disagreements arise after students have compared their answers with a partner's, replay the interview rather than giving the answer.

Expansion/Homework
Have students reread the vocabulary on page 125. Play the interview again, and have students raise their hands when they hear the vocabulary.

✪✪✪ MAKE INFERENCES   Suggested Time: 10–15 minutes

1. Give students time to read the exercise before you play the excerpts. Answer any vocabulary or comprehension questions. Because the excerpts are not linked, you can check answers after each one.

2. Play each excerpt and have students discuss their answers with a classmate. Encourage them to explain how they made their choices.

3. Go over the answers with the whole class. Replay the excerpts if necessary. You may wish to let students check the audioscript in the back of the student book and discuss the meaning of the excerpts.

✪✪✪ EXPRESS OPINIONS   Suggested Time: 15 minutes

1. Before students begin work in groups to discuss the opinion, tell them that it is not necessary for the groups to reach a consensus about whether they agree or disagree with the opinions. However, even when they agree, group members should support their opinions with reasons.

2. Call on volunteers from each group to share some of their group's ideas and experiences with the whole class.

Expansion/Homework
Have students discuss the topic in small groups or as a whole class: *There are other reasons that people do not eat food for periods of time, including trying to lose weight, going on a hunger strike, or because food is simply not available. Do you think people who go without food for these reasons gain any kind of spiritual benefit? That is, does*

fasting itself bring spiritual benefits, or does the faster need to have those specific motivations and intentions?

CRITICAL THINKING

Give students the following questions for discussion in small groups before discussing as a whole class:

1. What is fasting? Support your answers with evidence from the text.

   Answer: Refraining from food or other material things such as smoking.

2. According to the interview, why do people fast?

   Answers will vary, but the following responses are included in the interviews: to increase spirituality and come closer to the divine, to sharpen the heart's capacities, to foster humility and gratitude, to replenish the soul.

3. Have you or would you participate in fasting? Explain.

   Answers will vary, but students should support their responses with explanations or reasons.

4. What do you think Dr. Ahmed means when he talks about spiritual exhaustion?

   Answers will vary, but students should support their responses with information from the text and from their own experience and knowledge.

✪✪✪ B LISTENING TWO: Describing Monastic Life

Go to www.mynorthstarlab.com to listen to *Describing Monastic Life*.

Suggested Time: 10–15 minutes

Listening Two is a radio interview with journalist William Claasen who discusses his experiences with monasteries in three countries.

1. Read the introduction aloud to the class. Give students time to read the exercise. If you like, have students work with a partner to predict the answers and mark their predictions lightly in pencil.

2. Play the interview once while students listen with their eyes closed to focus their concentration.

3. Then play the interview and have students complete the exercise.

4. Have students compare answers with a partner's, and replay the audio if necessary to resolve differences of opinion. Then go over the answers with the class.

Expansion/Homework
(1) Discuss this question as a whole class: *This interview focuses on monasteries that have had many encounters with the mainstream world. Do you think these monasteries have too much contact with the mainstream world? Why? Why not?*

What is the purpose of a monastery? (**2**) Have students work in groups to discuss how members of a monastery might view the following types of visitors:

- Those who are wishing to find a new religion
- Those who are simply tourists
- Those who disapprove of the monastery's religion
- Those who are willing to pay an admission fee

 Link to NorthStar: Reading and Writing 5
Ask students to develop a definition of *monastery* using the guidelines for developing definitions in Unit 6 of the *Reading and Writing* strand.

✦✦✦ C   INTEGRATE LISTENINGS ONE AND TWO

◖ SKILLS

Organize, compare, and synthesize information from two audio segments; apply the information and ideas to other areas.

STEP 1: Organize   Suggested Time: 10–15 minutes

1. Have students work alone or with a partner to organize the ideas into the chart. Remind them to look back at their answers and notes from Listenings One and Two as a guide.

2. Go over the answers with the whole class.

STEP 2: Synthesize   Suggested Time: 20 minutes

1. Read the instructions aloud to the class. Have students work individually to prepare their mini-lectures. Allow them to make short notes if they wish (ideally written on note cards and not a full sheet of paper).

2. Have students practice their presentations out loud, quietly to themselves. Have them time themselves if possible.

3. Have groups present their ideas to the class. Let other class members ask questions.

Expansion/Homework
(**1**) Write the vocabulary from page 125 on the board while students are making notes for their mini-lectures. Ask students to try to use the words and expressions as they talk. If students are using the companion text, *NorthStar: Reading and Writing 5*, you may also want to include vocabulary from that unit's section 1C on the board. Alternatively, you could create a list integrating the vocabulary from both the *Listening and Speaking* and *Reading and Writing* strands. See the Word List for each unit at the end of the *Teacher's Manual.* (**2**) If possible, record or make a video of the mini-lectures. Play them back to the class, and ask students to write and submit to you a paragraph briefly describing what they feel they did well and what they wish to work on. If you like, allow students to re-record their mini-lectures if

they were not satisfied with their first performance. (**3**) Encourage students to follow this topic in the news or online. Have them bring to class any articles in which they find mention of monasteries or fasting.

 Link to *NorthStar: Reading and Writing 5*
Ask students to compare the notions on spiritual renewal in this unit and the definition of religion in the companion Unit 6. Ask: *Do these spiritual practices constitute a religion according to the definition you read? Is there a difference between religious practice and spiritual practice?*

Go to www.mynorthstarlab.com for *Notetaking* and *Academic Skills Practice*.

③ FOCUS ON SPEAKING

Ⓐ VOCABULARY

◀ SKILLS

Review vocabulary from Listenings One and Two; infer meaning of words from context; use vocabulary in semi-scripted questions and answers.

✪ REVIEW   **Suggested Time: 15 minutes**

Go to www.mynorthstarlab.com for *Review*.

1. Read aloud or have students read silently the information about Thomas Merton and the interview by Kenji Masaaki.

2. Have students work with a partner to read through the interview together. Have them read the complete interview, and then go back to figure out the meaning of the words. Remind them to use clues from the context and parts of speech.

3. Go over the answers with the class, checking pronunciation.

4. Call on pairs of students to read the interview aloud to the class again. Switch pairs after every few lines to give several students a chance to speak. Encourage students to read with expression.

Expansion/Homework
(**1**) Ask each student to choose three other words or expressions from the interview that are unfamiliar and check their meaning with you or in a dictionary. Then have students work in groups of 4–5 to teach the additional vocabulary. (**2**) If class time is limited, you may want to assign this exercise as homework, using class time to check answers and work on pronunciation.

Link to *NorthStar: Reading and Writing 5*

Ask students to imagine what the Dalai Lama and Thomas Merton discussed in their historical encounter in 1968. Ask: *What did these two men have in common?* As a follow-up, students could research the encounter online or in a library and report back to the class what they learned.

⊙⊙ EXPAND
Suggested Time: 15 minutes

1. Read the introduction aloud to the class. Ask students how many of them read or listen to blogs online and what the subjects of the blogs are.

2. Give students time to read the list of boldfaced expressions and the possible synonyms. Then have students follow along in their books as they listen to the blogs.

3. Have students work in pairs or alone to do the vocabulary exercise. Then go over answers with the whole class. If you wish, play the blogs one more time.

Expansion/Homework

Have students work alone to write their own blogs (about any subject). Ask them to use at least four of the target words or expressions. They can write their blogs and then turn them in to you or read them aloud to a group or to the whole class.

VOCABULARY EXPANSION: Words with Multiple Meanings

Remind students that many words in English have several meanings and the context of the sentence will help them to determine which meaning to choose. To explore multiple-meaning words in this unit, provide dictionaries and these words from the vocabulary: *back, divine, fast, foster, over time, royalties, trace,* and *will.* First, have students work in small groups to locate the various meanings for each word. Then assign colors or numbers to each student to reorganize groups (for example, all reds or all ones). After new group members have shared their information, ask students to have each new group select a word to display on poster board with multiple-word meanings and drawings to illustrate.

⊙ CREATE
Suggested Time: 15–20 minutes

1. Read the instructions to the class. Read the expressions for hesitation, slightly exaggerating a slow, thoughtful tone.

2. Call on two volunteers to model the example exchange.

3. Pair students of a similar fluency level, if possible, and have them ask and respond to the questions. Remind students to use a different expression for hesitation each time and to use them with expression.

4. If time permits, have students change partners and repeat the exercise, switching roles.

 Go to www.mynorthstarlab.com for additional *Vocabulary* practice.

📁 Go to www.mynorthstarlab.com for *Grammar Chart* and *Exercise 2*.

◖ SKILLS

Use quantifiers with count and non-count nouns.

Suggested Time: 35–40 minutes

1. Have students (of different fluency levels, if possible) work in pairs to examine the sentences in **Exercise 1** and respond to the two prompts that follow. Read or give students time to read the grammar chart. Point out to students that the logic that separates count and non-count nouns is not always easy to see, and certain nouns will just have to be memorized. When students learn a new noun, it is useful to check with a dictionary or native speaker to see if it is count or non-count. Remind students that the presence of a plural *-s* or other plural form is always an indication of a count noun.

2. For **Exercise 2** students can either fill in the answers individually and then check with a partner, or do each item together. Check answers to Exercise 2 with the whole class. Call on volunteers to give a sentence using each word with one of the quantifiers in the chart.

3. Have students do **Exercise 3** in pairs. Check answers by calling on volunteers to read the sentences aloud and say whether the nouns are count or non-count. Point out how the plural indicates the presence of a count noun.

4. Have students change partners to do **Exercise 4**. Ask students to read the whole interview once through before filling in the blanks. Then check answers by calling on pairs of volunteers to read portions of the dialogue. Ask the class to tell which nouns are being quantified in numbers 2 (interest) and 9 (avalanches). Point out how adjectives can separate the quantifier and the noun being quantified.

Expansion/Homework
(**1**) This whole section works well for homework. Students can go over the answers in class to work on pronunciation. (**2**) Using the pronunciation skills they learned in Unit 3, students could silently read through the completed interview and mark the thought groups before they read their roles aloud. (**3**) You may want students to further review this material by choosing one topic discussed in this unit (fasting, life in monasteries, spiritual practices, Thomas Merton, Tenzin Palmo) for a short (one-minute) extemporaneous speech. The students listening can write all the count and non-count nouns they hear. Review their lists as a class. (**4**) For further practice, offer exercises from *Focus on Grammar 5,* 3rd Edition or Azar's *Understanding and Using English Grammar,* 3rd Edition. See the Grammar Book References on page 267 of the student book for specific units and chapters.

📁 Go to www.mynorthstarlab.com for additional *Grammar* practice.

❚ SKILLS

Recognize and produce different vowel sounds in pairs of related words; tell an anecdote; integrate the concepts, vocabulary, grammar, pronunciation, and function from the unit to conduct a group discussion.

✪✪ PRONUNCIATION: Vowel Alternation

Suggested Time: 25 minutes

1. Remind students that working on pronunciation will help both listening comprehension and speaking. Then read the introductory passage aloud. For **Exercises 1** and **2**, have the class repeat after you or the audio. Remind students when they speak to lengthen the amount of time it takes to say the vowel sounds in the words in the left-hand columns (e.g, the word *keep* should take longer to say than the word *kept* because the /iy/ sound is longer).

2. Have students work with a partner (from a different language backgrounds if possible) to do **Exercise 3**. Make sure they say the words out loud. Then check answers with the whole class. If students aren't familiar with the pronunciation of these words, you will need to read each set aloud as they listen and identify the vowel sound pattern.

Expansion/Homework

Some additional verbs whose vowels change sound in the past tense are *sleep, bite, hide, deal, read, rise*. Write these words on the board and have students tell you the past tense. Correct their pronunciation if necessary. Point out that for the verb *dream,* the past tense traditionally was *dreamt,* but is changing these days to the more regular *dreamed.* Ask students to keep an eye out for this word in the past tense and notice which form is used.

✪✪ FUNCTION: Telling an Anecdote

Suggested Time: 25 minutes

1. Read or ask students to read (silently or aloud) the introductory paragraph and the questions in **Exercise 1** before listening to the excerpt. Remind students that expressive intonation also helps when telling an anecdote, and ask them to pay attention to Claassen's tone of voice as he relates the anecdote.

2. Have students listen to the anecdote and take notes for their answers. Replay the audio as necessary. Then go over the answers with the whole class.

3. Read aloud or call on a volunteer to read the expressions in the box for **Exercise 2**. Brainstorm other possible phrases or expressions and write them on the board. Play the anecdote again and ask the class to raise their hands when they hear one of the expressions.

4. Read the instructions for the first two steps of **Exercise 3**. Have students work individually to plan their anecdotes. If you wish, let them make brief notes, preferably on note cards and not full sheets of paper. Remind them not to read their notes as a script.

5. Have students work in pairs to tell each other their anecdotes. Remind the listeners to show that they are interested in the story by using both body language (making eye contact, leaning forward) and verbal backchannels (*Really? Wow. Mmm-hmmm*). Listeners should take brief notes.

6. Have students work in groups or with the whole class to retell the anecdotes they heard. Students can keep tallies of the number of times they hear *would*, or you or a volunteer can mark them on the board as students speak.

Expansion/Homework
(**1**) If possible, have students record these anecdotes and then listen to hear their own performance. They can listen for pronunciation and usage errors, which they may then correct, and also for use of the target expressions. (**2**) For a written assignment, students can write their anecdotes. In informal writing, the use of *would* is common. The expressions for "telling the story," however, are more spoken than written. Especially if you recorded the oral anecdotes, have the class compare differences between the written and spoken versions.

✪✪✪ PRODUCTION: Group Discussion

Suggested Time: 50 minutes

If you wish to assign a different speaking task that the one in this section, see page 145. The alternative speaking topics relate to the theme of the unit, but may not target the same grammar, pronunciation, or function taught in the unit.

1. Have students take turns reading the introductory information about Mepkin Abbey, or give the class time to read the information silently. If possible, show the students where the state of South Carolina is on a map before they begin reading.

2. To check comprehension, ask: *What is the monks' schedule? What shape was Mepkin in when the abbot arrived? How did the abbot revitalize Mepkin? What is the new proposal? Who supports the new proposal? Why? Who is against the new proposal? Why?*

3. Give students time to check back through the unit to remind themselves of the vocabulary, grammar, and punctuation they studied.

4. Have the class divide into two groups. Have members of each group take on roles specific to the case (monks, abbot, neighbors, visitors, the elderly, business owners, farmers). Have students develop their arguments and identify the pros and cons. Circulate while students are working to help out.

5. Then have the class conduct a debate. You could be moderator to ensure each side gets equal time in presenting and rebutting arguments.

Expansion/Homework

(1) During the debate, take note of the most salient usage and pronunciation errors, and comment on the content and delivery of ideas. You can then distribute these notes to the individual students. Have them return the papers to you with the usage errors corrected and the pronunciation words marked with stress marks over the stressed syllables. As a class, review the pronunciation of the most frequent errors. (2) For homework, students could write an opinion on the Mepkin case from the point of view of one of the characters and either submit it to you in writing or record it for you.

✪ ALTERNATIVE SPEAKING TOPICS

These topics give students an alternative opportunity to explore and discuss issues related to the unit theme.

✪ RESEARCH TOPICS

Suggested Time: 30 minutes in class

1. Have students turn to page 263. Decide whether the whole class will do the same research project or choose different ones.

2. For Topic 1, have students work with a partner to choose a topic from the box to research. If you like, have the class brainstorm additional topics and write them on the board.

3. Have students prepare their presentations outside of class as homework. Ask students to relate the presentation to material covered in class if possible.

4. Have students present their reports to the whole class. Encourage the audience to ask follow-up questions.

5. For Topic 2, have students work with a partner to research a spiritual retreat center or monastery in the area. Suggest that students use the Internet or a phone book to find the place. Have students brainstorm a list of questions to ask.

6. Have students conduct their research and prepare a presentation. In class, have students present their findings.

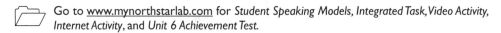 Go to www.mynorthstarlab.com for *Student Speaking Models, Integrated Task, Video Activity, Internet Activity*, and *Unit 6 Achievement Test.*

UNIT 7

Workplace Privacy

Theme: Business
This unit explores the issue of workplace privacy and the surveillance of employees by their employers.

Listening One: *Interview on Workplace Surveillance* is a radio interview with various experts about surveillance of employees.

Listening Two: *Managers and Employees Speak Out* is a radio broadcast in which managers and employees give different views on workplace surveillance.

Critical Thinking

Interpret a cartoon
Analyze editorial blogs and individual responses
Infer word meaning from context

Analyze and discuss different opinions
Frame arguments
Debate ideas and cases

Listening

Make predictions
Listen for main ideas
Listen for details
Make inferences based on tone and word choice

Organize and synthesize information from the listenings
Relate information in the listenings to one's viewpoints

Speaking

Use and check understanding of new words and expressions
Agree and disagree with opinions
Role-play scripted and semi-scripted conversations

Frame oral arguments
Conduct a debate on a case related to workplace privacy

Vocabulary

Use context clues to infer meaning
Identify and use synonyms
Identify and use idiomatic expressions

Grammar

Verb + gerund or infinitive—two forms, two meanings

Pronunciation

Stress on two-syllable words

 MyNorthStarLab
Readiness Check, Background and Vocabulary, Listenings One and Two, Notetaking and Academic Skills Practice, Vocabulary and Grammar, Achievement Test

 NorthStar: Reading and Writing 5
Unit 7 examines how a company's size and values influence corporate culture.

①FOCUS ON THE TOPIC

◖ SKILLS

Share opinions; predict content; preview vocabulary; infer the meaning of new vocabulary from context.

✪✪✪ Ⓐ PREDICT

Suggested Time: 10 minutes

1. Ask students to read the title and the cartoon and discuss the questions with a neighboring classmate or small group. Ask students to guess the meanings of *civil liberties* and *security* without checking their dictionaries. Then allow students two minutes to write down individually their associations with the word *privacy*.

2. Call on volunteers to share their ideas, and offer correct definitions if necessary. List the brainstormed topics and words on the board. Encourage students to give an example sentence with each word so that you can check for comprehension and usage.

✪✪ Ⓑ SHARE INFORMATION

Suggested Time: 15–20 minutes

1. Have students of varied cultural backgrounds, if possible, form the small groups to discuss the questions. Circulate while students are discussing to help out with vocabulary.

2. Call on volunteers from each group to share with the class any interesting insights from their group discussions.

Expansion/Homework
Have students design a short survey on privacy, beginning with the three situations in number 3 and adding at least three more of their own. Have students collect answers to the survey from friends, family, and acquaintances and report their answers back to the class. See if any generalizations can be drawn about how different cultures, genders, or age groups consider privacy.

Go to www.mynorthstarlab.com for *Background and Vocabulary*.

Suggested Time: 25 minutes

1. Read the introduction to the class. Ask the class, *Why do you think someone would keep a blog about workplace privacy? What kind of people would read and respond to such a blog?*

2. Ask students to follow along in their books while they listen to the blog and the responses. Point out that the boldfaced words and expressions are target vocabulary for the unit and the upcoming listening tasks.

3. Have students work with a partner to complete the vocabulary exercise. Remind students to reread the context sentence in the blog and responses, as well as the previous and subsequent sentences, for clues. Then go over the answers as a class. Make sure students know how to pronounce each word.

4. Check comprehension by asking, *What do most employees object to? How do most employers respond? Are the laws that protect workplace privacy generally weak or strong? What is the situation like in the other countries mentioned? Which of the people who responded to the blog agreed with the author's opinions? Which disagreed?*

Expansion/Homework

(**1**) Students could also read the blog and comments and complete the vocabulary exercise as homework. Then use class time to check answers and pronunciation. If time permits, have students listen to the blog and comments in class afterwards. (**2**) Have students work alone or with a partner to write responses agreeing or disagreeing with the blog and giving examples (you may wish to let them invent information to make their answers more creative), using at least three of the target words and expressions in their answers. (**3**) To help students memorize vocabulary, have them work in pairs to quiz each other on the definitions of the target vocabulary: one is the teacher; the other is the student. Then they switch roles.

Go to www.mynorthstarlab.com for additional *Background and Vocabulary* practice.

②FOCUS ON LISTENING

 SKILLS

Predict; understand main ideas and details; make inferences; express opinions.

❊❊❊ Ⓐ LISTENING ONE: Interview on Workplace Surveillance

📁 Go to www.mynorthstarlab.com to listen to *Interview on Workplace Surveillance*.

Suggested Time: 5 minutes

Listening One is a radio interview in which a reporter speaks to attorneys and experts in management about the prevalence and the purpose of workplace surveillance.

1. Read the title of Listening One and the introductory paragraph. Make sure that students know what *surveillance* means. To encourage use of the vocabulary learned in Section 1C, write the words on the board for students' reference.

2. Before students write their predictions, remind them that it's OK if their predictions are not correct. If you like, call on volunteers to share their predictions and write them on the board.

LISTENING STRATEGY: Point of View

Remind students that identifying points of view can help guide their understanding. For example, if we can identify a supportive point of view, we can anticipate the positive direction of comments to come. If we identify a point of view that is likely to oppose, we can anticipate the direction of their comments. Have students listen for different points of view presented in the interviews. Initially, as students listen to get the gist of the report, ask them to simply note the number of different perspectives. Then, during a second listening, ask students to begin to identify the different points of view, specifically focusing on who, what, and why. Then in a third listening, they can begin to evaluate the speakers' points.

REACHING ALL STUDENTS: Listening One

- **Less Proficient:** Have students create a three-column chart to list pros and cons for workplace surveillance before listening to the interview. As they hear items on their list, they can note the name and position/organization of the person who mentioned them in the third column.

- **More Proficient:** After students list pros and cons for workplace surveillance, ask them to provide a reason to support each position on their list.

✪✪✪ LISTEN FOR MAIN IDEAS

1. Read or give students time to read the instructions and exercise. Then play Part One of the audio. Have students compare their answers with a partner's. Play the audio a second time if necessary.

2. Check answers with the whole class and then repeat the procedure for Parts Two and Three.

Expansion/Homework
(1) To challenge more advanced students, convert Listening One into a notetaking activity. With books closed, have students take notes using a divided page: Main Ideas/Details. Then have students pair up with a neighboring classmate to compare notes. When finished, students can open their books and answer the questions.
(2) To test general comprehension, have students summarize each part in their own words. They may refer to their notes if necessary.

✪✪✪ LISTEN FOR DETAILS

1. Have students read the statements, marking answers they already know in pencil.

2. Play the interview again. Have students complete their responses and then compare their answers with a partner's. If disagreements arise, replay the interview rather than giving the answer. In some cases, students may even want to listen a third time. This is a particularly challenging text.

3. Go over the answers with the whole class. Students may have corrected false statements in more than one way; accept any reasonable corrections.

Expansion
(1) Have students reread the vocabulary on pages 149–150. Play the interview again and have students raise their hands when they hear the vocabulary. (2) Ask each student to write an additional true or false statement to present to the class. (3) With lower-level classes, play the interview again and have students raise their hands when they hear the answer to one of the questions. If necessary, students can check the audioscript in the back of the student book. However, if students read the script, afterwards have them listen one final time with their books closed.

✪✪✪ MAKE INFERENCES

1. Explain that making inferences involves drawing conclusions about what we hear from indirect information—for example, vocabulary choice and tone of voice. Because inferences depend on the listener as well as the speaker, opinions may vary. Reassure students that it's all right for them to disagree, as long as they can support their opinions.

2. Give students time to read the exercise before you play the excerpts. Because the excerpts are not linked, you can check answers after each one.

3. Play each excerpt and have students discuss their answers. Replay the excerpts as necessary. Then go over the answers with the whole class. Accept any reasonable answers that students can defend.

Expansion/Homework
If the class had a difficult time, let them check the audioscript in the back of the book and circle the word choices that support the answers. Play the excerpts again and have students underline words or phrases that were said with an emphatic or particularly expressive tone of voice. Then play the excerpts once more and have students listen with their books closed.

✪✪✪ EXPRESS OPINIONS   Suggested Time: 15–20 minutes

1. Read the instructions aloud to the class. Before students begin working in groups, make sure they understand that they need to support their answers with reasons. If they wish to say *It depends*, they must say what their answer depends on. Remind students that they can use examples as their reasons.

2. Call on volunteers to share their views with the whole class.

Expansion/Homework
(1) Have students work in pairs. Tell students that they will think of arguments that could be used to agree or disagree with the statements even if they do not personally believe those arguments. First, Student A will agree with the first sentence and Student B will disagree, then Student B will agree with the second sentence and Student A will disagree, and so on. (2) As homework, students could write one reason in favor and one reason not in favor of each position. Have students share their reasons with the whole class, and discuss which reasons are the most convincing for each side. (3) Have students consider the issue of a government's need to maintain national security and the rights of citizens concerned about their right to privacy. In pairs or small groups, have students create a similar exercise that expresses opinions about a government's right to monitor its citizens. Then have two pairs or groups join and discuss each other's statements. You may wish to bring in current articles discussing this issue in the United States.

CRITICAL THINKING

Give students the following questions for discussion in small groups before discussing as a whole class:

1. What are some examples of workplace surveillance?

   Answers will vary. Students can answer from the text, their experience, and their prior knowledge.

2. What is your opinion of this kind of surveillance?

   Answers will vary, but students should provide reasons for their opinions.

3. If you were an employer, would you monitor your workers? Give reasons to support your choice.

   Answers will vary, but they should be supported with reasons from the text and students' experience and knowledge.

4. Would you work for an employer who monitored your phone conversations? Your e-mail? Your activities at work? Give reasons to support your choices.

   Answers will vary, but they should be supported with clear reasons.

Go to www.mynorthstarlab.com to listen to *Managers and Employees Speak Out.*

Suggested Time: 20 minutes

Listening Two is a radio broadcast in which two managers and two employees give present differing views on workplace surveillance.

1. Tell the class that they will hear two managers and two employees give their views on workplace surveillance. Ask, *What do you think the employees will say? What do you think the managers will say?* If you like, write the predictions on the board.

2. Give students time to look over the chart. Point out that *position* here means *role in the workplace.* Then play the audio and have students complete the chart. They will not need to write in the last column. Pause after each speaker to give students time to write.

3. Have students compare their answers with a partner's, and replay the audio if necessary to resolve differences of opinion. Then go over the answers with the class.

4. Have students of different cultural and work backgrounds, if possible, form the small groups to discuss the questions in the final column. Call on volunteers to summarize their group's ideas.

Link to *NorthStar: Reading and Writing 5*
Ask, *How do you think Howard Schultz or a manager from Wal-Mart would feel about workplace privacy?* Ask students to write a paragraph statement from the perspective of one of these business people.

✪✪✪ **C** INTEGRATE LISTENINGS ONE AND TWO

◀ **SKILLS**

Organize, compare, and synthesize information from two audio segments; apply the information and ideas to other areas.

STEP 1: Organize   **Suggested Time: 15 minutes**

1. Read or give students time to read the introductory summary. Make sure students understand the meaning of *a fine line* (a very small difference; one side can arguably be confused with the other side).

2. Have students work alone or with a partner to organize the ideas into the chart and go over answers with the entire class. If you wish, let students suggest pros and cons that were not mentioned in the listenings as additional material for their discussion.

1. Read the instructions aloud to the class, and then have students form their groups of three. Encourage students to give reasons or justifications for their policies. If you wish, write phrases on the board for this, such as: *We decided to (. . .) in order to (. . .). We chose to (. . .) because (. . .).* Have one person in each group take notes from which the group can speak. Set a time limit (10 or 15 minutes) for the task.

2. Have groups in turn present their policies to the class. Let class members ask questions if they wish.

3. As a whole class, discuss similarities and differences among the policies.

Expansion/Homework
(**1**) Have students, alone or in pairs, interview members of the community about the privacy policies where they work and report their findings back to the class. (**2**) Have students investigate the privacy policies of the school where they are studying. For example, does the administration have the right to read student e-mails? Have students discuss their findings in class, and write one paragraph explaining the policy and another paragraph giving their reaction to it. (**3**) Encourage your students to follow this topic in the news or online. Have them bring to class any articles in which they find mention of workplace privacy and employee surveillance.

    Go to www.mynorthstarlab.com for *Notetaking* and *Academic Skills Practice.*

FOCUS ON SPEAKING

Ⓐ VOCABULARY

◖ SKILLS

Review vocabulary from Listenings One and Two; identify synonyms; infer meaning of words and expressions from context; use vocabulary in a role play.

✪ REVIEW   **Suggested Time: 15 minutes**

1. Read the instructions and complete the first item together with the whole class as an example. As students work in groups of three to complete the exercise, let them use dictionaries if available.

2. Go over the answers with the class, checking pronunciation and understanding of the similarities and differences among the synonyms.

Expansion/Homework
You may want to assign the exercise as homework and then use class time to check answers and correct pronunciation.

⦿⦿ EXPAND

 Go to www.mynorthstarlab.com for *Expand*.

1. Read the introduction and go over the vocabulary in the box with the class. If necessary, give example sentences with the words and expressions to help explain them. Some idiomatic expressions may not be in students' dictionaries.

2. Have students work with a partner to complete the exercise. Remind the class that they may need to change verb forms to agree with tense or person.

Expansion/Homework

(1) This section could be assigned as homework. If time allows, go over the answers and check pronunciation of vocabulary in class. (2) You may wish to check answers by calling on students to read several sentences at a time. Ask the class to think of the text as a radio broadcast and encourage students to read with expression. Different groups could also record themselves reading the text. Then play the recordings in class. Point out particularly expressive passages and good pronunciation.

 Link to *NorthStar: Reading and Writing 5*

Have students work in pairs to use the vocabulary in Review and Expand to write a similar newsletter article about a fictional case that could have taken place at Wal-Mart, Enron, or a similar company. Encourage students to be creative yet realistic.

VOCABULARY EXPANSION: Be the Expert

Have each student select one word from this group of ten that he/she will gain expert knowledge of: *surveillance, safeguards, eavesdropping, legitimate, scope, demeaned, dignity, driving, sinister, deter*. Students may use any resources available to learn all aspects of their word. They will need to know etymology, multiple meanings, parts of speech, differing forms of the word, prefixes/suffixes/roots, and be able to use the word accurately in conversation. Then group students who have the same word and have them compare their information before preparing a creative presentation for the class.

⦿ CREATE

1. Read the instructions to the class, and then have students work in pairs to create their dialogue. More proficient students could make notes, and less proficient students could write out the entire script. Remind students to use as much of the unit vocabulary in their script as they can, in addition to the cues provided.

2. Give pairs time to rehearse their presentations a few times. Circulate while students are working to help out. Encourage them to speak dramatically. Then have pairs present their conversations to the class.

Expansion/Homework

(1) If possible, bring in props to help set the mood; for example, a suit jacket and tie for the Nissan manager and a clipboard or a smartphone for Ms. Bourke. (2) Record students' presentations. Listen to them again as a whole class, and note the target vocabulary that was used. Students can also listen to their own role play and identify errors to correct. (3) If taping is not possible, take notes on pronunciation and usage as they perform their role plays. After commenting on the strengths of their role play, write the usage errors on the board (or overhead projector) and invite students to correct the errors. For pronunciation correction, write the words to be practiced on the board, invite the class to identify the stressed syllables, model the pronunciation, and encourage students to practice repeating each word or phrase until they are confident of their own pronunciation

Go to www.mynorthstarlab.com for additional *Vocabulary* practice.

✪✪ B GRAMMAR: Verb + Gerund or Infinitive—Two Forms, Two Meanings

Go to www.mynorthstarlab.com for *Grammar Chart* and *Exercise 2*.

◖ SKILLS

Understand the difference in meaning when certain verbs are followed by a gerund as compared to when they are followed by an infinitive.

Suggested Time: 35–40 minutes

1. Have students work with a partner to read the sentences in **Exercise 1**, or call on volunteers to read them aloud to the class. Then have students work in pairs to discuss the questions. Go over the answers with the whole class.

2. Read or give students time to read the grammar chart.

3. Have students complete **Exercise 2** in pairs. They can fill in the answers individually and then check with a partner or do each item together.

4. Go over the answers with the whole class. If mistakes were made, elicit further examples of the verbs followed both by a gerund and by an infinitive, write them on the board, and as a class discuss the differences in meaning.

5. Read the instructions for **Exercise 3** aloud. After partners have filled in the dialogue, go over the answers with the whole class.

6. Have pairs practice the conversation. Encourage them to read dramatically. If time permits, have each student practice both roles.

Expansion/Homework

(1) If class time is limited, Exercises 1 and 2 can be assigned for homework. In class, students compare answers and work on pronunciation. (2) Using the pronunciation skills they learned in Unit 3, students could silently read through Exercise 3 and mark the thought groups before they read their roles aloud.

(3) Students could further review this material by telling each other anecdotes using at least three of the underlined words in this section. Have students tell real anecdotes about work or privacy issues, or have students create fictional anecdotes. The students listening can write down all the verbs they hear from this section. Review the lists as a class. (4) For further practice, offer exercises from *Focus on Grammar 5*, 3rd Edition or *Azar's Understanding and Using English Grammar*, 3rd Edition. See the Grammar Book References on page 268 of the student book for specific units and chapters.

 Go to www.mynorthstarlab.com for additional *Grammar* practice.

C SPEAKING

◖ SKILLS

Understand and produce the stress patterns in two-syllable words; use language to frame an argument; integrate the concepts, vocabulary, grammar, pronunciation, and function from the unit to participate in a debate.

◐◑ PRONUNCIATION: Stress on Two-Syllable Words

Suggested Time: 25–30 minutes

1. Remind students that working on pronunciation will help both listening comprehension and speaking. Read the introductory statement aloud or have students read silently. Have students listen to the audio and identify the stressed syllables of the boldfaced words.

2. Model the pronunciation of the boldfaced words in **Exercise 1**. Point out that two-syllable nouns tend to receive the stress on the first syllable, whereas two-syllable verbs tend to receive the stress on the second syllable. Also point out how the stressed vowel tends to be a clear, open, and long vowel, and how the unstressed vowel tends to be reduced, closed, and short.

3. Have students (of different language backgrounds, if possible) form pairs to complete **Exercise 2**. Remind students that figuring out the part of speech will let them know where the syllable stress falls. Then play the audio for students to check their answers. If mistakes were made, play the audio again and have the class repeat the sentences in chorus.

4. Read the instructions for **Exercise 3**, and call on two volunteers to model the first example. Then have students complete the exercise in pairs. If time permits, have them switch roles, but this time ask the questions in a different order. Go over the answers with the whole class.

Expansion/Homework
(1) Some students can grasp stress better if it is accompanied with a gesture; the physical movement focuses attention on the cadence of the word. You can have

students swing their hands, shift their weight, or tap their feet or fingers to reflect the stressed syllable of a word. (2) Students can practice further by making their own statements about the theme of workplace privacy using the underlined words and reading them to a partner. As students listen, they can identify the words as nouns or verbs.

✪✪ FUNCTION: Framing an Argument

Suggested Time: 25 minutes

1. Read the title and the introductory information aloud. Make sure that students understand the use of *framing* here (introducing; highlighting). Read or call on volunteers to read the example sentences. Point out that these phrases are more common in spoken English and informal written English.

2. Give the class a few minutes to read through the information and prepare notes for reference. As they are reading, write the phrases on the board for students' reference.

3. As students work in pairs to complete the exercise, encourage them to make eye contact and use gestures to enhance the expression of opinion in these exchanges. Invite students to add their own points as they frame their arguments.

Expansion/Homework
Have each pair stand up in front of the class and deliver a dramatic exchange modeled on one of the points. Be sure they use stress, intonation, and gestures to strengthen the argument they present. Offer individual written corrections to each student.

✪✪✪ PRODUCTION: A Debate

Suggested Time: 45–50 minutes

If you wish to assign a different speaking task than the one in this section, see page 170. The alternative speaking topics relate to the theme of the unit, but may not target the same grammar, pronunciation, or function taught in the unit.

1. Read or have students to read the task and the introductory information about biometrics.

2. Have students skim back through the unit to review the vocabulary, grammar, pronunciation, and functions that they learned.

3. Call on volunteers to take turns reading paragraphs from the interview, or give the class time to read the interview silently. Answer any vocabulary questions.

4. Divide the class into the two teams. Give the teams about 10 minutes to develop their arguments. Students may write notes to speak from if they wish.

5. Have one student from each team present the opening arguments, and then have other team members present the additional arguments. Impose a time limit of about 3 minutes to present each argument. If you wish, allow students to cross-examine speakers as well, by asking them questions. Limit the question and answer exchanges to 3–5 minutes.

6. Have one student from each team summarize the team's arguments at the end.

7. During the debate, you can play the role of impartial timekeeper and protocol enforcer. Conduct a debriefing session after the debate to hear students' reactions to the case.

Expansion/Homework

(1) You may want to videotape the debate. Use it to have students appreciate and react to their work. You may want to ask for a written reaction paragraph: *How did you feel watching yourself speak English? What did you do well? What skills need work?* (2) During the debate, take notes of the most salient usage and pronunciation errors. When the debate is finished, present your notes—either for the class or for each individual student—and invite students to correct the errors. For pronunciation correction, write the words to be practiced on the board, invite the class to identify the stressed syllables, model the pronunciation, and encourage students to practice repeating each word or phrase until they are confident of their own pronunciation.

✪ ALTERNATIVE SPEAKING TOPICS

These topics give students an alternative opportunity to explore and discuss issues related to the unit theme.

✪ RESEARCH TOPICS

Suggested Time: 30 minute in class

1. Have students turn to pages 263–264. Read the scenario to the class.

2. For Step 1, have students work alone to choose people to interview. If possible, have them write down several choices in class. Encourage them to think of several possibilities in case their first choices are not available. You may choose to allow students to conduct their interviews by e-mail.

3. For Step 2, have students work with a partner to brainstorm and write down questions and discussion topics.

4. For Step 3, if you like, have students role-play asking their interview questions with a partner to work on their poise. Then have students conduct their interviews and take notes.

5. For Step 4, have students present their reports to the whole class. Encourage the class to notice similarities and differences among the different practices and policies related to workplace privacy. Which practices do they think are reasonable? Do any practices seem unreasonable?

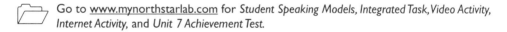 Go to www.mynorthstarlab.com for *Student Speaking Models, Integrated Task, Video Activity, Internet Activity,* and *Unit 7 Achievement Test.*

UNIT 8 Warriors without Weapons

OVERVIEW

Theme: The Military
This unit deals with the International Committee of the Red Cross (ICRC): its history, mission, services, and controversial position on wartime neutrality.

Listening One: *Warriors without Weapons* is a radio interview with Michael Ignatieff about the history and purpose of the ICRC.

Listening Two: *Michael Ignatieff's Views on War* is a continuation of the radio interview with Michael Ignatieff about how he personally responds to the mission of the ICRC.

Critical Thinking

Respond to pictures and symbols	Infer word meaning from context
Share experiences	Analyze and discuss different opinions
Gather background information	Distinguish between direct and indirect speech

Listening

Make predictions	Make inferences based on tone and word choice
Listen for main ideas	Organize and synthesize information from the
Listen for details	listenings

Speaking

Role-play a scripted conversation	Respond appropriately to complex and
Use direct and indirect speech when re-telling a	controversial questions
story	Create a public service announcement

Vocabulary

Use context clues to infer meaning
Identify and use synonyms and commonly
    confused words
Identify and use idiomatic expressions

Grammar

Direct and indirect speech

Pronunciation

Vowels

 MyNorthStarLab
Readiness Check, Background and
Vocabulary, Listenings One and Two,
Notetaking and Academic Skills Practice,
Vocabulary and Grammar, Achievement Test

 NorthStar: Reading and Writing 5
Unit 8 explores the experiences of
women in the military.

 ①FOCUS ON THE TOPIC

◀ SKILLS

Respond to pictures and symbols; share information; predict content; preview vocabulary; infer the meaning of new vocabulary from context.

✪✪✪Ⓐ PREDICT

Suggested Time: 5 minutes

1. Ask students to read the title, look at the pictures, and read the questions before forming small groups to discuss their responses. Have the groups share their ideas with the class.

2. You may choose to give some very basic information about the Geneva Conventions (*they are treaties that were signed in Geneva, Switzerland, that outline standards for international laws about humanitarian concerns in the four areas shown in the pictures*); however, let students know that they will find out more about the Geneva Conventions in the Background and Vocabulary Section.

✪✪Ⓑ SHARE INFORMATION

Suggested Time: 15 minutes

Give students time to read the information silently, or call on volunteers to read it aloud. Then have students work with a partner to check (✔) the statements. Students could also share answers in small groups. Call on volunteers to share experiences. Be careful not to press students for details of personal or sensitive information if they seem hesitant.

Expansion/Homework
(**1**) Have students interview someone outside of the classroom who has experienced one of the items and report their findings to the class. (**2**) Have students research the origins of the different symbols shown: the red cross, the red crescent, and the red crystal. When did each originate, and why? What other symbols have been used or proposed? Have students share and discuss their findings in class.

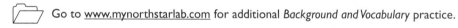

Go to www.mynorthstarlab.com for *Background and Vocabulary*.

Suggested Time: 20 minutes

1. Ask students to follow along in their books while they listen to the article. Point out that the boldfaced words and expressions are target vocabulary for the unit and the upcoming listening tasks.

2. Before partners complete the vocabulary exercise, remind students to reread the context sentence in the article, as well as the previous and subsequent sentences, for clues.

3. Go over the answers as a class. Make sure students know how to pronounce each word. Answer any additional vocabulary questions.

4. Check comprehension of the passages by calling on volunteers to paraphrase the main idea of each paragraph.

Expansion/Homework

(**1**) Students could also read the passage and complete the vocabulary exercise as homework. Then use class time to check answers and pronunciation. If time permits, have students listen to the passage in class afterwards. (**2**) Let students check comprehension by having pairs write true/false statements based on information in the passage. Then put two pairs together to quiz each other. (**3**) Have students work alone or with a partner to write new sentences with each of the vocabulary words. Call on volunteers to write their sentences on the board. Alternatively, put two pairs together to read their new sentences aloud, though without including the vocabulary word (they can say *blank* instead). The other pair guesses which vocabulary word completes the sentence. (**4**) To help students memorize vocabulary, have them work in pairs to quiz each other on the definitions in Exercise 2: one is the teacher; the other is the student. Then they switch roles. (**5**) Encourage your students to follow this topic in the news or online. Have them bring to class any articles in which they find mention of the ICRC.

Go to www.mynorthstarlab.com for additional *Background and Vocabulary* practice.

②FOCUS ON LISTENING

◖ SKILLS

Predict; understand main ideas and details; make inferences; express opinions.

Go to www.mynorthstarlab.com to listen to *Warriors without Weapons*.

Suggested Time: 10 minutes

Listening One is a radio interview, with author Michael Ignatieff who explains the history, purpose, and some of the modern roles of the International Committee of the Red Cross.

1. Read the introductory paragraph and the instructions aloud or have students read them silently. Ask the class what Ignatieff might mean by *unarmed warriors* and *warrior's honor.*

2. As students work in pairs to write their predictions, remind them that it's OK if their predictions are not correct, but that they should try to think of reasonable descriptions. If you like, call on volunteers to share their predictions and write them on the board.

3. Play the first part of the interview and have students check their predictions.

LISTENING STRATEGY: Adding Information

After a first or second listening, ask each student in the group to contribute one piece of information from what they heard. Continue in sequence until students cannot add more information. Then have students listen again, check off their information, and repeat the process. Finally, have students organize the information in complete sentences under specific headings.

✪✪✪ LISTEN FOR MAIN IDEAS   **Suggested Time: 15 minutes**

1. Read or give students time to read the instructions and exercise. Explain that they can write notes instead of complete sentences.

2. Play Parts One, Two, and Three, pausing after each part so students can complete their writing. If disagreements arise after students compared answers with a partner's, play each part again. Go over the answers with the whole class. You can check the answers after each part, or after all three parts are completed.

Expansion/Homework
Ask students to use the key phrases and their notes to orally summarize the listening.

 Link to *NorthStar: Reading and Writing 5*
Have students listen to the Part 3 again, and raise their hands when they hear words such as *his* and *men*. Ask students if they think that what Ignatieff says about men is also true about women, based on the information they learned in Reading One.

- **Less Proficient:** Have students practice notetaking by listening for words, phrases, and ideas to write as they listen. They can reconstruct information from any of those by discussing with a partner or group and then listening again for more information.

- **More Proficient:** Have students organize the information (words, phrases, ideas) as they listen by putting notes into main points and supporting reasons. These can be adjusted by discussing with a partner or group and then listening again for more information.

✪✪✪ LISTEN FOR DETAILS   Suggested Time: 10–15 minutes

1. First have students read the statements, circling the answers they already know.

2. Play the interview again. Have students complete their responses and then compare their answers with a partner's. If disagreements arise, replay the interview rather than giving the answer. Play the audio as often as necessary.

✪✪✪ MAKE INFERENCES   Suggested Time: 10 minutes

1. Explain that making inferences involves drawing conclusions about what we hear from indirect information—for example, vocabulary choice and tone of voice. In this section, then, the answers will not be given directly in the listening passages; rather, students must use context clues to figure out what the speakers intend.

2. Give students time to read the instructions and the statements before you play the excerpts. Because the excerpts are not linked, you can check answers after each one.

3. Play each excerpt. Give students time to think and write their answers. Replay the excerpts if necessary.

4. Have students share their answers and explanations in groups. Remind students that it is OK to disagree, as long as they can support their opinions.

5. Call on a volunteer from each group to summarize the group's positions. Replay the excerpts if there have been a lot of varying opinions.

✪✪✪ EXPRESS OPINIONS   Suggested Time: 15 minutes

1. Read the introductory paragraph for **Exercise 1** aloud to the class. Make sure students understand that now they are giving their own opinions, not Ignatieff's. Give students time to mark their answers. If they feel they must write "It depends," ask them to make notes on the relevant factors to prepare for their discussion.

2. Before students work in groups to discuss their opinions, tell them that it is not necessary for the groups to reach a consensus about whether they agree or disagree with the opinions. However, even when they agree, group members should support their opinions with reasons.

3. Call on a volunteer from each group to summarize the group's opinions. Ask, *Did anyone's opinion change after listening to the interview? In what ways?*

Expansion/Homework

Write the phrases for Framing Arguments from Unit 7 (page 166) on the board for students to use during their discussion.

CRITICAL THINKING

Give students the following questions for discussion in small groups before discussing as a whole class:

1. According to the interview, what is the Red Cross trying to do?

   Answer: The Red Cross is trying to make sure that "if people are going to fight [they] conduct the fighting according to certain rules."

2. What are the Geneva Conventions?

   Answer: According to the interview, the Geneva Conventions are rules pertaining to war, a document, which dates to 1864, revised in 1949, and which sets forth standards that countries agreed to follow in conducting wars. They deal with treatment of prisoners and civilians.

3. Some people believe that war itself is so uncivilized that it's absurd to try to civilize it with rules. What is your opinion?

   Answers will vary, but students should support their opinions with clear reasons based on their knowledge, experience, and the interview.

4. Imagine that you are an advanced society studying the people of the earth. What conclusions would you draw about cultures that have a document like the Geneva Conventions?

   Answers will vary, but students should be able to explain their opinions.

❀❀❀ B **LISTENING TWO: Michael Ignatieff's Views on War**

📁 Go to www.mynorthstarlab.com to listen to *Michael Ignatieff's Views on War*.

Suggested Time: 10 minutes

Listening Two is a radio interview with Michael Ignatieff who explains his personal views on war and how they have been influenced by his background and his study of the ICRC.

1. Read the introduction aloud to the class and give them time to read the statements. If you like, have students predict what the answers will be by discussing their guesses with a partner.

2. Play the interview once or twice and have students mark their answers. Have students check answers with a partner, and replay the audio if necessary to resolve differences of opinion. Then go over the answers with the class.

Expansion/Homework

Have students work in groups to discuss their own reactions to the statements in Parts Two and Four. Do they share Ignatieff's views? Why or why not?

✪✪✪ C INTEGRATE LISTENINGS ONE AND TWO

◀ SKILLS

Organize, compare, and synthesize information from two audio segments; apply the information and ideas to other areas.

STEP 1: Organize   Suggested Time: 15 minutes

1. Read or give students time to read the introductory summary. Then have students work alone or with a partner to organize the ideas into the chart.

2. Go over the answers with the entire class.

STEP 2: Synthesize   Suggested Time: 20 minutes

1. Read the instructions aloud to the class, and then have students work with a partner to prepare the address. Less proficient students can write a complete script and more proficient pairs can just make notes. Set a time limit (10 or 15 minutes) for the preparation.

2. Circulate while students are working to help out. If any pairs finish early, they can practice presenting their address.

3. Before pairs join to give feedback, remind students to make sure they listen for key points and views.

Expansion/Homework

(1) Write the vocabulary from pages 173–174 on the board while students are planning their address. Ask students to try to use the words and expressions as they talk. If students are using the companion text, *NorthStar: Reading and Writing 5*, you may also want to include vocabulary from that unit's section 1C on the board. Alternatively, you could create a list integrating the vocabulary from both the *Listening and Speaking* and *Reading and Writing* strands. See the Word List for each unit at the end of the *Teacher's Manual*. (2) If possible, record the summaries and play them back for the whole class. Listeners can compare the summaries and note down target vocabulary that was used. (3) The Gulf War soldiers sent letters home describing the "death and destruction" of war. Ask students: *What rules of war did they fear would be broken? One soldier gave an example of warrior honor. What was it?*

📁 Go to www.mynorthstarlab.com for *Notetaking* and *Academic Skills Practice*.

3 FOCUS ON SPEAKING

A VOCABULARY

◖ SKILLS

Review vocabulary from Listenings One and Two; distinguish between similar words; use vocabulary in scripted role plays.

✪ REVIEW

Suggested Time: 10–15 minutes

 Go to www.mynorthstarlab.com for *Review*.

1. Read the introductory information to the class. Ask, *Why do you think Dr. Martino wrote a letter to the newspaper? What might she hope to accomplish with her letter?* Accept any reasonable answers and write them on the board so that students can check their predictions after they read the letter.

2. Call on volunteers to read the letter aloud to the class. Go over pronunciation of the target vocabulary if necessary. If students need help with comprehension, paraphrase entire sentences or ideas instead of just offering a synonym for one word.

3. Have students work with a partner to complete the exercise. Let students use dictionaries if available.

4. Go over the answers with the class.

Expansion/Homework
You may want to assign the exercise as homework and then use class time to check answers and correct pronunciation.

 Link to NorthStar: Reading and Writing 5
Have students work alone or with a partner to write a letter to the editor from someone who believes that women should (or should not) serve in the military. Ask them to use as much of the target vocabulary as they can. Then have students share their letters with the class by reading them aloud.

✪✪ EXPAND

Suggested Time: 15 minutes

1 Read or call on a volunteer to read the sentences in **Exercise 1** aloud. Have students paraphrase them to show that they understand them. Then read the information below the sentences about confusing words.

2. Play the audio for **Exercise 1** while students follow along in their books and repeat the words. Have them circle the numbers of word pairs with the same sounds.

3. Have students work in pairs to complete **Exercise 2**. Then check the answers with the whole class.

4. Read the instructions for **Exercise 3** to the class. Call on a volunteer to model the first exchange with you; the student reads Student A and you read Student B. Make sure students realize that Student A has the correct answers. Student A should also check for correct pronunciation if necessary. When pairs have finished the first part, remind them to switch roles.

5. If time permits, have students change partners and repeat the exercise, switching roles.

Expansion/Homework

Have students work in pairs. Student A reads one of the sentences from Exercise 2, indicating which word is underlined by raising a hand or nodding. Student B, with book closed, spells the underlined word out loud or writes it down. Student A corrects if necessary. Then have students switch roles.

VOCABULARY EXPANSION: Examples and Non-Examples

Have students work in groups to list two examples and two non-examples for each vocabulary word (for example, *devastating*—examples: hurricane, tornado, divorce; non-examples: rain shower, light breeze, wedding). Then have student groups add to their lists by putting each word on the board or overhead projector and having groups add their choices. This activity may be extended by having students write a paragraph explaining the examples in a single category.

✪ CREATE

Suggested Time: 30 minutes

1. Read the instructions for **Exercise 1** to the class. Have partners work with a person with a different language background, if possible, to complete the letter. Model the first line so that students understand that Student A needs to read several words beyond the blank space for Student B to be able to identify the missing word. When they finish the first part, have the partners switch jobs.

2. Go over the answers with the whole class.

3. Have students discuss the questions in **Exercise 2** in pairs or small groups. Circulate and monitor the discussions.

Go to www.mynorthstarlab.com for additional *Vocabulary* practice.

✪✪ B GRAMMAR: Direct and Indirect Speech

Go to www.mynorthstarlab.com for *Grammar Chart* and *Exercise 1*.

◖SKILLS

Use direct quotations and indirect speech to relate a story.

Suggested Time: 35–40 minutes

1. Have the class examine the paragraph in **Exercise 1** and answer the two questions that follow. Ask students to read the grammar explanations silently or read them aloud to the class.

2. Pair students of similar fluency levels to do **Exercise 2**. Model the first sentence: *The Red Cross volunteer said hello and asked the POW how he was doing. He explained he was there to collect messages for the prisoner's family.* Point out that *POW* is read as *pee-oh-double-you*. Circulate as students are working to answer questions.

3. Check answers by reading one sentence at a time and calling on volunteers to change it to reported speech. Write the verb tense shifts on the board if necessary.

Expansion/Homework

(**1**) Students can complete Exercise 2 as written homework and then go over the answers in class. (**2**) For further practice, offer exercises from *Focus on Grammar 5,* 3rd Edition or Azar's *Understanding and Using English Grammar,* 3rd Edition. See the Grammar Book References on page 268 of the student book for specific units and chapters.

 Go to www.mynorthstarlab.com for additional *Grammar* practice.

C SPEAKING

◀ SKILLS

Distinguish among three distinct vowel sounds; respond to complex or controversial questions; integrate the concepts, vocabulary, grammar, pronunciation, and function from the unit to create and perform a public service announcement.

✪✪ PRONUNCIATION: Vowels

Suggested Time: 25–30 minutes

1. Remind students that working on pronunciation will help both listening comprehension and speaking.

2. For **Exercise 1**, play the audio or have students watch you as you model the words.

3. For **Exercise 2**, play the audio or say the words yourself. Encourage students to look at how your mouth forms each sound.

4. For **Exercise 3**, play the audio and have students circle the words they hear. If students are having trouble, say the words yourself and let students observe you carefully.

5. For **Exercise 4**, have pairs of students from different language backgrounds, if possible, listen to each other pronounce the words.

6. Model **Exercise 5** by writing the five patterns on the board and choosing several phrases for students to classify. Point out that in English the sound-symbol correspondence is not stable. For example, in the word *government* the *o* sounds like a short *u* /ə/.

7. Then have students return to their partners to pronounce the words and identify their vowel sound patterns. If students aren't familiar with the pronunciation of these words, you will need to read them aloud as they listen and identify the vowel sound pattern.

8. For **Exercise 6**, play the tongue twisters or model them for the class. Encourage students to have fun as they tackle these "vowel" twisters.

Expansion/Homework
(**1**) If students are having difficulty distinguishing the vowel sounds that they hear, say the words in Exercise 2 aloud. Say each word several times in a row before changing to the next word. Have students raise their hands when you change. For example, say *cat, cat, cat, cat, cat, cot* (students raise hands), *cot, cot, cut* (students raise hands), *cut, cut, cut, cot* (students raise hands), and so on. Then have students work in pairs to do the same thing. (**2**) You may want students to review one of the paragraphs in the Background text (Section 1C), to identify first all the vowels that sound like /æ/, then /ə/, and then /ɑ/. (**3**) If possible, bring several copies of the children's book *Fox in Socks* (Dr. Seuss), a classic book of tongue twisters, to class. Have students work in groups, taking turns to read each page aloud.

✪✪ FUNCTION: Responding to Complex or Controversial Questions

Suggested Time: 20–25 minutes

1. Read or ask students to read (silently or aloud) the introductory information, directions, and list of expressions. Call on two volunteers to read the example exchange aloud. Then read the opening and follow-up phrases aloud. Ask students to pay attention to your intonation, which should sound slow, thoughtful, and reasonable.

2. Before partners begin the exercise, give them a few minutes to read through the information and prepare notes for reference. Meanwhile, write the phrases on the board for easy reference. Encourage use of eye contact and gestures to enhance the interaction in these exchanges, and ask students to use different opening and follow-up phrases each time they respond.

Expansion/Homework
(**1**) If possible, have students record these exchanges and then listen to hear their own performance. They can listen for pronunciation and usage errors, which they may then correct. (**2**) If recording is not possible, circulate around the room listening in on the students' dialogues. Note any errors using a divided page: Usage/Pronunciation. Have students correct the usage errors and mark the pronunciation words with stress marks over the stressed syllables. Answer any student's questions. As a class you can review the pronunciation of the most frequent errors. (**3**) Review this exercise as a class. Ask individual students one of the tough questions. Encourage the student to buy time to compose a thoughtful answer.

Link to *NorthStar: Reading and Writing 5*

Have students work alone or with a partner to write complex or controversial questions based on the issues raised in the readings. Then have students read their questions aloud in class and call on a specific student to answer them. That student should then use the opening and follow-up phrases in the response.

✪✪✪ PRODUCTION: A Public Service Announcement

Suggested Time: 45–50 minutes

If you wish to assign a different speaking task than the one in this section, see page 195. The alternative speaking topics relate to the theme of the unit, but may not target the same grammar, pronunciation, or function taught in the unit.

1. Read or have students to read the introductory information about PSAs. If your class did Unit 4, remind students of the PSAs they created then.

2. Have students close their eyes as they listen to the PSA for the first time. Then have them answer the questions in **Exercise 1** with a partner.

3. Have students read the outline in **Exercise 2**, and play the PSA again. Have students complete the outline and check their answers with a partner. If necessary, replay the PSA.

4. Give students a few minutes to check back through the unit for vocabulary, grammar, pronunciation, and functions.

5. Make sure the class understands what is meant by *blood donation*, and have the class list reasons that people donate blood and reasons that blood donations are needed. Be sensitive to strong personal and/or cultural reactions to this topic. Ask if anyone in your class has donated blood before. If so, have them briefly describe the experience and explain why they donated.

6. Divide the class into small groups for **Exercise 3**. Give students a time limit of 15 or 20 minutes to create their PSA. Circulate while students are discussing to monitor and help out. Have students record their PSA if possible. If not, they will present it orally to the class.

7. Play or have groups deliver the PSAs. Have the rest of the class discuss the effectiveness of the PSA.

Expansion/Homework

(**1**) If your students will be able to incorporate sound into their PSAs, give them advance notice of this activity to allow them time to select and locate music and think about how to create sound effects. (**2**) When presenting the PSAs, have the class listen for the information outlined in this section. Encourage them to appreciate their classmates' work, giving constructive feedback on content. (**3**) As students present their PSAs, note pronunciation and usage errors. Concentrate on the target language from this unit (you may also wish to include language points from previous units). At the end of the presentations, present your notes—either for the class or for each group—and have students correct the errors. Help students work on pronunciation. (**4**) Students may be interested in finding out how to give

Warriors without Weapons 103

blood in their communities. Have them call their hospitals or the Red Cross and report their findings to the class.

 Link to *NorthStar: Reading and Writing 5*
Students could also develop a short radio advertisement to recruit women to the military, or a PSA advertising a support group or counseling service to women (or men) who have served in the military who need help coping with stress or injuries.

⊙ ALTERNATIVE SPEAKING TOPICS

These topics give students an alternative opportunity to explore and discuss issues related to the unit theme.

⊙ RESEARCH TOPICS

Suggested Time: 30 minutes in class

1. Have students turn to page 264. Have students work alone or with a partner.

2. For Step 1, have students choose a relief agency, or you may wish to assign agencies to different students to make sure that enough variety is covered in class.

3. For Step 2, go over with the class how to organize their research. Remind them to paraphrase or quote and credit the information that they find, and not to just copy information directly from websites. Make sure they read the information in Step 3 that describes what to include in their presentation.

4. For Step 3, have students present their reports to the whole class. Encourage the class to notice similarities and differences among the different agencies, their methods, and their effects.

 Go to www.mynorthstarlab.com for *Student Speaking Models, Integrated Task, Video Activity, Internet Activity,* and *Unit 8 Achievement Test.*

Boosting Brain Power through the Arts

OVERVIEW

Theme: The Arts

This unit investigates whether early exposure to music and music education can enhance children's cognitive abilities.

Listening One: *Does Music Enhance Math Skills?* is a radio interview with a researcher and psychologists about the positive effects of early music education.

Listening Two: *Music, Art, and the Brain* is a radio interview with a magazine's science editor on how music education can positively impact mathematical and spatial skills in infants and young children.

Critical Thinking

Interpret a cartoon
Analyze scientific experiments and studies
Infer word meaning from context
Analyze and discuss different opinions

Analyze figurative language
Compare and contrast results from experiments and studies

Listening

Make predictions
Listen for main ideas
Listen for details
Make inferences based on implied information

Organize and synthesize information from the listenings
Relate information in the listenings to others' viewpoints

Speaking

Recognize and use figurative language
Role-play a scripted and a semi-scripted conversation
Discuss experiments and studies

Use linking expressions to discuss similarities and differences
Role-play a public meeting

Vocabulary	Grammar
Use context clues to infer meaning	The passive voice and the passive causative
Distinguish between literal and figurative meanings	**Pronunciation**
Identify and use synonyms	
Identify and use idiomatic expressions	Joining final consonants

 MyNorthStarLab
Readiness Check, Background and Vocabulary, Listenings One and Two, Notetaking and Academic Skills Practice, Vocabulary and Grammar, Achievement Test

 NorthStar: Reading and Writing 5
Unit 9 explores the role of art in one's life, particularly its healing qualities.

 ①FOCUS ON THE TOPIC

◀ SKILLS

Analyze a cartoon; share background knowledge; predict content; preview vocabulary; infer the meaning of new vocabulary from context.

✧✧✧Ⓐ PREDICT

Suggested Time: 5 minutes

1. Ask students to read the title and the cartoon and discuss the questions with a neighboring classmate. Have the pairs share their ideas with the class. If the class has already heard of the "Mozart effect," they may understand that the cartoon is ironic; that is, that the cartoonist is making fun of people's belief in the power of classical music to enhance brain power.

2. If necessary, give some brief background about Mozart: He was an Austrian composer who lived from 1756–1791. He was also an accomplished performer who played the violin and piano. He began playing music from age four and composing from age five. His father was also a composer, and his older sister was possibly equally talented, but was discouraged from pursuing a musical career as an adult because it was considered unsuitable for women.

✧✧Ⓑ SHARE INFORMATION

Suggested Time: 20 minutes

1. Have students listen to the music. Encourage them to listen with their eyes closed to minimize distractions.

2. For **Exercise 1**, have students work individually to list their ideas before they join a partner or group to compare lists.

3. Brainstorm with the whole class different types of music and art that are present in their lives today. Write the list on the board. Encourage them to think in broader terms than formal lessons; for example, students might listen to music on an MP3 player or their cell phone, on the radio in a car, or as a film or television soundtrack; art could include photos of friends posted on a website, posters in their room, or cartoons they draw themselves. Then have students work in groups to discuss the questions in **Exercise 2**.

Expansion/Homework

Have students listen again to the Mozart excerpt. Ask them to try to listen to both the melody, which moves forward from note to note, as words do when spoken, and to the harmony, produced when two ore more notes sound together. Some researchers have suggested that the movement from one harmonic chord to another, which follows a logical progression, is analogous to the grammatical structure in language.

✿✿✿Ⓒ BACKGROUND AND VOCABULARY

Go to www.mynorthstarlab.com for *Background and Vocabulary.*

Suggested Time: 30 minutes

1. Read or call on a volunteer to read the introductory information. Then divide the class into groups of three.

2. For **Exercise 1**, ask students to follow along in their books while they listen to the studies. Point out that the boldfaced words and expressions are target vocabulary for the unit and the upcoming listening tasks.

3. For Step 1, have students summarize the studies on which they concentrated to their groups. Call on volunteers from different groups to share their summaries with the whole class. Circulate while groups are completing Step 2. Then go over the answers as a class. Make sure students know how to pronounce each word.

4. Have students discuss the questions in **Exercise 2** in small groups. If time allows, conduct a whole class discussion as well.

Expansion/Homework

(**1**) Students could also read the reviews and complete the vocabulary exercise as homework. Then use class time to check answers and pronunciation. If time permits, have students listen to the reviews in class afterwards. (**2**) Have students work alone or with a partner to write new sentences with each of the vocabulary words. Call on volunteers to write their sentences on the board. Alternatively, put two pairs together to read their new sentences aloud, though without including the vocabulary word (they can say *blank* instead). The other pair guesses which vocabulary word completes the sentence. (**3**) Encourage your students to follow this topic in the news or online. Have them bring to class any articles in which they find mention of arts programs in schools. (**4**) Students could work individually or with a partner to do additional research online or in a library about the three studies mentioned.

Go to www.mynorthstarlab.com for additional *Background and Vocabulary* practice.

2 FOCUS ON LISTENING

◖ SKILLS

Predict; understand main ideas and details; make inferences; express opinions.

 ✪✪✪ A **LISTENING ONE: Does Music Enhance Math Skills?**

📁 Go to www.mynorthstarlab.com to listen to *Does Music Enhance Math Skills?*

Suggested Time: 10 minutes

Listening One is a radio interview in which a reporter talks to a researcher and two psychologists about the impact that studying music and art can have on children's cognitive abilities.

1. To encourage use of the vocabulary learned in Section 1C, write the words on the board for students' reference as they work with their partners to list their ideas.

2. Have students listen to the excerpt and compare that list with their own. Ask students to share any reactions with the class.

LISTENING STRATEGY: Speaker's Purpose

Remind students that a speaker has a purpose for speaking just as the listener has a purpose for listening. Using the title, have students speculate on the speaker's intended purpose (to inform, to entertain, or to persuade). Then use each of these purposes to infer the students' purpose for listening (to understand, to be entertained, to evaluate). Have students work in small groups to determine how their listening strategies might be different for each of these purposes (for example, to learn/understand might involve taking detailed notes, to be entertained might involve simply listening appreciatively, and to evaluate might involve using a pro-con organizer).

✪✪✪ LISTEN FOR MAIN IDEAS   **Suggested Time: 10 minutes**

1. Read or give students time to read the exercise before they listen. Answer any vocabulary questions. If students wish, they can circle their guesses in pencil.

2. Play Parts One and Two, pausing after each part so students can complete their answers. After students compare answers, play each part again if disagreements arise. Then go over the answers with the whole class.

Expansion/Homework

To challenge more advanced students, convert this first listening into a notetaking activity. With books closed, have students take notes using a divided page: Main Ideas/Details. Then have students compare notes with a partner's. When finished, students can open their books and answer the questions using their notes.

✪✪✪ LISTEN FOR DETAILS   Suggested Time: 15 minutes

1. Go over the chart carefully with the class. Play the interview, stopping it at times to let students compare answers. If disagreements arise, replay the part rather than giving the answer. In some cases, students may even want to listen a third time.

2. Check answers with the whole class. You could photocopy the chart onto an overhead sheet and call on volunteers to come up and fill in the answers, or have one student ask a question for each area of the chart (e.g., *In Part One, what was the researcher's name?*) and call on another student to give the answer. Help students with the spelling of names as necessary.

✪✪✪ MAKE INFERENCES   Suggested Time: 15 minutes

1. Explain that making inferences involves drawing conclusions about what we hear from indirect or implied information. For this reason, answers may vary. Students need not agree on answers, as long as they can support their opinions.

2. Give students time to read the exercise before you play the excerpts. Have students read the items before listening to the excerpts. Allow students a few minutes to think about how they would rank the items before discussing their judgments in small groups.

3. Call on volunteers to share their rankings with the whole class. Remind them to support their opinions with reasons or examples. If practical, list any different rankings on the board for the whole class to see.

REACHING ALL STUDENTS: Make Inferences	
• **Less Proficient:** To help create a visual image for Excerpt One, have students draw a web as they listen to the information. The center circle of one web will be Standard Curriculum; the center circle of the other will be Special Curriculum.	• **More Proficient:** Have students create a Venn diagram to compare the two studies. Then have students compare the chart, the web, and the Venn diagram to determine the most effective method of organization for their use in this task.

✪✪✪ EXPRESS OPINIONS   Suggested Time: 20 minutes

1. Read the instructions for Step 1 aloud to the class. Then have students fill in their own answers and talk to three other classmates. Encourage them to get up and move about the room so that they can talk to people that they did not work with when doing the other exercises from Listening One if possible. Let students know when three minutes are up so that they can change partners.

2. Have students change groups and summarize their opinions and those of the other students they talked to. Encourage groups to note both similarities and differences among the class' opinions.

Expansion/Homework

(1) Listen in on groups, noting the most interesting ideas. Present these on the board and invite comments. (2) Have students ask modified versions of questions 2, 3, and 4 to people outside their class, and summarize the opinions they gathered to the class. Were opinions from people who hadn't heard Listening One very different from the students who had?

 Link to *Northstar: Reading and Writing 5*

Expand question 3 into a class discussion on the many levels on which music (and the arts) affects us. Ask: *In what other ways can music enrich us? How did it help in war-torn Sarajevo? How does it help people who are suffering? How can it enhance a person's self-expression?*

CRITICAL THINKING

Give students the following questions for discussion in small groups before discussing as a whole class:

1. In Part I, what was the experiment that was done with the first and second graders?

   Answer: Some classes had a special arts curriculum incorporated into their normal school week. Other classes continued with the standard curriculum, which gave students music and art lessons twice a month.

2. What was the result of the experiment?

   Answer: They learned that students in the special arts classes had improved in both reading and math.

3. What conclusions can you draw from this experiment?

   Answer: Studying art and music helps students in other academic areas.

4. How can you use this information for your own benefit?

   Answers will vary, but they might include taking music and art lessons or providing them for their children in the future.

✪✪✪ B LISTENING TWO: Music, Art, and the Brain

 Go to www.mynorthstarlab.com to listen to *Music, Art, and the Brain.*

Suggested Time: 20 minutes

Listening Two is a radio interview in which a scientist discusses how music education can help very young children develop better math and spatial skills.

1. Read the introduction aloud to the class. To accentuate the difference between the two steps—notetaking and summarizing—have students close their books as they listen to the interview, and take notes on a separate sheet of paper.

2. When the excerpt is finished, allow them to open their books, write their summaries, and compare them with a partner's. If necessary, replay the

interview. Remind students that their summaries will not be expressed in exactly the same words, but the main ideas should be the same.

3. Call on volunteers to present their summaries to the whole class.

Expansion/Homework
(1) With less proficient students, model the first part with the class before you ask students to work with partners. Write the notes that you take on the board so that students can see you write down main ideas and supporting information and not complete sentences. (2) At the end of this interview, the scientist editor suggested ways to boost your child's intelligence. Ask students: *If/when you have children, would you use anything you have learned from these listenings to boost your child's intelligence? Why? Why not?*

✪✪✪ C INTEGRATE LISTENINGS ONE AND TWO

◖ SKILLS

Organize, compare, and synthesize information from two audio segments; apply the information and ideas to other areas.

STEP 1: Organize   Suggested Time: 10–15 minutes

1. Give students time to look over the chart and the notes they took on Listenings One and Two. Then have students work alone or with a partner to organize the ideas into the chart.

2. Go over the answers with the entire class.

STEP 2: Synthesize   Suggested Time: 20 minutes

1. Have students work in groups of three to role-play the interview. Encourage students to review their notes from the listenings first. Set a time limit of 10–15 minutes.

2. Call on the education advisor in each group to explain to the class which proposals sounded best, and why.

Expansion/Homework
(1) Before beginning this section, you may want to have students orally restate each experiment in pairs, small groups, or as a class, to help strengthen their overall grasp of the material. (2) Have students write a few paragraphs about the art and music education they received as young children, both in and out of school. Do they think it had an effect on them? They can turn in the paragraphs to you or read them aloud in small groups in class. (3) Either write the vocabulary from pages 199–200 on the board while students are talking, or have one student in each pair keep a book open to pages 199–200. Ask students to try to use the words and expressions as they talk. If students are using the companion text, *NorthStar: Reading and Writing 5*, you may also want to include vocabulary from that unit's section 1C on the board. Alternatively, you could create a list integrating the

vocabulary from both the *Listening and Speaking* and *Reading and Writing* strands. See the Word List for each unit at the end of the *Teacher's Manual*. Have students check (✔) each word and expression as they use it. (4) Encourage your students to follow this topic in the news or online. Have them bring to class any articles in which they find mention of arts education (either being implemented or being cut) in the schools or for very young children.

 Link to *NorthStar: Reading and Writing 5*
Students using the companion text can write a paragraph from the point of view of the cellist of Sarajevo, Yo-Yo Ma, or the protagonist of *The Soloist,* arguing for or against music education for very young children.

 Go to www.mynorthstarlab.com for *Notetaking* and *Academic Skills Practice.*

③ FOCUS ON SPEAKING

 **Ⓐ VOCABULARY**

◖ SKILLS

Review vocabulary from Listenings One and Two; identify and use the literal and figurative meaning of words; use vocabulary in free discussions.

✪ REVIEW   Suggested Time: 15 minutes

 Go to www.mynorthstarlab.com for *Review.*

As pairs work to complete the exercise, let them use dictionaries if available. Then go over the answers with the whole class, checking pronunciation.

Expansion/Homework
(1) You may want to assign the exercise as homework and then use class time to check answers and correct pronunciation. (2) To help students memorize vocabulary, have them work in pairs to quiz each other on the definitions: one is the teacher; the other is the student. Then they switch roles.

✪✪ EXPAND   Suggested Time: 15 minutes

1. Read the introduction and example to **Exercise 1** aloud to the class. Explain that figurative expressions are usually cultural, although there are often surprising similarities among different cultures. As the class works with the figurative expressions in Expand, encourage them to note any cultural similarities to or differences with other languages they know.

2. As a class, practice pronouncing the boldfaced words and expressions.

3. Before partners complete the exercise, remind them to use context clues and the literal meaning of the words and expressions to help figure out the figurative meanings.

4. Go over the answers with the whole class. If necessary, give or call on volunteers to give additional examples of the figurative use of the words and expressions.

5. For **Exercise 2**, Student B can also use the Opening Phrases from Unit 8 (page 192) and the language for Framing an Argument from Unit 7 (page 166) if they wish.

Expansion/Homework

(**1**) Have students work alone or with a partner to write new sentences that use the words in a figurative sense. Have students check their sentences with you to make sure the usage is correct, and then share them with the class. (**2**) Convert the exercise into a listening exercise by having pairs of students take turns reading the sentences aloud. The student who listens must decide whether the word is used figuratively or literally.

Link to *NorthStar: Reading and Writing 5*

Give students using the companion text a list of words used figuratively in *The Cellist of Sarajevo* and have them explain their figurative use. Suggested words: *supercharged, moving* (paragraph 2), *pushed* (paragraph 4), *flew* (paragraph 5), *poured* (paragraph 6), *stealing* (paragraph 7), *framed* (paragraph 9). More proficient students could find figuratively used words on their own.

VOCABULARY EXPANSION: Words in Context

Remind students of the various ways context clues are provided in a text, lecture, or discussion (synonym, antonym, general clue, example, or definition). Have student partners work with the context in these sentences from the interview by substituting synonyms and/or identifying the context clue: (1) Just how music enhances mathematical skills is unknown. (2) It may be by the more general effect of increasing self-esteem. (3) Or maybe something neurological happens in the brain. (4) Studying music and art can significantly advance a child's reading skills and especially boost math proficiency. (5) Some classrooms had an extra hour of this special arts curriculum. (6) She found they scored significantly higher on a particular IQ test that measures abstract reasoning—a skill essential to mathematics. Then ask students to be aware of how often they "get" the meaning of a word/sentence without actually knowing the definition of the words in the sentence. This is especially helpful for students who tend to rely too heavily on dictionaries when they read.

✪ CREATE   Suggested Time: 25–30 minutes

1. Model the game for the whole class. Point out that students can use either the literal or the figurative meaning of the words and expressions. Have students form groups to set up the game. Then call out a start time.

2. Monitor teamwork to ensure students are focused on the prompts and not just running through a list of responses to find the right word. Award the winning team with applause. Then have the teams play again.

Expansion/Homework

When playing the word game, students can use prompts other than questions, for example: omitting the word from the sentence and having the team fill it in; using the word in the question so that it is repeated in the response, or having the whole team create a story using the words on the board.

📁 Go to www.mynorthstarlab.com for additional *Vocabulary* practice.

✪✪ B GRAMMAR: The Passive Voice and the Passive Causative

📁 Go to www.mynorthstarlab.com for *Grammar Chart* and *Exercise 2*.

◖ SKILLS

Understand and practice the use of the passive to emphasize the action in a sentence and the passive causative to talk about arranged actions.

Suggested Time: 35–40 minutes

1. Have students work with a partner to read the sentences in **Exercise 1**, or call on volunteers to read them aloud to the class. After pairs have discussed the questions, go over the answers with the whole class.

2. Read or give students time to read the grammar chart. Have students complete **Exercise 2** in pairs. They can either fill in the answers individually and then check with a partner, or do each item together. If students are having difficulty deciding when to use the active or the passive, ask them to answer the question *Who or what is (doing the action)?* If the actor is either missing or follows the verb and is preceded by a preposition such as *by*, then they should use the passive.

3. Go over the answers with the whole class. Then check comprehension of the passage by asking: *What is being researched by Frances Rauscher? What hypotheses was she testing? What were her results? According to this study, can children learn more form a computer keyboard or a piano keyboard? Why? Based on her studies, what does she recommend?*

4. Read the instructions for **Exercise 3** aloud. If you wish, have students leave the columns uncovered while two volunteers model #1. As students work in pairs to complete the exercise, encourage the conversational tone of this exercise by having students read the information in the book silently and then look up at their partners to speak. They may need to break the information into smaller pieces to retell it. It doesn't matter how frequently they refer to the book as long as they are looking at their partner when they speak. If time permits, have them switch roles and repeat the exercise with a new partner. They can repeat the exercise until Student A's questions and Student B's answers are comfortable and fluent.

Expansion/Homework
(**1**) Students can complete Exercise 2 as homework then go over the answers in class to work on pronunciation. (**2**) Have students work alone or in pairs to research real musical prodigies or performers whose musical careers began when they were still children. Have them write a few paragraphs about the person, using some passive and passive causative sentences, or have them write individual sentences in the passive or passive causative. Suggestions for people to research: Wolfgang Amadeus Mozart, Frederic Chopin, Franz Liszt, Felix Mendelssohn, Yo-Yo Ma, Vanessa Mae, Anne-Sophie Mutter, Charlotte Church, Midori, Lang Lang, Hilary Hahn, Joshua Bell, Miroslav Kultyshev. (**3**) You may want to mention some verbs in English that don't normally take the passive form: *appear, consist of, collide, disappear, emerge, happen, last, look, occur, resemble, seem, take place, vanish,* and *weigh.* (**4**) For further practice, offer exercises from *Focus on Grammar 5,* 3rd Edition or Azar's *Understanding and Using English Grammar,* 3rd Edition. See the Grammar Book References on page 268 of the student book for specific units and chapters.

 Go to www.mynorthstarlab.com for additional *Grammar* practice.

C SPEAKING

(SKILLS

Fluently join the final consonants of one word to the initial sounds of the following word; link sentences or ideas with transitions that show similarity or contrast; integrate the concepts, vocabulary, grammar, pronunciation, and function from the unit to role-play a school board meeting.

○○ PRONUNCIATION: Joining Final Consonants

Suggested Time: 20–25 minutes

1. Remind students that working on pronunciation will help both listening comprehension and speaking. Then read the introductory passage aloud or have students read it silently. Play the audio in **Exercise 1** or demonstrate the examples yourself. Then have students (of different language backgrounds, if possible) work in pairs to practice pronouncing these phrases. Circulate while students are practicing to give feedback.

2. For **Exercise 2**, review the pronunciation of the phrases by playing the audio or modeling them yourself. Have students mark the phrases before they complete the sentences. Have students work with a partner to compare answers and practice the phrases.

✪✪ FUNCTION: Expressions That Link Sentences or Ideas

Suggested Time: 25 minutes

1. Read or ask students to read (silently or aloud) the example sentences, explanation, and list of expressions.

2. Model the example. Then pair up students of similar fluency levels to make statements from the information in the chart. Encourage students to make eye contact while speaking. Circulate among the pairs, listening in and correcting.

3. Call on volunteers to read sentences aloud to check pronunciation and intonation. Make sure students pause after the comma that follows the words and phrases that begin a sentence.

Expansion/Homework
(1) Have students write sentences that compare and contrast the results from the experiments described in the Background and Vocabulary and Listenings One and Two. (2) If possible, have students record these exchanges and then listen to hear their own performance. They can listen for pronunciation, intonation, and usage errors, which they may then correct. (3) The exercise could be assigned for homework, with students writing down their sentences. Class time can be used to compare the sentences in small groups.

✪✪✪ PRODUCTION: A School Board Meeting

Suggested Time: 50 minutes

If you wish to assign a different speaking task than the one in this section, see page 223. The alternative speaking topics relate to the theme of this unit, but may not target the same grammar, pronunciation, or function taught in the unit.

1. Read or have students read the introductory information and the information in Step 1. Answer any vocabulary questions. To check comprehension, ask: *What is a school board? How are schools funded? What areas have already been proposed for cuts? How has the community reacted to the proposed art and music cuts?*

2. Have students form three groups: parents, teachers, and school board members, and one student volunteer to chair the meeting. Have each group read its role description and write out its position on the issue. Meanwhile, brainstorm with the "leader" phrases for opening, conducting, and closing a meeting.

3. Collect the editorial letters and let students read one another's or share them in small groups.

Expansion/Homework
(1) You may want to write expressions from the Vocabulary and Function sections on small pieces of paper and distribute them to students. As they speak, they must try to incorporate their assigned phrases. (2) During the meeting, take notes of the most salient usage and pronunciation errors. You can then distribute these notes to the individual students. Have them correct the usage errors and mark the

pronunciation words with stress marks over the stressed syllables. Then have them share their corrections with a student (of a different language background, if possible) for feedback. Circulate around the room answering students' questions. As a class, you can review the pronunciation of the most frequent errors. (**3**) After the meeting, have students reflect on the situation. Emphasize that education in the United States is controlled locally, so this is an authentic situation.

 Link to *NorthStar: Reading and Writing 5*
Students could write a letter from Yo-Yo Ma or the cellist of Sarajevo in support of music education in the schools to be read at the School Board Meeting or as a newspaper editorial.

✪ ALTERNATIVE SPEAKING TOPICS

These topics give students an alternative opportunity to explore and discuss issues related to the unit theme.

✪ RESEARCH TOPICS

Suggested Time: 30 minutes in class

1. Have students turn to pages 264–265. Read the scenario aloud to the class. You can use the excerpt of Mozart music from the audio portion of the student book or choose an excerpt from a different work if you have access.

2. For Step 1, divide the class into groups. Explain the experiment to the class, and make sure they understand that there will be a "treatment" group that will listen to the music and a "control" group that will not, but that each group is equally important.

3. For Step 2, send the two groups to different rooms so that the control group cannot hear the music. After 10 minutes, bring the two groups together again and administer the simple tests.

4. For Step 3, mark the students' tests for accuracy and compare the results.

5. For Step 4, show the results to the class and have students make statements about what is (or is not) shown by the experiment.

6. For Step 5, have students discuss the questions in small groups or as a whole class.

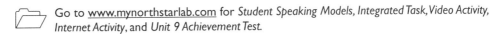 Go to www.mynorthstarlab.com for *Student Speaking Models, Integrated Task, Video Activity, Internet Activity*, and *Unit 9 Achievement Test.*

UNIT 10

Microfinance: Changing Lives $50 at a Time

<table>
<tr><td colspan="2" align="center">**OVERVIEW**</td></tr>
<tr><td colspan="2">

Theme: Poverty

This unit explores the institution of microfinance and discusses the impact it can make in developing nations.

Listening One: *Microfinance* is a radio interview with three leaders in the microfinance field.

Listening Two: *Interview with a Microfinance Director* is a radio interview that gives specific examples that illustrate how and why microfinancing can be successful.

</td></tr>
<tr><td colspan="2" align="center">**Critical Thinking**</td></tr>
<tr><td>

Interpret photographs
Share background knowledge and impressions
Analyze and evaluate aid programs

</td><td>

Identify and use supporting information
Infer word meaning from context
Analyze and discuss different opinions

</td></tr>
<tr><td colspan="2" align="center">**Listening**</td></tr>
<tr><td>

Listen for main ideas
Listen for details
Make inferences based on vocabulary choices
    and tone of voice

</td><td>

Paraphrase and relate information in the
    listenings to others' viewpoints
Organize and synthesize information from the
    listenings

</td></tr>
<tr><td colspan="2" align="center">**Speaking**</td></tr>
<tr><td>

Share predictions and opinions
Discuss proposals
Paraphrase and react to quotes
Role-play conversations

</td><td>

Add details and examples to support main
    ideas
Simulate a policy meeting

</td></tr>
<tr><td align="center">**Vocabulary**</td><td align="center">**Grammar**</td></tr>
<tr><td rowspan="3">

Use context clues to infer meaning
Identify and use word forms
Identify and use paraphrases and synonyms
Identify and use idiomatic expressions

</td><td>

Unreal conditionals—present, past, and mixed

</td></tr>
<tr><td align="center">**Pronunciation**</td></tr>
<tr><td>

Stress in two-word units used as nouns

</td></tr>
<tr><td>

 MyNorthStarLab
Readiness Check, Background and
Vocabulary, Listenings One and Two,
Notetaking and Academic Skills Practice,
Vocabulary and Grammar, Achievement Test

</td><td>

 NorthStar: Reading and Writing 5
Unit 10 focuses on methods of combating
poverty and why they may or may not be
effective.

</td></tr>
</table>

118

 FOCUS ON THE TOPIC

◖ SKILLS

Analyze photos; predict content; preview vocabulary; infer the meaning of new vocabulary from context.

✪✪✪ A PREDICT

Suggested Time: 5–10 minutes

1. Ask students to look at the photos and describe what they see. Provide any necessary vocabulary.

2. Have students work in groups to discuss the questions.

3. Have volunteers from different groups report their ideas to the class. Accept any reasonable ideas that students can support.

Expansion/Homework
If your students are not familiar with U.S. dollars, convert the amounts into local currency.

✪✪ B SHARE INFORMATION

Suggested Time: 15–20 minutes

1. Read the introductory information to the class. Then have students work with a partner to evaluate the ideas. Circulate while students are working to help out with vocabulary and understanding the ideas.

2. Call on volunteers to share some of their evaluations. You could also write the tally of responses on the board. Does the class mostly agree, or are opinions very different?

Expansion/Homework
Have students work individually or with a partner to research one of the organizations mentioned in the chart in terms of its program for dealing with poverty. Have them share the information they found with a small group or the whole class.

Go to www.mynorthstarlab.com for *Background and Vocabulary.*

Suggested Time: 30 minutes

1. Set the context for **Exercise 1** by explaining that some popular news magazines in the United States invite readers to send in questions for a person being profiled in the magazine. The person being profiled then writes direct answers to the questions. Explain that Transformation International is not real, although it is based on similar organizations, and the information presented in the answers is accurate.

2. Ask students to follow along in their books while they listen to the questions and answers. Point out that the underlined words and expressions are target vocabulary for the unit and the upcoming listening tasks. Make sure students notice the four footnotes at the bottom of the page.

3. Have students work with a partner to complete **Exercise 2**. Remind students to reread the context sentence in the interview, as well as the previous and subsequent sentences, for clues. Then go over the answers as a class. Make sure students know how to pronounce each word.

4. Check comprehension of the passages by calling on volunteers to paraphrase the main idea of each of the ten answers.

Expansion/Homework

(**1**) Students could also read the questions and answers and complete the vocabulary exercise as homework. Then use class time to check answers and pronunciation. If time permits, have students listen to the interview in class afterwards. (**2**) Have students work alone or with a partner to write new sentences with each of the vocabulary words. Call on volunteers to write their sentences on the board. Alternatively, put two pairs together to read their new sentences aloud, though without including the vocabulary word (they can say *blank* instead). The other pair guesses which vocabulary word completes the sentence.

Go to www.mynorthstarlab.com for additional *Background and Vocabulary* practice.

②FOCUS ON LISTENING

◖ SKILLS

Predict; understand main ideas and details; make inferences; express opinions.

Go to www.mynorthstarlab.com to listen to *Microfinance.*

Listening One is a radio interview in which three leaders in the field explain how microfinancing works and give some specific examples.

Read or call on volunteers to read the introductory paragraphs aloud. After students work in pairs to write their predictions, call on volunteers to share their predictions and write them on the board. How many basic needs were listed by almost everyone in the class?

LISTENING STRATEGY: Multiple Strategies

Remind students that these strategies are characteristic of good listeners: set a purpose; listen with pen in hand to help focus attention; make a listening frame or other graphic to organize information; write advance questions to anticipate information; and think/question as they listen. Suggest that students review the strategies they've studied and select several that they find helpful in listening and understanding. Then have them specifically use their preferred group of strategies as they listen to this piece.

REACHING ALL STUDENTS: Review and Summary

- **Less Proficient:** Have students work in small groups. One student in the group asks a question, the other group members will answer the question, and all will write the question and answer. Continue with the other group members each asking a question until all members have asked at least two questions.

- **More Proficient:** Have students complete the review process with student one asking, student two answering, student three writing, and student four locating the answer in the audio (e.g., That was in Part II when Raj talked about what happens to the kids). Student two then becomes the questioner and the process continues in order.

✪✪✪ LISTEN FOR MAIN IDEAS   Suggested Time: 10 minutes

1. Give students time to read the instructions and exercise.

2. Play the interviews and have students write the main ideas individually. Remind them to write complete sentences. Pause after each part to give students time to write. Then have students compare their answers with a partner's. If necessary, play the interview again. Check answers by calling on volunteers to share their answers.

✪✪✪ LISTEN FOR DETAILS   Suggested Time: 15 minutes

1. First have students read the prompts, writing in answers they already know. Point out that they do not need to write complete sentences here, just notes.

2. Play the interview again. Have students complete their responses and then compare their answers with a partner's. If disagreements arise, replay the interview rather than giving the answer.

Expansion/Homework

Have students reread the list of vocabulary on page 230. Play the interview again, and have students raise their hands when they hear the vocabulary.

✪✪✪ MAKE INFERENCES   Suggested Time: 15 minutes

1. Explain that making inferences involves drawing conclusions about what we hear from indirect or implied information. For this reason, answers may vary. Students need not agree on answers, as long as they can support their opinions.

2. Give students time to read the exercise before you play the excerpts. Because the excerpts are not linked, you can check answers after each one.

3. Play each excerpt and have students discuss their answers.

4. Go over the answers with the whole class. Remember to accept any reasonable answer that students can support with a reason. Replay the excerpts if necessary.

✪✪✪ EXPRESS OPINIONS   Suggested Time: 15–20 minutes

1. Before groups begin to paraphrase the quotes and discuss them, tell students that it is not necessary for the groups to reach a consensus about whether they agree or disagree with the opinions. However, even when they agree, group members should support their opinions with reasons. Circulate while students are working to help out.

2. Call on volunteers from each group to share their paraphrases and some of their group's opinions.

Expansion/Homework

Write these questions on the board. Have students discuss them in small groups.

1. Why do you think some countries are poorer than others?

2. Is it the responsibility of wealthier countries to assist poorer countries? Why or why not?

3. Who has responsibility to take care of poor citizens in a country? The government? Private organizations? Philanthropists? Everybody? Nobody?

4. What motivates some wealthy people to help others? Why do some wealthy people not donate money?

 Link to *NorthStar: Reading and Writing 5*

Students who are using the companion text could write a paragraph about whether Jeffrey Sachs would support microfinancing. Alternatively, two students could role-play a conversation between Jeffrey Sachs and an officer from a microfinancing institution.

Give students the following questions for discussion in small groups before discussing as a whole class:

1. What are some ways a loan of $60–$70 could benefit someone in extreme poverty?

   Answers will vary, but students should contribute ideas based on their own experience and knowledge as well as on information from the text. Encourage creative, problem-solving ideas.

2. According to the interview, what is the advantage of microfinancing?

   Answer: Microfinancing is sustainable, in that one can borrow and repay, and then another can borrow, etc. It can help more people over time.

3. Who might benefit from listening to this interview?

   Answer: Though anyone might benefit, student answers will vary and should include those people who currently contribute or are thinking about contributing to charities.

4. Would you prefer to give to microfinancing groups or to major charitable organizations? Give specific reasons to support your choice.

   Answers will vary, but students should be able to note the difference in approach and provide clear reasons in support of their choices.

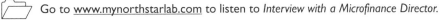

✪✪✪ B LISTENING TWO: Interview with a Microfinance Director

Go to www.mynorthstarlab.com to listen to *Interview with a Microfinance Director*.

Suggested Time: 20 minutes

Listening Two is a radio interview in which a microfinance officer gives a specific example of how lending a small amount of money can make a difference in someone's life.

1. Read the introduction aloud to the class. Ask students, *What do you think the story of this woman will show?* If you like, write the guesses on the board, and check them again after the class has listened to the interview.

2. Give students time to read the statements in Part One. Then play the interview and have students check (✔) the true statements and correct the false ones. Have students compare their answers with a partner's, and replay the audio if necessary to resolve differences of opinion. Then go over the answers with the class.

3. Have students listen again and check (✔) the answers to Part Two. Play the interview again if necessary. Go over the answers, and then repeat the procedure with Part Three.

Expansion/Homework

Students can listen to the entire Listening Two with their eyes closed (to focus attention) before they do either of the exercises; or, you could have students listen first to the section that corresponds to Part One, check answers, and then listen to the section that corresponds to Part Two, and then to the section that corresponds to Part Three.

✱✱✱ C INTEGRATE LISTENINGS ONE AND TWO

◖ SKILLS

Organize, compare, and synthesize information from two audio segments; apply the information and ideas to other areas.

STEP 1: Organize   Suggested Time: 10 minutes

Read or give students time to review their notes and answers from the two listenings. Then have students work with a partner to write the ideas into the chart. Students can write notes instead of complete sentences. Then go over the answers with the entire class.

STEP 2: Synthesize   Suggested Time: 20 minutes

1. Go over the instructions with the whole class. As students work to complete the exercise, make sure each student in a group chooses a different benefit to explain.

2. Have students practice their one-minute summaries a few times quietly, out loud, or in their heads. Then have them present their summaries to their group or the whole class.

Expansion/Homework
(1) With the whole class, brainstorm some phrases for beginning a presentation (*Thank you for coming. Today I'd like to explain . . .*), some phrases for linking the summaries (*The first/A second/An additional benefit is . . .*), and some phrases for ending a presentation (*Thank you for coming today. Do you have any questions?*). Then have each group give a presentation to the class in which they include all three summaries. Record the presentations if possible and play them back for the presenters. (2) Either write the vocabulary from page 230 on the board while students are talking, or have one student in each pair keep a book open to page 230. Ask students to try to use the words and expressions as they talk. If students are using the companion text, *NorthStar: Reading and Writing 5*, you may also want to include vocabulary from that unit's section 1C on the board. Alternatively, you could create a list integrating the vocabulary from both the *Listening and Speaking* and *Reading and Writing* strands. See the Word List for each unit at the end of the *Teacher's Manual*. Have students check (✔) each word and expression as they use it. (3) Encourage your students to follow this topic in the news or online. Have them bring to class any articles in which they find mention of microfinance, microlending, or poverty and development aid in developing countries.

Link to *NorthStar: Reading and Writing 5*

Students using the companion text can discuss specific ways in which microfinance can address or circumvent some of the barriers to eliminating poverty that were discussed in Reading One or the problems of the working poor that were discussed in Reading Two.

Go to www.mynorthstarlab.com for *Notetaking* and *Academic Skills Practice*.

3 FOCUS ON SPEAKING

A VOCABULARY

◀ SKILLS

Review vocabulary from Listenings One and Two; identify and use different word forms; use vocabulary in free discussions.

✪ REVIEW   Suggested Time: 15 minutes

Go to www.mynorthstarlab.com for *Review Exercise 1*.

1. For **Exercise 1**, go over the words in the box with the whole class. Make sure students know how to pronounce each one. Explain meanings or let students use dictionaries.

2. To set the context for the exercise, show students where Honduras is on a map or describe its location. Ask students to share any background knowledge or impressions they have of Honduras.

3. Have students work with a partner to complete the exercise. Circulate while students are working to help out.

4. Play the audio so students can check their answers. Then check comprehension by asking, *What were the economic conditions like in Honduras when the reporter visited? What does the Kiva.org do? How did Julia use her loan money?*

5. Have students work with a partner or a small group to discuss the questions in **Exercise 2**. Then call on volunteers from each group to share some of their group's ideas and opinions.

Expansion/Homework
(1) You may want to assign Exercise 1 as homework and then use class time to check answers and correct pronunciation. (2) Have students work in pairs to write example sentences that use the different word forms, if possible keeping the same context for each word family. Check pairs' sentences as they are working. Then put two pairs together to quiz each other. A student from each pair takes turns reading

the sentences aloud but letting a student from the other pair supply the missing word.

☾☾ EXPAND

1. As a class, practice pronouncing the boldfaced words and expressions. Explain vocabulary as necessary or let students use dictionaries.

2. Have students work alone or with a partner to complete the exercise, and then check their answers with a partner or another pair. Then go over the answers with the whole class.

Expansion/Homework
Have students review the pronunciation sections of previous units and choose a few points to work on. Then have students take turns reading the reactions aloud to a small group or the whole class. Encourage them to read with expression.

VOCABULARY EXPANSION: Match Game

To review all vocabulary from the units, have students play a game similar to *Concentration*, matching vocabulary words and definitions. To prepare, give index cards in two different colors to each group of students. Assign one or more units from the text to each group and ask them to write the vocabulary words on one color card and the definition on a card of the other color. Collect all cards and divide the sets equally among groups, ensuring that each set of cards has both words and definitions. Mix the cards, turn them face down on the table, and begin the game. Award points for matches. When a student completes a match, he/she can use the word in a sentence for an extra point. When a group completes their set of cards, they may exchange with another group and continue the game.

✪ CREATE

Read the instructions to the class. Model the example with a student. Then have students work in pairs to read and paraphrase the comments. If time permits, have students change partners and repeat the exercise, switching roles.

📁 Go to www.mynorthstarlab.com for additional *Vocabulary* practice.

✪✪ B GRAMMAR: Unreal Conditionals—Present, Past, and Mixed

📁 Go to www.mynorthstarlab.com for *Grammar Chart* and *Exercise 1*.

◖ SKILLS

Use conditionals to talk about unreal situations in the present and past.

Suggested Time: 35 minutes

1. Have students work with a partner to read the sentences in **Exercise 1**, or call on volunteers to read them aloud to the class. Then have students work in pairs to discuss the questions. Go over the answers with the whole class.

2. Read or give students time to read the grammar charts.

3. Have students do **Exercise 2** in pairs. More proficient students can cover each other's columns, and less proficient students can leave them uncovered or even write out the correct verb forms before they speak. However, if they take intermediary steps, have less proficient students then change partners and repeat the exercise, switching roles.

4. Check answers with the whole class by calling on pairs to read the question and respond. If the class had trouble, give the correct answer and have students repeat it chorally. Then have them change partners and repeat the exercise in pairs.

5. Read the instructions for **Exercise 3** aloud. Call on volunteers to give some example answers for question 1. Then have students finish the exercise in pairs.

Expansion/Homework

(1) Have students choose one or two questions from Exercise 3, and write a paragraph response, using unreal conditionals. They can turn in the paragraphs to you or read them aloud in a small group. (2) For further practice, offer exercises from *Focus on Grammar 5*, 3rd Edition or Azar's *Understanding and Using English Grammar*, 3rd Edition. See the Grammar Book References on page 268 of the student book for specific units and chapters.

 Link to NorthStar: Reading and Writing 5
Students using the companion text can work in pairs to write sentences about the conditions Barbara Ehrenreich encountered in Reading Two. Then they can take turns making unreal conditional sentences to comment on the information.

 Go to www.mynorthstarlab.com for additional *Grammar* practice.

⒞ SPEAKING

◖ SKILLS

Correctly stress the first syllable in the initial word of a compound noun phrase; use details and examples to support ideas; integrate the concepts, vocabulary, grammar, pronunciation, and function from the unit to participate in a simulation.

☺☺ PRONUNCIATION: Stress in Two-Word Units Used as Nouns

Suggested Time: 25–30 minutes

1. Remind students that working on pronunciation will help both listening comprehension and speaking. Read the explanation to the class. Play the audio or read the words slowly so that students can focus on the stress in each word. Have students repeat the phrases after the audio.

2. Give students time to study the chart. Explain that all of the words and expressions are used as nouns. (Sometimes nouns made up of more than one word are called *noun phrases* or *nominals*.) Point out that while this is a very common intonation pattern, students will also encounter exceptions.

3. Play the audio for **Exercise 1** and have the class repeat the words in chorus. Remind students that stressed syllables are longer in time, higher in pitch, and slightly louder than unstressed syllables. Repeat the audio if necessary.

4. After students have completed **Exercise 2**, go over the answers with the whole class, and write the answers on the board so that students can see which are written as one word and which are written as two words.

5. Have students continue working with the same partners for **Exercise 3**. They can look back through the unit to find further examples of noun combinations. Have them share their lists with the class by reading their expressions aloud.

Expansion/Homework

(**1**) Students can tap their fingers or feet or raise their hands when they pronounce the most stressed syllable to help them give it enough emphasis. Have the class do this in unison so students don't feel embarrassed at first. (**2**) Point out to the class that any noun can be used as an adjective for another noun. Give a few examples. Then have students work in pairs to challenge each other to think of noun phrases, stressing the first syllable of the first noun appropriately. The game could also be played in a circle, with the student who gives the noun phrase then choosing the next noun. A: table, B: table top; A: mountain, B: mountain resort; A: love, B: love interest. (**3**) Have students look for these compounds in the Background and Vocabulary section and circle them. Then have them practice reading the sentences that contain those phrases to a partner or the whole class. Compounds: *handouts, making textiles, raising cows* (you may need to point out that *making* and *raising* here are gerunds, and therefore nouns), *village lenders, interest rates, banking services, future generations, health emergencies, biotech consultant.*

Link to *NorthStar: Reading and Writing 5*

For homework, have students bring in five examples of noun compounds from the readings. Have students take turns reading their compounds aloud, and have the rest of the class repeat in chorus.

☺☺ FUNCTION: Supporting Ideas with Details and Examples

Suggested Time: 20–25 minutes

1. Read or ask students to read (silently or aloud) the introductory information and example. Point out that these kinds of expressions are particularly

important for longer speeches because they help the listener understand the speaker's organization and because they highlight the coming detail or example.

2. Model the beginning of the exercise with a student. Then have students work with a partner to ask and answer the questions. Tell students to read and think about the information in the chart before they begin their answer. You may want to write the expressions on the board so that students don't refer back to their books. Encourage students to make eye contact while speaking. Circulate among the pairs, listening in and correcting.

Expansion/Homework
If possible, have students record these exchanges and then listen to hear their own performance. They can listen for pronunciation and usage errors, which they may then correct.

 Link to *NorthStar: Reading and Writing 5*
Students using the companion text can work in pairs to create a similar chart of questions, main ideas, and supporting details from one or both of the readings, and then practice asking and responding to the questions in class.

✪✪✪ PRODUCTION: Simulation

Suggested Time: 45–50 minutes

If you wish to assign a different speaking task than the one in this section, see page 254. The alternative speaking topics relate to the theme of the unit, but may not target the same grammar, pronunciation, or function taught in the unit.

1. Read or have students read the introductory information. Then have them complete Step 1 as a class.

2. Divide the class into four groups, assign each one to a role, and have them study the chart. If your class has students of mixed ability, make sure that there are some students of each ability level in each of the four groups. Give students a few minutes to check back through the unit for vocabulary, grammar, pronunciation, and functions.

3. Give students a time limit of 15 minutes to prepare their plans, or to prepare questions for the other groups. Circulate while students are discussing to monitor and help out. Encourage students to make notes to speak from, but not to write out their entire speech.

4. Have the students from Group 4 invite the other groups to present their plans and then ask them questions. If you like, you could also let members of Groups 1–3 question one another. Wrap up the simulation by asking Group 4 to select the plan they feel is the most viable.

Expansion/Homework
(1) As students present their plans and question one another, note pronunciation and usage errors. Concentrate on the target language from this unit (you may also wish to include language points from previous units). At the end of the presentations, present your notes—either for the class or for each group—and have students

correct the errors. Help students work on pronunciation. (2) Have the members of Groups 1–3 write up their plans for the Opinion section of a newspaper. Have members of Group 4 summarize and critique the three plans they heard.

✪ ALTERNATIVE SPEAKING TOPICS

These topics give students an alternative opportunity to explore and discuss issues related to the unit theme.

✪ RESEARCH TOPICS

Suggested Time: 30 minutes in class

1. Have students turn to page 266. Decide whether the whole class will do the same research project or choose different ones.

2. Read through each of the options with the class, and make sure they understand each one. Have students work in groups to brainstorm how they will conduct their research. Encourage them to write down their ideas so they don't forget them, and then have them conduct their research as homework.

3. Have students present their reports to the whole class. Encourage the audience to ask follow-up questions and discuss the findings and information with one another.

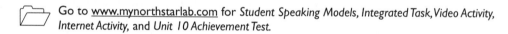 Go to www.mynorthstarlab.com for *Student Speaking Models, Integrated Task, Video Activity, Internet Activity,* and *Unit 10 Achievement Test.*

Student Book Answer Key

UNIT 1

1C BACKGROUND AND VOCABULARY

2, page 3

1. h	3. k	5. b	7. i	9. f	11. d
2. j	4. g	6. a	8. e	10. c	

LISTEN FOR MAIN IDEAS, page 4

Kandell's view of Internet addiction: It is not a new addiction. Some people may have been addicted for a while. Internet use is more widespread now, so Internet addiction is growing, especially on college campuses.

Chief symptoms/warning signs: When too much Internet use begins to affect other parts of students' lives.

Possible treatments: Support group for Internet addiction.

LISTEN FOR DETAILS, page 4

Examples of addictions: gambling, sex, shopping, video games, online chat rooms.

Evidence for this view: Students are coming to Kandell more often for help with relationship problems or problems with their grades, but the real problem is not relationships or grades but rather their overuse of the Internet.

Other symptoms/warning signs: When computer use affects work performance or school performance or relationships; when students start losing some of the skills that make relationships successful; when friends begin to comment on Internet overuse.

Reasons this treatment is helpful: Students have a chance to talk and deal with people face to face; they leave the isolation of their room; they help each other strategize on the best way to break the pattern and figure out what is causing these problems.

MAKE INFERENCES, page 5

Excerpt One
By using the word "groupies" he wants to attract the attention of a particular group in the audience—people who are technology enthusiasts. The word implies that Internet enthusiasts "follow" the technology trend of using the Internet, just as music enthusiasts ("groupies") follow popular singers or bands.

Excerpt Two
"Well . . . uh . . . I mean . . . for some people . . ." He doesn't seem to want to make a firm statement that Internet addiction is a definite problem on college campuses. That would be a very controversial stance for a psychologist, and he would most likely need more scientific and medical proof. Instead, he is tentative and gives an anecdotal observation that "they" are seeing more cases of kids being addicted.

Excerpt Three
He is skeptical and a little cynical. He addresses Kandell very informally and almost jokingly. He says amusingly, imitating a student, "Doc, you gotta help me!" This implies that he is taking the topic less seriously than he could be or that he is imitating the informality of college students' speech in order to be funny.

2B LISTENING TWO, page 6

MAIN IDEAS	DETAILS
Brook's view of communication and information: We are exposed to so much information that it affects our personality.	Cell phone, computers, laptops, personal organizers, every advance and technology create more communications at us; we are overwhelmed by the information flow
Advantages of so much information	It makes the brain work better and faster. Ability to make fast decisions and to fill out SAT type tests
Disadvantages of so much information	No time for playful noodling or for reading a book
Effect on Brooks	Always wondering if he got a voicemail

STEP 1: Organize, page 7

PROBLEMS	SOLUTIONS
1. Brooks	1. Kandell
2. Brooks	2. Brooks
3. Kandell	3. Kandell
4. Kandell	4. Brooks
5. Kandell	5. Kandell
6. Kandell	6. Kandell

REVIEW

1, page 9

NOUN	VERB	ADJECTIVE
1. addict	—	1. addicted
2. addiction	—	2. addictive
anxiety	—	anxious
1. compulsiveness	—	compulsive
2. compulsion		
depression	depress	1. depressed
		2. depressive/depressing
enhancement	enhance	enhanced
fulfillment	fulfill	1. fulfilling
		2. fulfilled
isolation	isolate	isolated/isolating
	overwhelm	1. overwhelmed
		2. overwhelming
problem	—	problematic
strategy	strategize	strategic
support	support	1. supportive
		2. supporting
symptom	—	symptomatic
therapy	—	therapeutic

2, pages 10–11

1. compulsive
2. overwhelmed
3. problem
4. anxiety
5. symptoms
6. fulfilled
7. depressed
8. strategies
9. addicted
10. isolating
11. supportive
12. therapeutic

EXPAND, pages 11–12

1. f
2. k
3. c
4. d
5. b
6. e
7. h
8. a
9. i
10. j
11. l
12. g
13. m
14. n
15. o

3B GRAMMAR

2, pages 15–16

1. would
2. wouldn't
3. weren't
4. could have
5. had known
6. hadn't been
7. wouldn't
8. weren't
9. did
10. hadn't
11. could have
12. had

PRONUNCIATION

1, page 17

1. huge
2. thousands
3. Nothing
4. totally
5. Fifteen / only
6. Totally / five
7. and / complete
8. fast

2, page 17

A: Workaholism isn't <u>really</u> an addiction. Some people <u>have</u> to work long hours.

B: But <u>others</u> are workaholics because they <u>love</u> their work.

A: Agreed, but success at <u>any</u> cost may not be such a <u>good</u> thing.

B: Yeah, that makes me think of my <u>father</u>. He was so <u>hooked</u> on work. When he <u>drove</u>, he was on his <u>cell</u> phone; at a red <u>light</u>, he checked his <u>e</u>-mail.

A: You <u>must</u> be joking. That is multi<u>tasking</u> at its <u>best</u>!

B: Well, not <u>exactly</u>. He lost his <u>driver's</u> license after his <u>third</u> accident, which was also his <u>fifth</u> ticket.

UNIT 2

1C BACKGROUND AND VOCABULARY

1, pages 26–27

a. 3	d. 10	g. 9	j. 4
b. 12	e. 7	h. 1	k. 6
c. 5	f. 8	i. 2	l. 11

LISTEN FOR MAIN IDEAS, page 28

(See next section)

LISTEN FOR DETAILS, page 29

Liars are narcissistic.
- can lie so cleverly that they won't get caught
- define themselves through responses of others

Liars are preoccupied with the moment.
- a way to avoid criticism or anger
- trapped in lies, confirming there's nothing there

A lie is a very particular form of deception.

Two criteria
- a deliberate choice to mislead others

Ways to lie
- falsify information
- tell the truth in a mocking fashion

Nine reasons for telling lies

1. To avoid punishment
2. To get a reward
3. To protect another person from getting punished
4. To protect yourself from physical harm
5. To win admiration of others
6. To get out of an awkward situation
7. To avoid embarrassment
8. To maintain privacy
9. To get power over other people

There is a high price to pay for telling lies.

- destroys trust between people

MAKE INFERENCES, page 30

Answers will vary. Suggested answers:

Excerpt One
1. b
2. a. serious
   b. slow, deliberate
   c. "relentless erosion of trust," "trapped in his lies," "deep down believes to be true."

Excerpt Two
3. c
4. *Answers will vary.*

Excerpt Three
5. b
6. a. sarcastic
   b. fast
   c. "Gee, officer."

2B LISTENING TWO

2, page 31

2, 4, 8, 3, 1, 7, 5, 6

STEP 1: Organize, page 32

Concealments	Possible Reasons

Answers will vary. Suggested answers:

Rapaport's father didn't tell his family about his son.	To maintain privacy To protect others
Rapaport's father didn't tell his family about his time in France or Romania.	To avoid punishment To protect others To avoid physical harm
Pierre didn't tell his father's family about who or where he was.	To protect others

REVIEW, pages 32–34

1. put one over
2. relentless
3. finely honed
4. put the pieces together
5. inflated
6. pervasive
7. conceal
8. tattling
9. mislead
10. preoccupation
11. mull over

EXPAND

1, pages 34–35

1. d   2. a   3. b   4. e   5. c

2, page 35

1. d   2. a   3. b   4. c

3B GRAMMAR

2, page 38

1. should be able to tell
2. can't / couldn't get away with
3. must want
4. might be paying / may be paying / could be paying
5. should be relieved
6. couldn't have deceived
7. must have cut corners
8. might have concealed

3, page 39

1. must have
2. couldn't have
3. could / might / may 've been
4. must have
5. might have / may have / could have
6. should have
7. couldn't have been
8. must've known

PRONUNCIATION

2, page 40

Molly: should've kept

Anton: shouldn't've said

Molly: would've thought

Anton: could've said

Molly: would've been

UNIT 3

IC BACKGROUND AND VOCABULARY

2, page 48

1. f	4. h	7. l	10. e
2. c	5. d	8. i	11. b
3. j	6. a	9. g	12. k

LISTEN FOR MAIN IDEAS, page 49

Part One

1. Forty-eight percent of Americans label themselves as shy, and the number is growing.
2. **Cultural factors:** competition, testing, emphasis on individual merit
Social factors: electronic revolution isolates people, smaller families, fewer extended families that give children the opportunity to learn social interaction skills

Part Two

3. **Situation shyness:** momentary shyness based on the situation
Dispositional shyness: chronic shyness that exists regardless of the situation
4. Shy people should admit their shyness.
5. People make false assumptions that they are aloof or condescending. Rather, they are simply shy.

LISTEN FOR DETAILS, pages 50–51

Part One	Part Two
1. a	7. c
2. c	8. c
3. a	9. b
4. c	10. b
5. a	11. a
6. a	12. b

MAKE INFERENCES, pages 51–52

Excerpt One

1. He is ironically telling the radio listeners not to worry. He uses the word *friends* to create a sort of mock intimacy between him and the audience before approaching the rather personal topic of shyness.
2. He is making fun of the topic and doesn't really take it too seriously.

Excerpt Two

3. He places stress on the word *amazement*. He also paraphrases his data to indicate his emphasis on the research.

Excerpt Three

4. He might feel a bit embarrassed initially by the question. First, we hear a hesitation in his voice; but then, we hear a smile in his tone of voice once he starts to explain.

2B LISTENING TWO, pages 53–54

1. c	2. e	3. a	4. b	5. d

STEP 1: Organize, page 54

Answers will vary. Suggested answers:

Personality Type	Pos. Attributes	Neg. Att.	Ways to Cope
Dispositionally shy		• always uncomfortable	
Situationally shy		• physically tense	• say to self "that's not me; it's the situation"
		• not prepared to perform	
Optimist	• cheery • find silver lining	• unrealistic	
Pessimist	• realistic	• grouchy	• assert self to optimist
		• cranky	• ignore optimist

REVIEW, pages 55–56

1. virtually	7. mark
2. grouchy	8. think of
3. outlook	9. wind up
4. take things as	10. drawing out
5. widespread	11. fill the void
6. carried away	12. break the ice

EXPAND

1, page 57

Introvert
bashful / inhibited / petrified / reserved / reticent / self-conscious / shrinking violet / standoffish / timid / wallflower

Extrovert
assertive / bold / gregarious / life of the party / open/ outgoing / sociable / social butterfly / talk a blue streak

Pessimist
gloomy / killjoy / negative / whiny

Optimist
open / Pollyanna / positive / upbeat

3B GRAMMAR

2, page 61

The Palo Alto Shyness Clinic was founded by Dr. Philip
Zimbardo, (who) is a professor at Stanford University, in Palo
Alto, California. The clinic provides group and individual
therapy for people (who) are trying to overcome loneliness
and shyness. The clinic, (which) is currently directed by
psychologist Dr. Lynn Henderson, uses a specialized
treatment model called the Social Fitness Model (that) trains
people in social skills in much the same way (that) people get
trained in physical fitness. Dr. Henderson, (who) invented the
Social Fitness Model, believes that problems of shyness,
(most of which) can be overcome, must be explored in a
supportive, positive, environment.

PRONUNCIATION

1, page 62

1. We discovered that about 40 percent of all Americans
   label themselves as currently shy.

2. Over the past 10 years, that figure has increased to
   about 48 percent.

3. Do you find these days that it's more difficult
   meeting people?

4. Two out of every five people you meet think of
   themselves as shy.

5. There are just many things in a culture, our culture,
   which lead a lot of people to be shy.

6. Children don't see . . . don't have the opportunity to
   see their parents and relatives relating in a natural,
   easy, friendly way.

7. When you're at a party, or just in a conversation with
   someone anywhere and you recognize that they're shy,
   what do you do to draw them out or try to make
   them more comfortable?

8. Admitting your shyness is really an important first
   step because if you don't, people make
   misattributions.

2, page 63

1. a   2. b   3. a   4. b   5. a   6. a

ALTERNATIVE SPEAKING TOPICS

1, page 68

Left of Center
If you want me
You can find me
Left of center
Off of the strip
In the outskirts
In the fringes
In the corner
Out of the grip
When they ask me
"What are you looking at?"
I always answer
"Nothing much" (not much)
I think they know that
I'm looking at them
I think they think
I must be out of touch
But I'm only
In the outskirts
And in the fringes
On the edge
And off the avenue
And if you want me
You can find me
Left of center
Wondering about you
I think that somehow
Somewhere inside of us
We must be similar
If not the same
So I continue
To be wanting you
Left of center
Against the grain
If you want me
You can find me
Left of center
Off of the strip
In the outskirts
In the fringes
In the corner
Out of the grip
When they ask me
"What are you looking at?"
I always answer

"Nothing much" (not much)
I think they know that
I'm looking at them
I think they think
I must be out of touch
But I'm only
In the outskirts
And in the fringes
On the edge
And off the avenue
And if you want me
You can find me
Left of center
Wondering about you
Wondering about you

2, page 69

1. b   2. a   3. c   4. a   5. c

UNIT 4

IC BACKGROUND AND VOCABULARY

2, page 74

1. h	4. d	7. e	10. f
2. i	5. j	8. g	11. k
3. c	6. b	9. l	12. a

LISTEN FOR MAIN IDEAS, page 75

1. Connectors are people who know a lot of people, are extraordinarily social, and can spread ideas to a lot of people they know.
2. Mavens are people who have specialized knowledge. They are experts in a particular field.
3. Salesmen are people who are incredibly persuasive.

LISTEN FOR DETAILS, pages 75–76

1. F; They are transmitted by a small number of exceptional people.
2. T
3. F; Only a few recognize between 120 and 130 names.
4. T
5. T
6. T
7. F; She is not a professional critic. She is just a maven.
8. F; Many are filled with friends of Ariel's, but not Gladwell's.
9. T
10. T
11. T
12. T

MAKE INFERENCES, pages 76–77

Excerpt One

1. b

Excerpt Two

2. d

Excerpt Three

3. c

Excerpt Four

4. b

2B LISTENING TWO

1, pages 78–79

1. b	4. c	7. c
2. c	5. b	8. b
3. a	6. c	9. c

STEP 1: Organize, pages 80–81

The Law of the Few
A connector calls the maven to ask about a new restaurant.
The connector tells a salesperson and many other people about a restaurant.
The salesperson tells a few people, including another connector, about the new restaurant.
The restaurant quickly becomes a very popular.

The Power of Context
The city sanitation department cleans up the garbage and graffiti.
The police arrest people for jumping turnstiles and other minor crimes.
Criminals understand that someone is paying attention to the subway.
The number of serious crimes drops dramatically.

REVIEW, page 83

NOUN	VERB	ADJECTIVE
	transmit	transmittable
generation		generated
consumption	consume	
profile		profiled
	root	
contagion		
	trigger	triggered
vandal		vandalized
	mess	messy
immunity/immunization	immunize	
infection		infected/infectious

1, page 84

Metaphors Related to Illness
Band-Aid® solution
be immune to an idea
contagious idea
infected
a social epidemic
viral marketing

Metaphors Related to Water or Weather
float an idea
a flood of ideas
make a splash
a ripple effect
swim against the tiede
the tied is turning
wave

CREATE, pages 86–88

2. contagious	9. sneezers
3. transmit	10. ripple effect
4. viral marketing	11. trigger
5. come around	12. infected
6. get a hold of	13. went through the roof
7. epidemic	14. "ideavirus"
8. immune	15. went a long way

3B GRAMMAR

2, pages 90–91

1. so	5. so	9. So	13. such
2. that	6. that	10. that	14. that
3. such	7. so	11. such	15. so
4. that	8. that	12. that	16. that

3, pages 91–92

1. such popular shoes that
2. so few . . . that
3. such a powerful tool that
4. so anonymous that
5. such an influential theory that
6. so contagious that
7. such a failure that
8. so strongly . . . that

PRONUNCIATION

1, page 93

1. a. sensitívity   c. responsibílity
   b. criminálity   d. populárity
2. a. energétic   c. realístic
   b. fantástic   d. apologétic
3. a. transmíssion   c. decísion
   b. organizátion   d. documentátion
4. a. fináncial   c. commércial
   b. artifícial   d. influéntial
5. a. lógical   c. crítical
   b. músical   d. theorétical

2, page 93

1. a. áble   b. póssible   c. públic
2. a. invíte   b. inóculate   c. cómplicate
3. a. président   b. bénefit   c. óffice
4. a. cátegory   b. cháos   c. sýmbol

3, page 93

1. b. possibílity
   c. publícity
2. a. invitátion
   b. inoculátion
   c. complicátion
3 a. presidéntial
   b. benefícial
   c. official
4. a. categórical
   b. chaótic
   c. symbólic

UNIT 5

1C BACKGROUND AND VOCABULARY

1, pages 101–102

a. 5	d. 2	g. 8	j. 9
b. 1	e. 6	h. 7	k. 4
c. 12	f. 3	i. 11	l. 10

LISTEN FOR MAIN IDEAS, pages 103–104

Part One

2. Feng shui is important in Asia. Lagatree doesn't know if knowledge of feng shui exists in Scandinavia, but clean designs there may reflect feng shui.
3. He uses feng shui to design and build his buildings.
4. Her home office is arranged according to feng shui.

Part Two

5. Mirrors are not desirable in the bedroom, but they are terrific in every other room.
6. She likes it and says it works and, at the very least, it couldn't hurt.
7. Everyone has experienced good feng shui.

LISTEN FOR DETAILS, pages 104–105

Part One

1. It sounds so superstitious.
2. The three examples are: the architecture of buildings, how staircases go up, how buildings are aligned.
3. Norway and Ireland. Her name is Scandinavian because she was named after a Norwegian opera singer, but she identifies as Irish.
4. Having an arrow (the one-way street sign) pointing at your house is unfavorable feng shui.
5. She would have had her back to the door and anyone who came into her office could surprise her. That is bad feng shui.
6. Feng shui has benefited her designs. She has a better floor plan than she would have had if she had designed her office herself.

Part Two

7. Mirrors could scare you if you wake up at night or mirrors could also frighten your spirit.
8. They reflect ch'i; they help chi'i circulate; in the dining room or kitchen, mirrors can double your abundance because everything appears twice.
9. She was also skeptical.
10. She would tell them that she didn't believe in feng shui but that they shouldn't tell anyone.
11. Anytime you walk into a room, you get an instinctive feeling about whether you feel good about being there or not.

MAKE INFERENCES, page 105

Answers will vary. Suggested answers:

Excerpt One

1. only a superstition
2. silly and ignorant

Excerpt Two

3. feng shui is popular and respected in the United States since Donald Trump is a wealthy and well-known businessman
4. not a feng shui expert; Thomson is being sarcastic

Excerpt Three

5. She didn't want anyone to know that perhaps she didn't believe in feng shui entirely, but she was also perhaps a bit embarrassed by her growing interest in it.

Bagua Chart

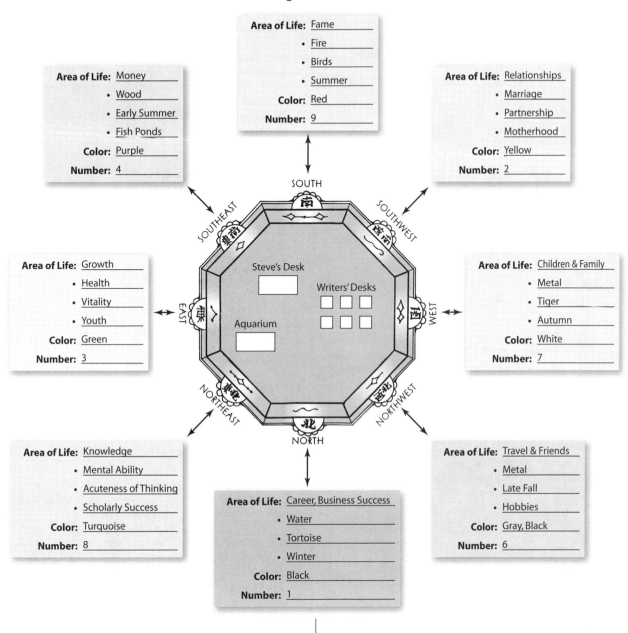

Area of Life: Fame
- Fire
- Birds
- Summer
Color: Red
Number: 9

Area of Life: Money
- Wood
- Early Summer
- Fish Ponds
Color: Purple
Number: 4

Area of Life: Relationships
- Marriage
- Partnership
- Motherhood
Color: Yellow
Number: 2

Area of Life: Growth
- Health
- Vitality
- Youth
Color: Green
Number: 3

Area of Life: Children & Family
- Metal
- Tiger
- Autumn
Color: White
Number: 7

Area of Life: Knowledge
- Mental Ability
- Acuteness of Thinking
- Scholarly Success
Color: Turquoise
Number: 8

Area of Life: Career, Business Success
- Water
- Tortoise
- Winter
Color: Black
Number: 1

Area of Life: Travel & Friends
- Metal
- Late Fall
- Hobbies
Color: Gray, Black
Number: 6

Steve's Desk

Writers' Desks

Aquarium

SOUTH
SOUTHEAST
SOUTHWEST
EAST
WEST
NORTHEAST
NORTH
NORTHWEST

REVIEW, pages 108–109

	NOUN	VERB	ADJECTIVE
			abundant
			acute
	alignment	align	
	digression	digress	
			frowned upon
1.	government	govern	governing
1.	quotation	quote	quotable
			scholastic / scholarly

2. sensation

1. sense
2. sensitize   sensible / sensitive / sensuous

1. skeptic
2. skepticism
     transcendence   transcendental
     vitality   vitalize
                       anecdotal

EXPAND, pages 109–111

1. got into
2. at heart
3. sharp
4. make a move
5. in the midst of
6. talked . . . into
7. work around
8. clean
9. hard-bitten
10. huge
11. rise or fall
12. scared the heck out of
13. keep out
14. peppier
15. caught off guard
16. can't hurt

3B GRAMMAR

2, page 113

1. Plus / In addition / On top of that
2. So / As a result
3. But / However
4. In addition / On top of that
5. So / As a result
6. Plus / In addition / On top of that
7. So / As a result

PRONUNCIATION

1, page 115

2. Of course
3. Well,
4. And
5. Actually,
6. Anyway,
7. And then,
8. However,
9. Now,
10. But

2, page 115

B: Actually
A: Well / Plus
B: So

UNIT 6

1C BACKGROUND AND VOCABULARY, pages 124–126

a. 2	d. 11	g. 6	j. 9	m. 1
b. 5	e. 3	h. 13	k. 7	n. 8
c. 14	f. 12	i. 10	l. 4	

LISTEN FOR MAIN IDEAS, page 127

| 1. d | 3. a | 5. e |
| 2. e | 4. c | 6. b |

LISTEN FOR DETAILS, page 127

1. The prophets of the old Testament
2. A break from our attachment to material things
3. Although fasting can be stressful, being able to endure a fast can make you stronger spiritually
4. The first Sunday of every month
5. They give it to poor people
6. From sunrise to sunset during the month of Ramadan
7. For spiritual well-being
8. Most people don't haves time to withdraw from their hectic lives

MAKE INFERENCES, page 128

Excerpt One

1. c
2. a
3. b

Excerpt Two

4. a
5. b

Excerpt Three

6. b
7. c

LISTENING TWO, pages 129–130

| 1. a, c | 3. b, d | 5. a, b, e, f |
| 2. c, d, e | 4. a, b | |

STEP 1: Organize, page 130

Spiritual Goals	Personal	Communal
• foster humility and gratitude	skip meals	give money to the hungry
• replenish spirituality	withdraw from hectic life	
• spiritual discipline	chanting / praying	help the sick
• less materialistic		help refugees

REVIEW, pages 131–133

a. 14	d. 7	g. 6	j. 9	m. 11
b. 12	e. 4	h. 1	k. 10	n. 8
c. 3	f. 2	i. 13	l. 5	

EXPAND, pages 133–134

1. disagreeing with
2. not understanding
3. problem or difficulty
4. positions in society
5. in extremely difficult situations
6. personal distress
7. peacefulness
8. stuck in the same place
9. understand something
10. agree

3B GRAMMAR

2, page 137

Count

discipline	monastery	stress
effort	notion	will
faith	pilgrimage	work
fast	quest	
journey	soul	

Non-Count

consumption	gratitude	spirituality
discipline	humility	stress
effort	impact	will
faith	soul	work

3, pages 137–138

2. a. NC / a great deal of
   b. C / X
3. a. NC
   b. C / fewer
4. a. C / a great many
   b. NC / very little
5. a. NC / quite a bit of
   b. C / a large number of
6. a. C / certain / many
   b. NC / a great deal of
7. a. NX / X (the)
   b. C / X (their)

4, pages 139–140

1.	a little	6.	a few	11.	little
2.	little	7.	little	12.	few
3.	a little	8.	little	13.	a little
4.	few	9.	a few		
5.	little	10.	Few		

PRONUNCIATION

3, page 141

1.	3	4.	—	7.	—	10.	—
2.	—	5.	1	8.	3	11.	2
3.	1	6.	2	9.	1	12.	—

FUNCTION

1, page 142

1. . . . but more or less how would the day start, when would it start, how would it unfold for you in retreat?
2. 14 times
3. It puts an emphasis on a routine in the past.

UNIT 7

1C BACKGROUND AND VOCABULARY, pages 148–150

a.	7	**e.**	6	**i.**	16	**m.**	2
b.	14	**f.**	15	**j.**	13	**n.**	5
c.	11	**g.**	12	**k.**	10	**o.**	9
d.	1	**h.**	4	**l.**	8	**p.**	3

LISTEN FOR MAIN IDEAS, pages 151–152

Part One

1. It is very common.
2. He warns that any employee may be under surveillance at any time.
3. They have the right to know how equipment is being used, if rules are being obeyed, and if employees are getting the job done.

Part Two

4. Monitoring can deter theft and also protect workers.
5. Surveillance practices demean workers.
6. Employees should be informed when monitored and there should be no monitoring in private places.

Part Three

7. It prohibits eavesdropping on private phone calls.
8. It can raise levels of worker stress and lead to lower productivity.

LISTEN FOR DETAILS, pages 152–153

Part One

2. F; nearly two-thirds
3. T
4. F; by 100%
5. F; He does not believe it is morally wrong.
6. F; The U.S. Postal service monitors the length of time to deliver the mail.

Part Two

7. F; They keep a log so that employees can pay for personal calls.
8. F; They monitor e-mail to protect employees from sexual harassment and racial slurs.
9. T
10. F; She concedes there are some legitimate reasons.
11. F; They should always be told.

Part Three

12. F; Most states allow surveillance in private places.
13. T
14. F; Employers do have the right to monitor the length of personal phone calls.
15. T
16. T

Excerpt Two

3. [circle #1]
4. He uses the phrase "Big Brother is watching and whatever." He also says . . . "That's a cheap shot."

Excerpt Three

5. [Circle # 5]
6. She uses "certainly" and "do not need." Her tone is firm and decisive.

Excerpt Four

7. [Circle #5]
8. She uses "whatsoever." Her tone is commanding and resolute.

2B LISTENING TWO, page 155

2. Attorney at large law firm | Supports | Employers have the right to safeguard their businesses | Just like homeowners protect their homes, employers have a right to protect their businesses
3. Chemist in large pharmaceutical company | Opposes | Right to private communication | Everyone has to make a few calls; workers take work home; invasion of privacy
4. Owner of small video production company | Supports | His company is his responsibility | He owns everything; should be able to check anything work related

STEP 1: Organize, page 156

Answers will vary. Suggested answers:

TYPES OF SURVEILLANCE TOOLS	PROS	CONS	EXPLANATORY NOTES
Monitoring e-mail	Can protect workers	Workers feel demeaned	Might reduce some abuses by employees, but they need to feel respected
Listening in on phone calls	Reduces time spent on personal calls	Invades privacy of employees	Although some personal calls are made during work hours, cannot totally separate job and home

TYPES OF SURVEILLANCE TOOLS	PROS	CONS	EXPLANATORY NOTES
Video surveillance in lounge or locker room	Can reduce criminal activity	Deprives people of dignity	Employees have a right to relax and change clothes in private
Secret monitoring of employees with various devices	Employers know what's happening	Violates workers' right to privacy	Employers can know what's going on in the company, but some people feel it's sneaky and sinister, especially without specific reasons
Looking at work on computers when workers aren't there	Assures employer that computer is used for work	Workers feel they're not trusted; increases stress	Owner might feel he has a right because everything belongs to him or his company, but employees have rights to privacy, too. Increased stress decreases productivity

REVIEW, pages 157–158

2. legal, justifiable
3. surrender, give up
4. spirit, confidence
5. watching, observing
6. discourage, put down
7. threatening, evil
8. discourage, prevent
9. compel, force
10. spy on, listen in on
11. at random, haphazardly

EXPAND, pages 158–159

1. going that extra mile
2. fine line
3. thought twice about
4. snooped on
5. stepped up
6. bugged
7. kept tabs on
8. foolproof
9. 24-7
10. cheap shot
11. subject to
12. leave . . . at the door
13. slippery slope
14. didn't have a leg to stand on

3B GRAMMAR

2, pages 162–163

1. a b	3. a b	5. b a	7. b a
2. b a	4. b a	6. a b	

3, pages 163–164

1. matching / to match
2. hiring
3. reading
4. testing
5. interviewing
6. to provide
7. to ask
8. to question
9. to make
10. administering
11. applying
12. asking
13. taking
14. revealing

PRONUNCIATION

2, page 165

1. íncrease (N), incréase (V)
2. condúct (V), cónduct (N)
3. óbject (N), objéct (V)
4. suspécts (V), súspect (N)
5. pérmit (N), permít (V)
6. récord (N), recórd (V)
7. insúlt (V), ínsults (N)
8. prógress (N), progréss (V)
9. cónflict (N), conflíct (V)
10. projécts (V), prójects (N)

UNIT 8

IC BACKGROUND AND VOCABULARY, pages 172–174

a. 3	d. 5	g. 1	j. 2	m. 13
b. 10	e. 8	h. 7	k. 4	n. 11
c. 12	f. 9	i. 14	l. 6	

LISTEN FOR MAIN IDEAS, page 175

Part One

2. ICRC's position of neutrality
3. International human rights and the laws of war

Part Two

4. ratified by hundreds of countries; basic rules of war
5. United States subscribed to Geneva Conventions
6. not white, Western European values; human universals

Part Three

7. one of the oldest moral traditions, warrior's honor and responsibility to protect community
8. task is dangerous, men must learn to restrain aggression and use war for benefit of community
9. war is so devastating; now equated with barbarism; morality cannot prevail
10. every culture contains elements of warrior's honor, which should restrain people

LISTEN FOR DETAILS, pages 176–177

Part One

1. a   2. a   3. c   4. c   5. b

Part Two

6. b   7. a   8. b   9. b   10. b

Part Three

11. a   12. c   13. b   14. c

MAKE INFERENCES, page 178

Excerpt One

1. D; He talks about how the CRC is trying to get people fighting in war to follow the rules of war.
2. D; He says that they are very "different traditions."

Excerpt Two

3. D; He admits that some people think it's absurd.

Excerpt Three

4. A; He says if you look deeply enough into your own culture, they are there.

Excerpt Four

5. A; The Red Cross is trying to remind people that this element of restraint is in every culture.

2B LISTENING TWO, page 179

Part One

1. T   2. F   3. T

Part Two

4. T   5. F   6. T

Part Three

7. F   8. T   9. F   10. T

Part Four

11. F   12. F   13. T

STEP 1: Organize, page 180

Answers will vary. Suggested answers:

2. war is sometimes necessary — there must be ways to "tame" it
3. simple rules of humanity — don't degrade bodies; don't torture prisoners
4. distinction between barbarism and war — sense of morality

REVIEW, page 181

a. 9	d. 14	g. 12	j. 8	m. 10	o. 6
b. 5	e. 3	h. 2	k. 16	n. 7	p. 13
c. 11	f. 1	i. 4	l. 15		

EXPAND

2, pages 182–184

1.	b	3.	a	5.	b	7.	b	9.	a
	a		b		a		a		b
2.	b	4.	b	6.	a	8.	b		c
	c		a		b		c	10.	b
	a		c				a		a

PRONUNCIATION

3, page 190

1. cot   2. cap   3. luck   4. nut   5. hot   6. lag

5, page 191

CUP-CUP
a bloody struggle
love of country

CAP-CAP
natural disasters
savage attack
a challenging task

CUP-COP
public controversy
gun shots
a tough job
combatant's conduct

CUP-CAP
cultural values
floods and famines
a bloody battle

CAP-CUP
lack of money
a practical discovery

UNIT 9

1C BACKGROUND AND VOCABULARY

1, pages 198–200

a.	12	d.	10	g.	5	j.	1
b.	6	e.	9	h.	8	k.	2
c.	4	f.	1	i.	3	l.	7

LISTEN FOR MAIN IDEAS, pages 201–202

Part One

1. b   2. c   3. a   4. c

Part Two

5. c   6. b   7. a

LISTEN FOR DETAILS, pages 202–203

Part One

Researcher's Name: Martin Gardiner
Experiment Location: Rhode Island
Research Subjects: 6- and 7-year-olds
Purpose of Study: impact of arts training on reading and math
Frequency of Classes, Control Group: Standard curriculum music: 2x/month
art: 2x/month
Frequency of Classes, Experimental Group: Special arts classes: 2x/week
Style of Instruction, Control Group: music lessons were passive
Style of Instruction, Experimental Group: arts program was active
Skills Taught: Art and Music, Control Group: listened to concerts, talked about music
Skills Taught: Art and Music, Experimental Group: sang together, drew shapes
Results: 1. Kids who started below average caught up to average in reading. 2. Kids were ahead in math. 3. Kids continued to improve in math.

Part Two

Researcher's Name: Frances Rauscher
Experiment Location: University of Wisconsin
Research Subjects: 3-year-olds
Purpose of Study: impact of arts education on math ability
Skills Taught: Art and Music, Experimental Group: piano and singing lessons
Results: 1. Children scored higher in IQ test of abstract reasoning. 2. Children understand proportions and ratios.

2B LISTENING TWO, page 206

Answers will vary. Suggested answers:

Part Two

Restate: So, in short, one of the reasons that math and music are so similar is that the same part of the brain is used for both functions.

Part Three

Restate: In other words, Sharon and Warren feel that it's important for parents to play an active role in their children's development in order to tap their children's full abilities.

Part Four

Restate: In other words, Sharon suggests that you simply give your child a lot of attention.

REVIEW, pages 208–209

1. e	4. f	7. g	10. j	13. m
2. d	5. k	8. a	11. i	
3. c	6. h	9. b	12. l	

EXPAND, pages 209–211

2. a. F applause
   b. L large-sized hands
3. a. L arranged the music (of)
   b. F strategically planned
4. a. L thin, thread-like metal to conduct electricity
   b. F neural (brain) connections
5. a. L glass or screen opening in a wall that lets in light and air
   b. F opportunities for learning and stimulation
6. a. F failed
   b. L stopped the electricity
7. a. F get angry
   b. L explode
8. a. L physically marked (on the skin)
   b. F emotionally or psychologically hurt or damaged

3B GRAMMAR

2, pages 214–215

1. are being researched
2. is being studied
3. appeared
4. can be enhanced
5. can be improved
6. were involved
7. were divided
8. received
9. was provided
10. were given
11. had been given (were given)
12. consisted
13. had . . . collected
14. had . . . analyzed
15. emerged
16. had been instructed (were instructed)
17. concluded
18. had been used (was used)
19. scored
20. seemed
21. may be simulated
22. are strengthened
23. appear
24. are fired
25. are performed
26. had . . . repeated

3, page 216

Student A

2. was . . . sparked
3. was . . . pushed
5. was told; had . . . made; was sent
6. has . . . been done
7. have been chosen
8. will be selected; will be printed

Student B

2. might have been inspired; was given
3. was encouraged; pushed; was identified
4. should have been noticed
5. was asked
6. are handled; have . . . repaired; get . . . dry cleaned; have . . . taken; must be done
7. is being considered; is chosen; have been invited

PRONUNCIATION

2, page 218

1. typical lesson
2. self-esteem
3. research challenge
4. standard)curriculum
5. art)classes
6. critical ingredients
7. boost)brain power
8. an interactive approach
9. logical)thinking

UNIT 10

IC BACKGROUND AND VOCABULARY

2, page 230

1. home-based business
2. able to continue
3. dangers
4. owing too much money
5. interesting
6. description
7. suffer the worst
8. for all future time
9. lessen
10. negative reaction
11. help in times of trouble
12. destroyed
13. sudden
14. solution

LISTEN FOR MAIN IDEAS, page 231

Part One

1. it triples the capital of their simple business and becomes a pathway to break the cycle of poverty

Part Two

2. it can have very positive outcomes for the children and for the next generation

Part Three

3. it is a gift that can keep on giving

Part Four

4. a shift from extreme poverty to moderate poverty

LISTEN FOR DETAILS, pages 232–233

I.
  A.
    1. you get overextended
    2. you don't own anything; the bank owns it
  B.
    1. don't haves access to jobs
  C.
    1. doing things the same way
    2. get a micro loan
  D.
    2. sometimes chickens would get wiped out
  E.
    1. have 12 or 13 chickens
    3. end up with a poultry farm of 500 chickens

II.
  A.
    1. improved weight and height outcomes
    3. payment of school fees
  B: a third to 40% of clients

III.
  A. gift / giving

IV.
  A.
    1. takes years
    2. not a panacea
  B.
    1. having minimal foodstuff for everyone in the family
    2. being able to send all kids to school

MAKE INFERENCES, pages 233–234

Excerpt One

1. b. He goes on to explain how there are few options for the extremely poor: either to starve or continue doing the same thing.

Excerpt Two

2. c. Giving the poor a small sum of money to start their own business is an "option that people should have."

Excerpt Three

3. a. He says that money for microfinancing is "money that might go to another program that might help people in poverty."

Excerpt Four

4. b. He realizes his audience may not be aware of the extremes of poverty when he says "it's probably a bigger life change financially and socially than any of your listeners are ever going to have over the course of their entire lives."

Excerpt Five

5. c. He's showing the impact of such a small amount of money on poor people's lives when he points out that some of the women "ultimately end up four years later having a poultry farm of 500 chickens."

2B LISTENING TWO, page 235

Part One

1. False. Only her ninth child was malnourished.
2. True
3. True
4. False. Another client gave her the money.
5. False. The money was a test loan to see what she would do with it.
6. True
7. True
8. False. She was allowed into the assembly after she paid back the woman.
9. False. She became successful after joining the assembly.
10. False. She became the vice president of the assembly.

Part Two

12. education
13. confidence

Part Three

17. sell very similar things
18. should sell things that bring them more money

REVIEW

1, pages 237–238

1. the world over
2. malnourished
3. wiped out
4. took a hit
5. sustainable
6. compelling
7. had fallen
8. elaborate
9. diminish
10. kicker
11. hit a ceiling
12. panacea
13. pitfalls
14. anecdote

EXPAND, pages 239–240

a. 10
b. 13
c. 2
d. 7
e. 1
f. 11
g. 4
h. 9
i. 12
j. 3
k. 6
l. 8
m. 5

PRONUNCIATION

2, page 248

1. backlash
2. profit margin
3. broadcast
4. livestock
5. safety net

Unit Word List

The **Unit Word List** is a summary of key vocabulary from the student book. The words are presented by unit, in alphabetical order.

UNIT 1

addiction
anxious
bombard with
clean slate
come out
compulsiveness
depressed
devote
driven
engage in
enhance
feed (verb)
feel empty
fulfillment
go on
go on a binge
go through

isolate
multitask
out of the woods
overwhelm
present with
problematic
put together
shape (verb)
strategy
support group
surf (verb)
symptom
therapy
turn into
turn someone in
vicious cycle

UNIT 2

bluff (verb)
conceal
deceptive
erosion
failure
fess up
finely honed
fudge (verb)
head toward disaster
honest
inflated
intrusive
lie
manipulate
mislead
mull over
pervasive

preoccupation
pull the wool over
 someone's eyes
put one over
put the pieces together
recipe for disaster
relentless
slippery slope
tattle on someone
tell
trick (verb)
trivial
two-faced
up front
veneer
whopper

UNIT 3

adverse
aloof
assertive
bashful
bold
break the ice
carried away
chronic
condescending
draw out
extroverted
fill the void
gloomy
gregarious
grouchy
handicap
inhibited
killjoy
kindred souls
life of the party
mark (verb)
merit
methodical
misattribution
negative (adjective)

open (adjective)
outgoing
outlook
petrified
phobia
Pollyanna
positive (adjective)
reserved
reticent
self-conscious
shrinking violet
sociable
social butterfly
standoffish
syndrome
take things as
talk a blue streak
think of
timid
upbeat
virtually
wallflower
whiny
widespread
wind up

UNIT 4

a flood of ideas
a ripple effect
a social epidemic
Band-Aid solution
be immune to an idea
consumed by
contagious idea
epidemic (noun)
float an idea
generate
get a hold of
go a long way toward
hold (verb)
immune
infect

make a splash
maven
mess
profile
root
swim against the tide
the tide is turning
transmission
trigger
vandalize
viral marketing
wave (noun)
win (someone) over
word-of-mouth

UNIT 5

abundance
acuity
acuteness
align
anecdote
at heart
can't hurt
catch off-guard
circulate
clean
digression
frown upon
get into
governance
hard-bitten
huge

in the midst of
keep out
make a move
peppy
quote (verb)
rise or fall
scare the heck out of
scholar
sense
sharp
skeptically
talk (someone) into
transcendent
vital
work around

UNIT 6

ascetic
at odds with
catch on
divine
draw (someone) out
enact (a law)
fasting
foster
gain insight
gratitude
hectic
humility
in a rut
in dire straits
inner turmoil
notion (of)
out of touch with

over time
prophet
pull back
quest
refrain from
replenish
royalties
see eye to eye
serenity
stumbling block
take on
trace back
vibrant
walks of life
well-being
will (noun)

UNIT 7

24-7
bug (verb)
cheap shot
concede
demean
deter
dignity
drive (verb)
eavesdrop
employee
employer
fine line
foolproof
go that extra mile
(not) have a leg to
  stand on
keep an eye on

keep tabs on
leave . . . at the door
legitimate
log (noun)
morale
racial slur
safeguards (noun)
scope (noun)
sinister
slippery slope
snoop on
step up
subject to
surveillance
think twice about
willy-nilly

UNIT 8

accept
access
advice
advise
affect
alternative ethic
assure
barbarism and savagery
code (noun)
council
counsel
counterintuitive
devastating
disinterested
disseminate
do without
draft evader
drawn to
effect
eminent
ensure
equate
except

excess
get at
house-and-garden
human universals
identify with
imminent
imply
infer
institutionalize
legitimacy
live by
prevail
principal
principle
ratify
restrain (verb)
spare (verb)
subscribe to
tame
uninterested
unleash
volatile

UNIT 9

abstract reasoning
advance (verb)
as a whole
attack
big hand
blow something
blow up
boost (verb)
building blocks
catch up to
curriculum
do more for
enhance
find (verb)
hallmark
have nothing to do with

intervention
neurological
orchestrate
prime (verb)
proficiency
reap benefits
regardless (of)
scar (verb)
self-esteem
sequential
underscore (verb)
well-rounded
windows
wiring
work in progress

UNIT 10

anecdote
as opposed to
backlash
bear the brunt of
bottom of the pyramid
characterization
compelling
cottage industry
diminish
elaborate (verb)
gift that keeps on giving
grassroots
have faith in
hit a ceiling
in perpetuity
kicker
make do

malnourished
niche market
non-monetary
overextend
overnight
panacea
pitfall
profit margin
pull themselves up by
   their bootstraps
safety net
sustainable
take a hit
the world over
top-down aid
upward mobility
wipe out

Achievement Tests
Unit 1

Name: _____

Date: _____

PART 1: LISTENING

1.1 CD 7 *Listen to the beginning of a talk show. Check (✔) the best prediction of what the listening is about. There is only one right answer.*

_____ **A.** definitions of communication technology

_____ **B.** reasons why people listen to new kinds of technology

_____ **C.** reasons why people don't talk to each other directly

_____ **D.** beliefs about the dangers of using certain kinds of technology

1.2 CD 7 *Now listen to the entire interview. Use the information to choose the correct answers. Check (✔) the answers.*

1. Why is Carlos Jimenez talking to people in the subway station?

_____ **A.** He is interviewing people who have invented new technologies.

_____ **B.** He hopes to find out how computers affect people's intelligence.

_____ **C.** He is taking a survey about the kinds of people who ride the subway.

_____ **D.** He wants to learn why people use iPods® and other devices.

2. The first person Mr. Jimenez interviews says listening to her iPod

_____.

_____ **A.** makes her work faster

_____ **B.** inspires her creativity

_____ **C.** helps her concentrate

_____ **D.** improves her computer skills

3. What does this woman think is not a problem?

_____ **A.** getting a new iPod

_____ **B.** interfering with work

_____ **C.** increasing intelligence

_____ **D.** using a BlackBerry®

(continued on next page)

4. The man who is not listening to a cell phone thinks _____.

       _____ **A.** they bother other people

       _____ **B.** some cell phones are dangerous

       _____ **C.** such devices damage people's hearing

       _____ **D.** they make people less intelligent

🔘 *Listen again to part of the interview. Then answer the question.*

5. What does Mr. Jimenez mean when he says, "Well, how can I argue with that?"

       _____ **A.** He thinks the woman is intelligent.

       _____ **B.** He does not agree with the woman.

       _____ **C.** He thinks the woman has a good point.

       _____ **D.** He does not want to argue with the woman.

6. How does the last man Mr. Jimenez interviews feel about people who talk on cell phones or iPods?

       _____ **A.** He wishes they wore ear plugs.

       _____ **B.** He thinks they bother other people.

       _____ **C.** He thinks they should listen to music.

       _____ **D.** He wishes they would get more space.

1.3 🔘 *Listen to "Time to Do Everything Except Think" from* NorthStar: Listening and Speaking 5, *Unit I. Use the information from this listening and the listening from Part 1.2 to complete the activity. Check (✔) the name of the person who says each idea. The first one has been done for you.*

Ideas	David Brooks	Carlos Jimenez	Young Woman
People are plugged into their own reality.		✓	
1. Technology shapes our personalities.			
2. Multitasking increases intelligence.			
3. Creativity comes when I am not listening to anything.			

PART 2: VOCABULARY

2.1 *Read the interview. Use the words and phrases from the box to fill in the blanks. Not all of the words and phrases will be used.*

addict	devote	fulfillment	overwhelming
blog	driven to	google	went through
bombarded with	engaged in	IM-ing	what's going on
compulsiveness	enhance	multitasking	

PATIENT: Doctor, I don't know what's wrong with me. I can't take my attention off the computer screen for even five minutes. My wife's about to leave me. She sees me in the study all day and wonders _____ in there.
1.

DOCTOR: Are there other activities you're _____?
2.

PATIENT: No. The minute I get up I turn on the computer and make a cup of coffee. Then I check into my _____ site and try to keep it
3.
up-to-date. The problem is, I don't have anything to update it with.

DOCTOR: And what about friends? Have you lost contact with other people?

PATIENT: Not at all. We're always _____ each other.
4.

DOCTOR: What you have is not uncommon these days. The _____ of
5.
Internet users like you is similar to the behavior of alcoholics or other drug abusers.

PATIENT: What?! Are you saying I'm an _____?
6.

DOCTOR: People who are _____ seek one thing at the risk of losing
7.
everything else have many of the symptoms of addiction.

PATIENT: I remember when the Internet was new and _____. It was
8.
too much to figure out. I took the first step toward addiction. It all began

(continued on next page)

when I learned to _____ and search for anything I wanted
                              9.

to look at. Soon I found myself looking at the computer screen while

talking on the phone and eating my breakfast at the same time.

DOCTOR: Well, learning the skill of _____ is very important in
                                              10.

today's world. But for now, you're going to have to stop everything related

to your former life. I'm going to give you the number of a group called

Internet Anonymous. Going to their meetings is the first step to saving

yourself from further addiction.

PART 3: SKILLS FOR SPEAKING

3.1 *Match the statements and questions with their responses. Write the correct letter on the line. The first one has been done for you.*

___E___   Is that weird guy still IM-ing you?

_____ **1.** Your husband has bought that expensive new computer, hasn't he?

_____ **2.** Can your friend go to your first Internet Anonymous meeting with you?

_____ **3.** Was your friend with you when you went to buy your computer?

_____ **4.** Will your father come to your 1-year anniversary of Internet Anonymous?

A. Yes, but I wish he hadn't.

B. No, but I wish he would.

C. Yes, but I wish he could.

D. No, but I wish he had been.

E. Yes, but I wish he weren't.

F. No, but I wish he will.

G. No, but I wish he could.

3.2 CD 7 *Listen to the sentences. Circle the word that is stressed. The first one has been done for you.*
(6)

I've sent her (three) e-mails, but she still hasn't answered.

1. Why don't you try calling her?

2. But she still doesn't have a cell phone.

3. They still make home telephones, don't they?

3.3 *Read the interview. Underline the expressions that the speakers use to build on each others' opinions. The first one has been done for you.*

HOST: Tonight our two distinguished guests are Dr. Green from the Center for Communication Studies and Dr. Chandra from the Sociology Department. Let's start of with you, Dr. Green. How will communication change in the next ten years?

DR. GREEN: I foresee an explosion of completely new forms of communication. It's impossible to imagine how technology will affect our daily lives. You're talking about ten years from now, but <u>I assume that</u> you've noticed how radically technology has transformed our lives in the past ten years.

1. DR. CHANDRA: Allow me to enter the discussion here. Yes, over the past ten years, TV, stereo, and telephones have been very rapidly disappearing. Another thing I'd like to add is that these changes are making the differences between socio-economic classes even more evident.

2. DR. GREEN: Not only that, but at some point communication between the classes will be difficult if not impossible. Unless the new technologies are to be made available to everyone around the world, there will be millions of people in developing countries who will not have the means to keep up with the ever-changing modes of communication.

3. DR. CHANDRA: I also see this as a grave problem. And to add to Dr. Green's point, any changes toward solving this problem must be made through a cooperative effort by governments and the companies that invent the new technology.

HOST: Thank you, gentlemen, for that very informative discussion.

PART 4: SPEAKING

4.1 *Say one thing that Carlos Jimenez from Part 1.2 found out from someone he interviewed. You may listen again to Part 1.2.*

4.2 *Think about what you said in 4.1. Do you agree with the person? Use an expression that builds on what you said in 4.1.*

4.3 *Changes in Technology*

Speak for 1 to 2 minutes about recent and future changes in communication technology.

- Before you speak, take notes about new forms of communication technology you currently use, for example, cell phones, iPods, IM, etc.
- Say what the positive and negative effects of these new technologies are.
- Talk about what changes might occur in the next ten years.
- Stress important words.
- Use the vocabulary and grammar from Unit 1.

Unit 1 Vocabulary Words				
addict	compulsiveness	engaged in	google	overwhelming
blog	devote	enhance	IM-ing	went through
bombarded with	driven to	fulfillment	multitasking	what's going on

Unit 1 Grammar: *Wish* Statements—Expressing Unreality
• Do you have an iPod? **No, but I wish I did.**
• Can Jim come to the Internet Anonymous meeting with you? **No, but I wish he could.**
• Your husband isn't addicted to the Internet, is he? **Yes, but I wish he weren't.**

Achievement Tests
Unit 2

PART I: LISTENING

1.1 🎵 *Listen to the beginning of a radio talk show. Check (✔) the best prediction of what the listening is about. There is only one right answer.*

_____ **A.** discussion about why people lie

_____ **B.** definitions of four kinds of lies

_____ **C.** suggestions on how to stop lying

_____ **D.** techniques to find out who is lying

1.2 🎵 *Now listen to the entire talk show. Use the information to choose the correct answers. Check (✔) the answers.*

1. What is the topic of Dr. Smith's talk show?

_____ **A.** why people tell lies

_____ **B.** why people shouldn't lie

_____ **C.** why lies can hurt

_____ **D.** what the consequences of lies are

2. What was Arlette wondering?

_____ **A.** what else her daughter might be keeping from her

_____ **B.** why her daughter was at Starbucks

_____ **C.** why her daughter doesn't study more

_____ **D.** where her daughter can get more peer guidance

3. Dr. Smith probably thinks that Arlette should be less _____.

_____ **A.** insecure

_____ **B.** secretive

_____ **C.** intrusive

_____ **D.** concerned

4. Why isn't Tim going to go to Harvard?

_____ **A.** He doesn't want to go.

_____ **B.** He didn't get accepted.

_____ **C.** His parents don't want him to go.

_____ **D.** His friends aren't going to be there.

(continued on next page)

5. Why did the girl in Baton Rouge feel bad?

    _____ **A.** The boy she liked didn't tell her the truth.

    _____ **B.** The boy who liked her lied about going to New Orleans.

    _____ **C.** She wasn't truthful when she talked to the boy who liked her.

    _____ **D.** She didn't want to visit her aunt in New Orleans.

6. Dr. Smith thinks that telling lies is sometimes _____.

    _____ **A.** trivial

    _____ **B.** painful

    _____ **C.** confusing

    _____ **D.** understandable

1.3   CD *Listen to the excerpt from "Interview with a Psychiatrist" from* NorthStar: Listening
9 *and Speaking 5, Unit 2. Use the information from this listening and the listening from
Part 1.2 to complete the activity. Match the reasons for lying that Dr. Ekman discussed
with the situations that Dr. Smith discussed. The first one has been done for you.*

Reasons People Lie	Situations that Dr. Smith Discussed
_D_ To avoid embarrassment	A. A girl lies to her mother about where she is going.
_____ **1.** To win the admiration of others	B. A girl lies to a boy in her math class.
_____ **2.** To get out of an awkward social situation	C. A boy lies to his friends about being accepted at Harvard.
_____ **3.** To maintain privacy	~~D. A boy says a university is too far away.~~

PART 2: VOCABULARY

2.1   *Read the sentences. Use the words and phrases from the box to fill in the blanks. Not
all of the words and phrases will be used.*

concealing	preoccupation	slippery slope
erosion	pull the wool over his eyes	tattle
inflated	put one over on	trivial
intrusive	put the pieces together	up front
mislead	relentless	

1. I don't know how to tell John I want to break up with him. I guess I should just be _____ with him.

2. My daughter lied again to cover up for her friend. I know it's not uncommon for kids that age to tell a lie rather than _____ on a friend.

3. I just told Antonio I was sick and couldn't see him even though that's not true. It's just a little lie, but my sister says there's no such thing as a _____ lie.

4. If you forget the lie you told someone, you might have to tell another lie to explain yourself. It's a _____.

5. Parents should be careful that they're not too _____ into their teenagers' lives. Teenagers need to have some privacy.

6. Arturo believes whatever people tell him. It's easy to _____.

7. Sasha's mother found out that he was at his friend's house when he had told her he would be at the library. Now she wonders what else he might be _____ from her.

8. The school tried to _____ people. It advertised that you could learn English in three weeks if you completed the courses.

9. Do you really think John believed that story? It's not that easy to _____ him.

10. Narcissists have a very _____ opinion of themselves.

PART 3: SKILLS FOR SPEAKING

3.1 *Read the conversations. Check (✔) the correct word or phrase to complete the sentence. The first one has been done for you.*

SILVIA: They all say they were at home when the crime was committed, but someone is lying.

MARY: Well, it _____ be my roommate Tara. We were both in our room studying for an exam all day. And I talked to Ahmed. He was at his house with his girlfriend all day, so it wasn't him. But I did see Joseph leaving the dormitory.

   ✔ **A.** couldn't   ____ **B.** shouldn't   ____ **C.** should

SILVIA: Then Joseph _____ be lying.
            1.

   ____ **A.** ought to   ____ **B.** must   ____ **C.** should

TEACHING ASSISTANT: The students _____ already known what
                  2.

plagiarism is, but apparently one or two didn't understand. A

couple of the papers were copied almost word for word from

an article on the Internet.

   ____ **A.** could have   ____ **B.** must have   ____ **C.** should have

PROFESSOR SRITA: They _____ heard my talk about the
           3.

seriousness of plagiarism.

   ____ **A.** could have   ____ **B.** shouldn't have   ____ **C.** must not have

DAVID: Do you think Markus was lying when he said he had never had a traffic

violation?

RICHARD: He _____ been telling the truth. I saw a speeding ticket on
             4.

his desk.

   ____ **A.** couldn't have   ____ **B.** might not have   ____ **C.** shouldn't have

3.2 ᶜᴰ⁷ ⑩ *Listen to the conversation. Check (✔) the sound of the underlined auxiliary you hear, **have** or [əv] (reduced). The first one has been done for you.*

A: I need your advice.

B: Sure. What's up?

A: Well, I saw Jane yesterday with someone and it wasn't her boyfriend, James. Then today I saw James, and he asked if I had seen Jane last night. Should I <u>have</u> said anything to him?

B: (1) I wouldn't <u>have</u> if I were you.

A: I didn't, but I feel guilty.

B: Well, it (2) might not <u>have</u> been what you think.

A: You're right. The guy (3) could <u>have</u> been her brother.

should I have said

_____ **A.** have

___✓___ **B.** [əv]

1. I wouldn't have

_____ **A.** have

_____ **B.** [əv]

2. might not have been

_____ **A.** have

_____ **B.** [əv]

3. could have been

_____ **A.** have

_____ **B.** [əv]

3.3 *Read the conversation. Use the phrases from the box to fill in the blanks. The first one has been done for you.*

and another point might be	on the other hand
if you look at it from the angle of	one way to think about it
it depends on	~~there are several things to consider~~

TOMO: Today the professor talked about the issue of downloading music files.

MARIAH: But everyone does it. What's the big deal?

TOMO: Well, ___there are several things to consider___. Of course

_____ whether you're a musician or a
                        1.

consumer who wants access to free music. Many musicians feel that

downloading is like stealing. When music is downloaded, they don't get

paid, the song writers don't get paid, and the people who hold the

copyrights don't get paid.

MARIAH: Yeah, but _____ a consumer like me, I'm
                        2.

not really buying music, I'm sharing it. You shouldn't have to pay for

sharing. _____ that when music is
                        3.

shared, the musicians have a larger audience.

TOMO: Yeah, but the audience doesn't pay the price of the ticket. They're seeing a

free concert.

PART 4: SPEAKING

4.1 *Say one thing that Dr. Smith from Part 1.2 told her listeners about their problems. You may listen again to Part 1.2.*

4.2 *Show another side to what Dr. Smith said. Begin your response with an introductory expression or an expression of additional response.*

4.3 *Consequences of Telling Lies*

Speak for 1 to 2 minutes about a time when you or someone you know told a lie.
- Before you speak, take notes about what happened.
- Discuss what you think the reason(s) might have been for telling the lie.
- Use expressions that show multiple sides of the issue.
- Use the reduction of the auxiliary *have*.
- Use the vocabulary and grammar from Unit 2.

<table>
<tr><td colspan="3" align="center">**Unit 2 Vocabulary Words**</td></tr>
<tr>
<td>concea(ling)
inflated
intrusive
mislead(ing)
preoccupation</td>
<td>pull the wool over somebody's eyes
put one over on somebody
put the pieces together
relentless
slippery slope</td>
<td>tattle
trivial
up front</td>
</tr>
<tr><td colspan="3" align="center">**Unit 2 Grammar: Modals—Degrees of Certainty**</td></tr>
<tr><td colspan="3">• My friend **must have** forgotten the tickets.
• You **shouldn't have** told that lie.
• I **might have** lost the paper, but I did write it.</td></tr>
</table>

Achievement Tests
Unit 3

Name: _____

Date: _____

PART 1: LISTENING

1.1 *CD 7*
(11) *Listen to the beginning of the discussion. Check (✔) the best prediction of what the listening is about. There is only one right answer.*

_____ **A.** a talk about social anxiety

_____ **B.** group therapy about kindred souls

_____ **C.** a therapy session for shy people

_____ **D.** a lesson on how to break the ice

1.2 *CD 7*
(12) *Now listen to the entire discussion. Use the information to choose the correct answers. Check (✔) the answers.*

1. What is this listening mainly about?

   _____ **A.** people's misperceptions of shy people

   _____ **B.** the good and bad aspects of shyness

   _____ **C.** ways people can overcome shyness

   _____ **D.** reasons why shyness is a handicap

2. What did the people in the group survive?

   _____ **A.** speaking to a group

   _____ **B.** introducing themselves

   _____ **C.** admitting their handicap

   _____ **D.** having social problems

3. We can infer that Gloria _____.

   _____ **A.** is actually not timid

   _____ **B.** is not happy at her job

   _____ **C.** doesn't want to talk to people

   _____ **D.** doesn't think that she is aloof

4. One of the positive aspects of shyness is _____.

    _____ **A.** observing situations

    _____ **B.** having better friendships

    _____ **C.** speaking in front of others

    _____ **D.** enjoying others' conversations

5. We can assume that Dr. Mendez _____.

    _____ **A.** understands shyness

    _____ **B.** was once shy himself

    _____ **C.** thinks shy people are popular

    _____ **D.** thinks shy people are standoffish

6. What are the people supposed to do before their next meeting?

    _____ **A.** be good listeners

    _____ **B.** meet more people

    _____ **C.** think more positively

    _____ **D.** practice breaking the ice

1.3 _Listen to part of "Americans Are Getting Shyer" from_ NorthStar: Listening and Speaking 5, _Unit 3. Use the information from this listening and the listening from Part 1.2 to complete the activity. Check (✔) the person who says each idea. The first one has been done for you._

Ideas	Dr. Zimbardo	Dr. Mendez	Both
Shy people are less popular.	✓		
1. People think shy people are not interesting.			
2. Shy people can be good listeners.			
3. People think shy people are dumb.			

PART 2: VOCABULARY

2.1 *Read the conversation. Use the words from the box to fill in the blanks. Not all of the words will be used.*

adverse	handicap	merits	petrified
extroverted	killjoy	misattributions	standoffish

DONALD: Did you go to the psychology lecture about shyness? It was fascinating.

CRISTINA: Yeah. I never realized what a _____ it must be to suffer
_____**1.**_____
from shyness. People think you're _____ because you're
_____**2.**
afraid to speak to them.

DONALD: People make all kinds of _____ about people who suffer
_____**3.**
from shyness. Practically everyone thinks being shy is an undesirable
quality. They think shy people lead boring lives and don't have many
friends.

CRISTINA: I know, but no one seems to realize that there are some

_____ to being shy. Shy people are usually good listeners.
_____**4.**
Most people need to have a friend who listens to them.

DONALD: Well to tell you the truth, I used to be extremely shy. I would be

_____ if I had to speak in front of the class.
_____**5.**

CRISTINA: That doesn't really surprise me. You still get petty quiet in group
situations.

2.2 *Match the words with their definitions. Write the correct letters on the lines. You will not use all of the definitions.*

_____ **1.** timid

_____ **2.** aloof

_____ **3.** kindred souls

_____ **4.** extrovert

_____ **5.** wallflowers

A. people who share the same traits

B. a person who is very sociable

C. gloomy

D. people who stay by themselves in social situations

E. shy

F. emotionally distant

G. valuable

PART 3: SKILLS FOR SPEAKING

3.1 *Read the paragraph. Write **I** on the line before the underlined clause if it is an identifying adjective clause. Write **N** if it is a nonidenifying adjective clause. Write **Q** if it is a quantifying expression. The first one has been done for you.*

Many people __I__ who are not usually shy have experiences of situational shyness.

This type of behavior, ____ which can happen when people have to perform in
   1.

front of a group, does not carry over into other parts of their lives. People ____
   2.

who are chronically shy, however, are often severely affected by this character trait.

It can affect their work, their friendships, even their intimate lives. To avoid these

problems, shy people often avoid places ____ where they have to interact with
   3.

groups. The chronically shy, ____ many of whom suffer from social phobia, can
   4.

have a difficult time adjusting throughout their lifetime.

3.2 CD ⁊ *Listen to the sentences. Check (✔) the sentence you hear. The first one has been done for you.*
10

_____ **A.** The report published in 1999 said that genetics play a large role in chronic shyness.

___✓___ **B.** The report, published in 1999, said that genetics play a large role in chronic shyness.

1. _____ **A.** The evidence which suggests that environment is an important factor is inconclusive.

_____ **B.** The evidence, which suggests that environment is an important factor, is inconclusive.

2. _____ **A.** The professor said shyness is treatable.

_____ **B.** The professor said, "Shyness is treatable."

3. _____ **A.** The clinic where the therapy was offered is now closed.

_____ **B.** The clinic, where the therapy was offered, is now closed.

3.3 *Read the conversation. Write the letter of the social skill on the line. You will not use all of the skills. The first one has been done for you.*

A. Volunteer information.   **D.** Ask open-ended questions.

~~**B.** Comment on something shared.~~   **E.** Listen actively.

C. Change the topic.   **F.** Introduce yourself.

                RINA: Hi, I'm Rina.

                KATYA: Oh, hi. I'm Katya.

___B___   RINA: Is this the first session you've come to?

_____ **1.** KATYA: Yes. How do you like the group?

                RINA: I think it's really helped. I'm not nearly as shy in social situations as I used to be.

_____ **2.** KATYA: Really?

_____ **3.** RINA: Oh, yeah. I never would have been able to carry on a conversation like this before I started coming to these sessions.

PART 4: SPEAKING

4.1 *Say one thing a member of the group from Part 1.2 said about a problem related to being shy. You may listen again to Part 1.2.*

4.2 *Say something that would keep a conversation going if the person in 4.1 had said that to you.*

4.3 *Shyness*

Speak for 1 to 2 minutes about shyness.
- Before you speak, take notes about some characteristics of shy people.
- Talk about what shy people can do to overcome their shyness.
- Group words together.
- Use the vocabulary and grammar from Unit 3.

Unit 3 Vocabulary Words				
aloof	handicap	misattributions	reserved	standoffish
bashful	kindred souls	outgoing	reticent	timid
extroverts	merit	petrified	self-conscious	wallflowers

Unit 3 Grammar: Adjective Clauses and Quantifying Expressions	
• Identifying Adjective Clause:	Many musicians **who are very introverted** come alive on stage.
• Nonidentifying Adjective Clause:	Dr. Mendez, **who runs the group therapy sessions**, is actually a very extroverted person.
• Quantifying Expression:	The patient had a number of symptoms, **all of which** were related to his difficult childhood.

Achievement Tests
Unit 4

PART I: LISTENING

1.1 *CD 7* (15) *Listen to the beginning of a talk show. Check (✔) the best prediction of what the listening is about. There is only one right answer.*

_____ **A.** three types of crimes

_____ **B.** a new perspective on crime

_____ **C.** different viewpoints on crime

_____ **D.** the profile of a person who commits crimes

1.2 *CD 7* (16) *Now listen to the entire talk show. Use the information to choose the correct answers. Check (✔) the answers.*

1. The main idea of this listening is to _____.

_____ **A.** discuss a theory about crime

_____ **B.** explain how crimes are committed

_____ **C.** show a criminal's reaction to an explanation of crime

_____ **D.** show how the conscience of a criminal's mind works

2. Mr. Mitchell believes crime can be reduced by _____.

_____ **A.** arresting more criminals

_____ **B.** cleaning up dangerous areas

_____ **C.** having more police on the street

_____ **D.** making citizens responsible for crime

3. What does the ex-criminal say about the subways in the 1980s?

_____ **A.** There were many people stabbed there.

_____ **B.** It was easy for a thief to steal there.

_____ **C.** Criminals were seen robbing children.

_____ **D.** People were trying to improve the subways.

4. The ex-criminal believes that crime in the subways decreased because

_____.

_____ **A.** the subways were cleaner

_____ **B.** fewer people jumped the turnstiles

_____ **C.** there was less graffiti in the subways

_____ **D.** more police were in the subway stations

5. What is Ms. Sanchez's theory about people who commit crimes?

_____ **A.** Parents are responsible for raising criminals.

_____ **B.** People who are morally corrupt commit crimes.

_____ **C.** The criminal mind is influenced by the environment.

_____ **D.** A strong desire to get something makes someone become a criminal.

6. Mr. Sorrell most likely does not agree with _____.

_____ **A.** Mr. Mitchell

_____ **B.** Ms. Sanchez

_____ **C.** Mr. Kelling

_____ **D.** the ex-criminal

1.3 🅒🅓 Listen to "Tipping Points in Fighting Crime" from NorthStar: Listening and
Ⓐ⑰ Speaking 5, *Unit 4. Use the information from this listening and the listening from Part 1.2 to complete the activity. Match the speakers with their opinions. Not all of the opinions will be used. The first one has been done for you.*

Speakers	Opinions
_C_ Mr. Sorrel	A. Cleaning the subways does not make them safe.
_____ **1.** Mr. Mitchell	B. A well-cared for neighborhood is a safe neighborhood.
_____ **2.** Ms. Sanchez	C. Parents have influence on their children's behavior.
_____ **3.** Ex-criminal	D. Crime occurs only in poor neighborhoods.
	E. Safety is not possible in today's world.
	F. Crime is caused because people have criminal minds.

PART 2: VOCABULARY

2.1 *Read the sentences. Use the words and phrases from the box to fill in the blanks. Not all of the words and phrases will be used.*

epidemic	goes a long way	mess	tide turned	vandalism
generate	hold	profiled	transmission	word of mouth
get a hold of	mavens	root		

1. The crime wave had reached _____ proportions by the time the city had it under control.

2. Before the scandal was even in the paper, it had spread by _____.

3. Even though the proposal to cut down on crime is popular, many sociologists think it won't _____ when considering violent criminals.

4. After the mayor spoke, the _____ toward approving the money to fight crime.

5. When kids _____ an idea, it's impossible to change their minds.

6. What is really at the _____ of crime?

7. The investigators _____ the criminal as a young, white female who came from a wealthy family.

8. On Halloween night _____ almost doubles.

9. The police had made such a _____ of the crime scene that none of the evidence could be used.

10. A poor economy can _____ crime.

PART 3: SKILLS FOR SPEAKING

3.1 *Read the sentences. Use the word or phrase in parentheses in an adverb clause to complete each sentence. The first one has been done for you.*

Central Park was once __so dangerous that__ people could enjoy it only during
                                     (dangerous)

daylight.

1. The crime wave spread _____ it soon reached epidemic
                                 (quickly)

   proportions.

2. John was _____ he convinced the audience to donate half their
                  (powerful speaker)

   income to the church.

3. The vandals were _____ they escaped every time the police tried
                     (clever)

   to catch them.

4. During the Los Angeles riots, there was _____ Los Angeles
                         (much vandalism)

   became a war zone.

3.2 🔊 *Listen to the sentences. Circle the syllable that has primary stress. The first one has been done for you.*

The criminal used very (com)pli ca ted tactics to fool the police.

1. In the end the **com pli ca tions** confused even him and led to his downfall.

2. When he was finally caught, the criminal had become so **po pu lar** that he was a hero.

3. Soon his **po pu lar i ty** made him one of the most famous criminals in history.

3.3 Read the paragraph. Replace the words in parentheses with metaphors from the box.
The first one has been done for you.

contagious	go through the roof	triggered
epidemic	immune	turn the tide
float an idea	infected	

As the economy worsened, people became angry. The recession

_____triggered_____ a sharp rise in crime. As more people lost their jobs, a feeling
     (caused)

of hopelessness _____ the country. In several months, the
     1. (spread through)

hopelessness had become an _____. There was nothing the
     2. (uncontrollable force)

government could do to _____ until the economy turned around.
     3. (change the course)

PART 4: SPEAKING

4.1 *Say one thing that a speaker from Part 1.2 said about crime. You may listen again to Part 1.2.*

4.2 *Use a metaphor in a sentence related to what you said in 4.1.*

4.3 *Crime*

Speak for 1 to 2 minutes about Kelling's theory that a well-cared-for environment discourages vandalism.

- Before you speak, take notes about the theory.
- Tell whether you agree or disagree with this theory.
- Make a point with a metaphor.
- Use correct primary stress in words.
- Use the vocabulary and grammar from Unit 4.

<table>
<tr><td colspan="5" align="center">Unit 4 Vocabulary Words</td></tr>
<tr>
<td>contagious
crime wave
epidemic
generate</td>
<td>get a hold of
go through the roof
goes a long way toward
holds</td>
<td>immune
infect
mess
profile</td>
<td>root
transmission
trigger
turn the tide</td>
<td>vandalism
win someone over</td>
</tr>
<tr><td colspan="5" align="center">Unit 4 Grammar: Adverb Clauses of Result</td></tr>
<tr><td colspan="5">

- The measures taken to reduce crime were **so effective that** the city became one of the safest cities in the country.
- The city had earned **such a bad reputation that** the tourist industry went bankrupt.
- The criminal ran **so quickly that** the police couldn't catch him.

</td></tr>
</table>

Achievement Tests
Unit 5

Name: _____

Date: _____

PART 1: LISTENING

1.1 *CD 7* (19) *Listen to the beginning of a conversation. Check (✔) the best prediction of what the listening is about. There is only one right answer.*

_____ **A.** the problems of a family

_____ **B.** the principles of feng shui

_____ **C.** a quote by Margaret Meade

_____ **D.** a metaphor for the nuclear family

1.2 *CD 7* (20) *Now listen to the entire conversation. Use the information to choose the correct answers. Check (✔) the answers.*

1. What is the main idea of this listening?

_____ **A.** Family problems might be helped by feng shui.

_____ **B.** Therapy can help align the energy in a household.

_____ **C.** Families cannot live in harmony.

_____ **D.** The mother is responsible for keeping the family together.

2. What is being compared in the quotation the therapist mentions?

_____ **A.** a family and a box

_____ **B.** tension and suffocation

_____ **C.** air circulation and energy

_____ **D.** rocky times and family problems

3. What is Kimberly complaining about?

_____ **A.** the flow of energy in her house

_____ **B.** tension at work

_____ **C.** the lack of interaction in her family

_____ **D.** her son and daughter's relationship

4. How does Nicole probably feel about her brother?

_____ **A.** She worries that he will miss her.

_____ **B.** She feels bad because he is depressed.

_____ **C.** She is tired of living in the house with him.

_____ **D.** She is afraid that she interferes with his studying.

5. What do most therapists probably think about feng shui?

_____ **A.** They think that it is harmful to their patients.

_____ **B.** They believe that it shouldn't be used in therapy.

_____ **C.** They are afraid that its principles are dangerous.

_____ **D.** They worry that it will take away their patients.

6. Matthew thinks feng shui is about _____.

_____ **A.** energy and harmony

_____ **B.** the alignment of feelings

_____ **C.** transcendent principles

_____ **D.** communication problems

1.3 🔊 *Listen to "Feng Shui in the Newsroom" from* NorthStar: Listening and Speaking 5, *Unit 5. Use the information from this listening and the listening from Part 1.2 to complete the activity. Check (✔) the box that indicates the direction that might help each person's problem.*

	1. **Kimberly** **(family)**	2. **Nicole** **(money)**	3. **Matthew** **(school)**
Northwest			
Southwest			
Northeast			
Southeast			

PART 2: VOCABULARY

2.1 *Read the conversation. Use the words and phrases from the box to fill in the blanks. Not all of the words and phrases will be used.*

abundance	anecdotes	digression	hard-bitten	skeptical
acute	caught off guard	frowned upon	quote	transcendent
aligned	circulating	govern	sense	

ARCHITECT: My client insists that all of the rooms be _____

1.

so that energy flows freely through them. Please don't

_____ me on this, but I have no idea which way
2.

the energy is flowing. I just draw up the design and add some

arrows to show which direction the air is _____.
3.

POLICE OFFICER: I'm pretty _____ too, but people expect that
4.

from a _____ police officer like me.
5.

INTERIOR DESIGNER: Well, I can imagine that you and your friends don't sit around

after work and look for _____ reasons for a
6.

criminal's behavior. Even in my field, feng shui is

_____ by many of the old school designers. But
7.

when I walk into a client's house, I can usually

_____ whether a room is filled with bad energy,
8.

like tension, or nice, calming energy. There are some ideas in

feng shui that all of you would agree with, I bet.

POLICE OFFICER: You've got to be kidding.

INTERIOR DESIGNER: A police officer especially wouldn't sit at a desk with his back

to the door. Think how easy it would be for someone to sneak

in. You'd be _____ and unable to defend
                          9.

yourself.

POLICE OFFICER: That's pretty obvious. What else would feng shui tell me that I

don't already know?

ARCHITECT: My client had dozens of _____ about friends
                                      10.

who painted the southeast corner of their living room purple

and suddenly their financial problems disappeared.

PART 3: SKILLS FOR SPEAKING

3.1 *Read the conversation. Use the discourse connectors from the box to fill in the blanks.
You will not use all of the words. The first one has been done for you.*

~~as a result~~	however	on top of that	so
but	on the other hand	plus	

WIFE: I paid for the most expensive designer because she's known for her

knowledge of feng shui. ____As a result____, we're bankrupt. We spent

all that money to make sure the energy was flowing smoothly so our

lives would be more relaxed. Now all we do is argue. And

_____, our house is hideous. Why did we let her convince
          1.

us to paint that room yellow?

HUSBAND: Honey, that's the color that goes with relationships. It's supposed to

enhance our marriage. _____, it doesn't seem to be
                            2.

working in our case.

(continued on next page)

WIFE: In fact, we can't agree on anything. So now we're broke.

            _____ our marriage is falling apart.
                    3.

HUSBAND: I guess that ugly purple wall isn't working either. We can't even afford to

            pay her bill.

WIFE: Why should we pay her? She redesigned our house, _____
                                                                          4.

            we have an ugly house, a ruined marriage, and an empty bank account.

3.2 ᶜᴰ₁ *Listen to the sentences. Add a comma after the introducer if it is separated from*
       ⌢ *the following sentence. The first one has been done for you.*
       ②②

        You know, it's a good idea to read a book about feng shui.

    1. So you'll get a lot of great ideas.

    2. Plus you'll learn from design experts.

    3. Anyway I think you should take my advice.

3.3 *Read the sentences. On the line write the letter of the correct explanation for the*
       underlined expression. You will not use all of the explanations. The first one has been
       done for you.

    A. add an explanation

    B. make an exclamation

    C. clarify meaning

    D. emphasize a point

    E. ~~say something unreasonable~~

    __E__   Shawna <u>would no more</u> paint her living room purple <u>than</u> she would

              wear a hot pink bikini.

    _____ **1.** Ever since we put that aquarium in the lobby, <u>I'd have to say</u> our business

              has doubled.

    _____ **2.** <u>Boy,</u> did his luck change since he had a feng shui master design his house!

    _____ **3.** <u>I wouldn't say</u> he doesn't believe in the principles of feng shui, <u>but I would

              say</u> he's skeptical.

PART 4: SPEAKING

4.1   *Say one piece of advice a feng shui master would give the family in Part 1.2 to help the energy in their house. You may listen again to Parts 1.2 and 1.3.*

4.2   *Use an exclamation to say what you think of the advice the feng shui master gave.*

4.3   *Feng Shui*

Speak for 1 to 2 minutes. Imagine that you have read several books about feng shui. Give a friend advice about how to design her home based on the principles of feng shui.

- Before you speak, take notes about your ideas.
- Use expressions to emphasize your points.
- Pronounce reductions with *have* correctly.
- Use the vocabulary and grammar from Unit 5.

Unit 5 Vocabulary Words			
acute	anecdotes	govern	sense (verb)
abundance	caught off guard	hard-bitten	skeptical
aligned	circulating	quote	transcendent

Unit 5 Grammar: Spoken Discourse Connectors

- Contrast: The woman didn't believe in feng shui, **but** her husband did.
- Addition: The new house was beautiful, and **on top of that**, it wasn't very expensive.
- Result: The couple painted the room red, and **as a result**, they had good luck.

Achievement Tests
Unit 6

Name: _____

Date: ____ _____

PART 1: LISTENING

1.1 CD 7 (23) *Listen to the beginning of an interview. Check (✔) the best prediction of what the listening is about. There is only one right answer.*

_____ **A.** life in the Himalayas

_____ **B.** a description of well-being

_____ **C.** the lifestyle of the monks

_____ **D.** the effect of leaving the hectic city

1.2 CD 7 (24) *Now listen to the entire interview. Use the information to choose the correct answers. Check (✔) the answers.*

1. This interview is mainly about the _____.

   _____ **A.** role of fasting in the monks' lifestyle

   _____ **B.** events in a Buddhist monastery

   _____ **C.** changes in the guest's lifestyle after visiting a monastery

   _____ **D.** monastery in the Himalayas where monks get spiritual renewal

2. How did John feel after returning from his trip?

   _____ **A.** He felt grateful for his chance to get away from the city.

   _____ **B.** He realized that he was out of touch with his body.

   _____ **C.** He seemed to be free of his inner turmoil.

   _____ **D.** He had a feeling of well-being.

3. John thought that the monks did not have to rely on material things because _____.

   _____ **A.** their monasteries compensated for the lack of material objects

   _____ **B.** refraining from eating or drinking was a ritual in their culture

   _____ **C.** their religion did not allow them to own things

   _____ **D.** having material goods was spiritually taboo

4. After his return home, John will most likely _____.

_____ **A.** live in a monastery

_____ **B.** get rid of all of his material things

_____ **C.** leave the hectic city

_____ **D.** learn how to do yoga

5. What did John most likely think about the Buddhist monks?

_____ **A.** They do not have very much inner turmoil.

_____ **B.** Through yoga, they develop a free mind.

_____ **C.** They are out of touch with their bodies.

_____ **D.** Their spiritual life is very complex.

6. According to the interview, the monks' ultimate goal is to _____.

_____ **A.** climb the mountains

_____ **B.** free their minds

_____ **C.** visit other monasteries

_____ **D.** rid themselves of stress

1.3 CD 7 25 *Listen to "The Religious Tradition of Fasting" from* NorthStar: Listening and Speaking 5, *Unit 6. Use the information from this listening and the listening from Part 1.2 to complete the activity. You will not use all of the answers. The first one has been done for you.*

A. Ramadan

B. to free the mind

C. first Sunday of every month

D. to foster humility

E. to replenish the soul

F. full moon days

Religious Group	When They Fast	Why They Fast
Muslims	A	2.
Buddhists	1.	3.

PART 2: VOCABULARY

2.1 *Read the paragraphs. Use the words and phrases from the box to fill in the blanks. Not all of the words and phrases will be used.*

divine	fasting	in a rut	refrain from	well-being
enact	hectic	out of touch	replenish	

In pagan religions, _____ is a ritual that lasts about forty days. In
1.

some sects of paganism, people _____ eating certain foods during
2.

this period. This ritual is performed to celebrate the union of certain gods who

_____ the earth with an abundance of food.
3.

For many people, the _____ pace of living in a large city is
4.

exhausting. They find that the constant pressure of work makes them feel

_____ with the important things in life. The practice of yoga or
5.

meditation helps some people relax and feel a sense of _____.
6.

2.2 *Match the words with their definitions. Write the letter of the correct definition on the line. You will not use all of the definitions.*

_____ **1.** ascetic	A. someone who goes without eating for religious reasons
_____ **2.** serenity	B. disturbing feelings of great emotional suffering
_____ **3.** will	C. the ability to feel strong emotions
_____ **4.** inner turmoil	D. the determination to take action
	E. a person who denies him or herself most pleasurable things
	F. a feeling of peace and calmness

PART 3: SKILLS FOR SPEAKING

3.1 *Read the sentences. Check (✔) **A** if the underlined noun is a count noun. Check (✔) **B** if the underlined noun is a non-count noun. The first one has been done for you.*

People who decide to live a monastic life have a great deal of <u>faith</u>.

_____ **A.** count noun

___✓___ **B.** non-count noun

1. It doesn't take much <u>effort</u> to eat instead of fast.

_____ **A.** count noun

_____ **B.** non-count noun

2. It requires a lot of <u>self-discipline</u> to become a yoga master.

_____ **A.** count noun

_____ **B.** non-count noun

3. An ascetic needs very few <u>material things</u> to get by in life.

_____ **A.** count noun

_____ **B.** non-count noun

4. Many disciplines require much <u>self-sacrifice</u>.

_____ **A.** count noun

_____ **B.** non-count noun

3.2 *CD 7* *Listen to the pairs of words. Check (✔) the vowel alternation you hear. The first* **26** *one has been done for you.*

sacrifice / sacrificial

___✓___ **A.** ay—ɪ

_____ **B.** iy—ɛ

_____ **C.** ey—æ

1. serene / serenity

_____ **A.** ay—ɪ

_____ **B.** iy—ɛ

_____ **C.** ey—æ

(continued on next page)

    2. describe / description

         _____ **A.** ay—ɪ

         _____ **B.** iy—ɛ

         _____ **C.** ey—æ

    3. profane / profanity

         _____ **A.** ay—ɪ

         _____ **B.** iy—ɛ

         _____ **C.** ey—æ

3.3   *Read the conversation. Write the letter of the phrase on the line where it best fits in the conversation. You will not use all of the phrases. The first one has been done for you.*

Phrases

  A. Let me know about . . .

  B. I want to draw you out on the subject . . .

  C. Well, I'll . . .

  D. I'll pull in one example . . .

  E. I can't imagine what . . .

  ~~**F.** Why don't you talk briefly about . . .~~

HOST: I'm here with John Saunders, who is back in hectic New York City after having spent three years living a very ascetic life in a quest for inner peace and harmony. _____F_____ your lifestyle during this quest?

JOHN: _____ tell you about how a spent a typical day. First, I would
1.
get up at sunset. I would then meditate for an hour before eating anything. My breakfast was a bowl of brown rice and broccoli. For the remainder of the day until sunset, I walked through the forest to regain a sense of our basic instincts. I would try to see the world through the eyes of the animals in the forest, say a deer or a bird.

HOST: _____ of our basic animal nature. Did you gain any insight
2.
into the profound question concerning human vs. animal?

JOHN: Yes. As I began to feel like an animal and live life at the survival level, I had

so many life-changing experiences. _____ of an early life-
                                            3.

changing experience.

PART 4: SPEAKING

4.1 *Tell which part of John Everly's trip he thought was the best experience. You may listen again to Part 1.2.*

4.2 *Respond to your answer to 4.1 with an expression that encourages John to tell more about this experience.*

4.3 *A Different Lifestyle*

Speak for 1–2 minutes. Imagine that you took a trip to experience a lifestyle that was very different from your own. You are now being interviewed on a talk show about the experiences you had on this trip and how they affected you.

- Before you speak, take notes about your imagined experiences.
- Use some phrases that begin an anecdote.
- Pronounce vowel sounds correctly.
- Use the vocabulary and grammar from Unit 6.

Unit 6 Vocabulary Words				
ascetic	gratitude	in a rut	refrain from	well-being
enact	hectic	inner turmoil	replenish	will
fasting	humility	out of touch with	serenity	

Unit 6 Grammar: Count and Non-Count Nouns and Their Quantifiers
• Count noun: I had **many** amazing **experiences** on my vacation.   • Non-count noun: **Quite a bit of effort** is needed to do well.

Achievement Tests
Unit 7

Name: _____

Date: _____

PART I: LISTENING

1.1 *CD 7* *Listen to the beginning of a talk show. Check (✔) the best prediction of what the listening is about. There is only one right answer.*

_____ **A.** the use of technology to monitor employees

_____ **B.** changes in the way business is conducted

_____ **C.** the ways technology has improved the workplace

_____ **D.** employees' right to monitor their work environment

1.2 *CD 7* *Now listen to the entire talk show. Use the information to choose the correct answers. Check (✔) the answers.*

1. The two people who call in to the talk show _____.

_____ **A.** think that monitoring employees is legitimate

_____ **B.** made calls to foreign countries

_____ **C.** feel that electronic communication is demeaning

_____ **D.** have been affected by surveillance systems

2. Jim's company _____.

_____ **A.** eavesdropped on employees' phone conversations

_____ **B.** recorded the number of calls employees made

_____ **C.** kept a log of which phones an employee used

_____ **D.** listened for racial slurs employees made on the phone

3. How did Jim prove that he didn't make the calls to Ankara?

_____ **A.** He told his company he had never been to Ankara.

_____ **B.** His company didn't have any clients in Turkey.

_____ **C.** Some of the calls were made when he wasn't in the office.

_____ **D.** Some employees said they didn't see him make the calls.

4. Jim's tone of voice indicates that he is _____.

_____ **A.** uncertain

_____ **B.** angry

_____ **C.** relieved

_____ **D.** encouraged

5. An employee that Anne supervises was upset because _____.

_____ **A.** she didn't like the idea of Big Brother monitoring her

_____ **B.** Anne was keeping track of the e-mails the employee sent

_____ **C.** someone sent her e-mails that contained racial slurs

_____ **D.** she felt that the surveillance system was an invasion of privacy

6. Anne would probably agree with which statement?

_____ **A.** It could be sinister to use technology to monitor the workplace.

_____ **B.** Monitoring employees in the workplace is demeaning.

_____ **C.** Employees must never use company phones for private calls.

_____ **D.** It can be beneficial to monitor employees' work.

1.3 ᶜᴰ⁊ 🔘29 *Listen to the excerpt from "Managers and Employees Speak Out" from* NorthStar: *Listening and Speaking 5, Unit 7. Use the information from this listening and the listening from Part 1.2 to complete the activity. Write the letter of the reason why each person agrees or disagrees with the statement. Not all of the reasons will be used. The first one has been done for you.*

A. separation of workplace from home

B. case of mistaken identity

C. safeguards business

D. material at workplace is not private

E. finds source of demeaning material

~~**F.** issue of trust~~

Statement: Technology can be used to monitor the workplace.

	Reason
Speaker 1	F
1. Speaker 2	
2. Jim Tate	
3. Anne Winslow	

PART 2: VOCABULARY

2.1 *Read the paragraph. Use the words and phrases from the box to fill in the blanks. Not all of the words and phrases will be used.*

a log	driving	legitimate	step up
Big Brother	eavesdrop	racial slur	surveillance
demeaning	employers	safeguarding	willy-nilly
deter	keeping an eye on	scope	

In an effort to _____ employees from using company time for
                                1.

personal matters, _____ may monitor their employees at the
                            2.

workplace. Some people feel that this is exactly what Orwell predicted—a place

where _____ is always _____ them. There are various
            3.   **4.**

kinds of _____ systems used, some that _____ on
                5.   **6.**

employees' conversations and others that keep _____ of how much
                                                          7.

time workers spend and for what purpose they use the company's telephone or

computer. While many employees find this situation _____, the
                                                              8.

owners of businesses feel this is a way of _____ their company. The
                                                    9.

real question is, what is a _____ use of new technologies used to
                                    10.

monitor people in their workplace?

PART 3: SKILLS FOR SPEAKING

3.1 *Read the sentences. Fill in the blanks with the gerund or infinitive form of the verb in parentheses. The first one has been done for you.*

Before she left work, Ms. Freeman stopped ____*to check*____ the surveillance
                                                      (check)

camera to see if anyone had misused company property.

John was caught using the Internet to shop for electronics. He knew this was against

company policy, but he didn't know it meant _____ fired.
                                                      1. (get)

Angela wonders why she didn't get the job she had applied for. She remembers

_____ the personality questionnaire, but now she realizes she might
        2. (turn in)

have forgotten _____ the drug test.
                        3. (take)

Tom was always uncomfortable at work because he felt like Big Brother was

watching everything he did. Now he regrets _____ the job.
                                              4. (accept)

3.2 CD 7 *Listen to the sentences. The underlined syllables are stressed. Check (✔) the*
        30 *correct stress and part of speech you hear. The first one has been done for you.*

Robert did not want to _____ his co-worker, so he did not
mention the gossip.

_____ **A.** <u>in</u>sult / noun

_____ **B.** <u>in</u>sult / verb

_____ **C.** in<u>sult</u> / noun

__✓__ **D.** in<u>sult</u> / verb

1. We did not plan well for the _____ and could not meet the
deadline.

_____ **A.** <u>pro</u>ject / noun

_____ **B.** <u>pro</u>ject / verb

_____ **C.** pro<u>ject</u> / noun

_____ **D.** pro<u>ject</u> / verb

2. The employee's continuing _____ with his boss led to his
eventual dismissal.

_____ **A.** <u>con</u>flict / noun

_____ **B.** <u>con</u>flict / verb

_____ **C.** con<u>flict</u> / noun

_____ **D.** con<u>flict</u> / verb

3. My manager _____ that Lola sent the offending e-mail.

_____ **A.** <u>sus</u>pects / noun

_____ **B.** <u>sus</u>pects / verb

_____ **C.** sus<u>pects</u> / noun

_____ **D.** sus<u>pects</u> / verb

3.3   *Read the conversations and speeches. Circle the letter in front of the underlined phrase that frames an argument. The first one has been done for you.*

JOSEPH: Did you know that employers can see what's on your computer screen? (A) <u>Not only that</u>, they can even get into the hard drive of your computer.

MARK: I just read about that. It really doesn't surprise me. Ⓑ <u>I mean, you have to agree that</u> when you're on the company's computer, you should be doing your work. (C) <u>Why should it bother you if</u> someone sees what's on your computer if you're not doing anything wrong?

1. SARAH: Now there's a software program that can keep track of how many keystrokes you make. (A) <u>I can't believe how</u> easy it's getting for your boss to know everything you do.

    TIM: (B) <u>I see what you mean</u>. It's like Big Brother is always keeping an eye on you. It's such an invasion of privacy.

    SARAH: I know. (C) <u>But the real question is</u>, what can be done so we don't lose what little privacy we have left?

2. **Organizer of National Office Workers Union**
    I know most of you are here to learn more about the recent rules that have been established in your places of work. (A) <u>Of course I understand that</u> you are worried about how these rules will affect you personally. The new surveillance system will make it possible for all of our phone calls to be monitored. (B) <u>That means that</u> we have to think carefully about what we discuss and who we talk to when we make a phone call. However, (C) <u>the point I want to make</u> is that it is our right to know when the new monitoring system is put in place.

3. **Psychologist speaking to management staff**
    I have been asked to speak with you about the effects of monitoring workers' phone calls and computer use. (A) <u>I would like to say specifically that</u> constant monitoring is adding a new layer of stress to an already stressful work environment. In the last month, more than twenty-five employees have come to my office with stress-related problems. (B) <u>I must ask</u>, what benefits do you get from the new surveillance system? (C) <u>Could the benefits</u> possibly outweigh the cost to your company? There has been a ten percent increase in the number of sick days taken by your employees.

PART 4: SPEAKING

4.1 *Say a reason in favor of monitoring employees at work. You may listen again to Part 1.2.*

4.2 *Use an expression that frames an argument to state the reason in favor of monitoring employees at work.*

4.3 *Monitoring Employees*

Speak for 1 to 2 minutes. Take a position for or against monitoring employees in the workplace. Make an argument that supports your position.

- Before you speak, take notes about your ideas.
- Use expressions to frame your argument.
- Use correct stress in nouns and verbs.
- Use the vocabulary and grammar from Unit 7.

Unit 7 Vocabulary Words				
a log	deter	employers	racial slur	sinister
Big Brother	driving	keeping an eye on	safeguard	surveillance
demeaning	eavesdrop	legitimate	scope	willy-nilly
Unit 7 Grammar: Verb + Gerund or Infinitive—Two Forms, Two Meanings				

- Verb + gerund: Celia **remembered speaking** to her boss about her phone calls, but her boss forgot the conversation.
- Verb + infinitive: Ms. Santos **remembered to check** the surveillance camera to see if all employees had been working at their computers.

Achievement Tests
Unit 8

Name: _____

Date: _____

PART I: LISTENING

1.1 CD7 (31) *Listen to the beginning of a lecture. Check (✔) the best prediction of what the listening is about. There is only one right answer.*

_____ **A.** the evolution of war

_____ **B.** the complexity of war

_____ **C.** the legitimacy of war

_____ **D.** the volatility of war

1.2 CD7 (32) *Now listen to the entire lecture. Use the information to choose the correct answers. Check (✔) the answers.*

1. What is the main idea of this lecture?

   _____ **A.** views about the legitimacy of war

   _____ **B.** reasons for the complexity of war

   _____ **C.** the institutionalization of war

   _____ **D.** the pacifist view of war

2. The professor most likely thinks that _____.

   _____ **A.** war is institutionalized mass murder

   _____ **B.** there is no good reason for war

   _____ **C.** war is a human universal

   _____ **D.** there is only one good reason for war

3. People who believe in human universalism think that war _____.

   _____ **A.** cannot be avoided

   _____ **B.** is always legitimate

   _____ **C.** is institutionalized murder

   _____ **D.** is accepted by everyone

4. Welzer and other Just War theorists believe the only just reason to start a war is to _____.

   _____ **A.** transition to peace

   _____ **B.** train soldiers

   _____ **C.** resist aggression

   _____ **D.** support a just cause

5. The question of just conduct during war considers all of the following issues EXCEPT _____.

 _____ **A.** the weapons that are used

 _____ **B.** the targets of soldiers' weapons

 _____ **C.** the treatment of prisoners of war

 _____ **D.** the just cause of war

🎧 CD 7 **33** *Listen again to part of the lecture. Then answer this question.*

6. Why does the professor say "So what *is* a legitimate reason to start a war?"

 _____ **A.** to admit that he doesn't know the answer

 _____ **B.** to make a transition to the next topic

 _____ **C.** to ask the students a question

 _____ **D.** to emphasize a point

1.3 🎧 CD 7 **34** *Listen to "Michael Ignatieff's Views on War" from* NorthStar: Listening and Speaking 5, *Unit 8. Use the information from this listening and the listening from Part 1.2 to complete the activity. Write the letter of the statements in the correct column. Not all of the statements will be used. The first one has been done for you.*

A. War is so savage that it is never justified.

~~**B.** There can be just causes of war.~~

C. Oppressed groups use war to free themselves.

D. Use right conduct while fighting a war.

E. You should not equate war with barbarism.

F. War is institutionalized mass murder.

Just War Theory (general concepts)	Ignatieff's Views on War (supporting details)
B	2.
1.	3.

PART 2: VOCABULARY

2.1   *Read the paragraphs. Use the words from the box to fill in the blanks. Not all of the words will be used.*

barbarism and savagery	disseminate	legitimate	subscribe
codes	identify	restrained	tame

For people who _____ to pacifist ideals, there is never a

1.

_____ or just cause for war. Strict pacifists reject violence of any

2.

kind. Many people, however, recognize that _____ are a part of war,

3.

but believe that in some cases war cannot be avoided.

When a nation resorts to war, it is inevitable that horrific acts of violence are

committed. However, the _____ of war embodied in the Geneva

4.

Conventions prohibit certain violent acts from occurring. For example, it is

important that soldiers are _____ from harming civilians.

5.

2.2   *Match the words with their definitions. Not all of the definitions will be used.*

_____ **1.** unleash	A. very unstable; likely to cause harm
_____ **2.** institutionalized	B. get rid of
_____ **3.** prevailing	C. true for every culture
_____ **4.** human universal	D. established; commonly accepted
_____ **5.** volatile	E. values or characteristics that are shared by all
	F. most widely accepted
	G. release

PART 3: SKILLS FOR SPEAKING

3.1 *Read the sentences. Check (✔) the correct words to complete each sentence. The first one has been done for you.*

In an interview about the concept of just wars, _____ if he could say something about how the criticisms were connected to the account of Just and Unjust Wars.

____✓____ **A.** a reporter asked Welzer

_____ **B.** Welzer said,

1. _____ "In the study of the wars the U.S. has been involved in, I cannot label one as a . . . war that had everyone's support."

    _____ **A.** The historian Robert Alotta said,

    _____ **B.** The historian Robert Alotta feels that the

2. When Dumant was helping the wounded, _____ "Would it not be possible, in time of peace and quiet, to form relief societies for the purpose of having care given to the wounded . . . ?"

    _____ **A.** he asked if

    _____ **B.** he wondered,

3. _____ "Throughout history, those who have the tendency to 'grow too fond of war,' in most cases have never fought in it."

    _____ **A.** Michael Gaddy said,

    _____ **B.** Michael Gaddy thinks that

3.2 🔘 *Listen to the sentences. Check (✔) the sound you hear in the underlined syllable. The first one has been done for you.*

Is there such a thing as a <u>just</u> war?

_____ **A.** /æ/

_____ **B.** /ɑ/

____✓____ **C.** /ə/

1. The reporter <u>asked</u> Mr. Welzer a question.

    _____ **A.** /æ/

    _____ **B.** /ɑ/

    _____ **C.** /ə/

(continued on next page)

2. The Red Cross brought <u>supplies</u> to the soldiers.

_____ **A.** /æ/

_____ **B.** /ɑ/

_____ **C.** /ə/

3. The reporter traveled to <u>vo</u>latile regions to gather news about the war.

_____ **A.** /æ/

_____ **B.** /ɑ/

_____ **C.** /ə/

3.3 *Read the conversations. Check (✔) the description of the underlined phrase. The first one has been done for you.*

SPEAKER: Professor Welzer, could you tell us how this war is different?

WELZER: <u>Well, that's a complicated issue</u>. You might say that technology has changed the way wars are fought.

___✓___ **A.** opening phrase

_____ **B.** follow-up phrase

_____ **C.** neither

1. SPEAKER: Mr. Alotta, could you tell us why most wars haven't received support from everyone?

MR. ALOTTA: Well, there's no simple answer to that. <u>You could say</u> that most wars benefit only a specific part of the population.

_____ **A.** opening phrase

_____ **B.** follow-up phrase

_____ **C.** neither

   2. SPEAKER: Mr. Gaddy, in your story about the young boy asking his father about World War I, how do you think the father felt?

       GADDY: <u>Hmm . . . that's a tough one</u>. You have to realize that every soldier experiences war in a different way.

_____ **A.** opening phrase

_____ **B.** follow-up phrase

_____ **C.** neither

   3. SPEAKER: Technology is changing the way wars are fought. Do you think that is a good thing or a bad thing?

       GADDY: Hmm . . . that's a tough one. <u>I don't think anything will</u> change the fact that war is unjust.

_____ **A.** opening phrase

_____ **B.** follow-up phrase

_____ **C.** neither

PART 4: SPEAKING

4.1 *Say one of the three questions the professor lists about the Just War Theory in Part 1.2. You may listen again to Part 1.2.*

4.2 *What would you say if you were asked the question about the Just War Theory that you stated in 4.1? Begin your answer with an opening phrase that is used to respond to a complex or controversial question.*

4.3 *Just and Unjust Wars*

Speak for 1 to 2 minutes. Discuss your opinions about just and unjust wars.

- Before you speak, take notes about your ideas.
- Use follow-up phrases when you explain your ideas.
- Pronounce vowels correctly.
- Use the vocabulary and grammar from Unit 8.

Unit 8 Vocabulary Words				
codes	do without	identify	legitimate	subscribe
devastating	equate	institutionalized	prevailing	unleash
disseminate	human universal	legitimacy	restrain	volatile

Unit 8 Grammar: Direct and Indirect Speech
• Direct speech: **My professor said,** "I don't think that war can be just."   • Indirect speech: **She said that** she didn't think that war could be just.

Achievement Tests
Unit 9

Name: _____

Date: _____

PART 1: LISTENING

1.1 CD7 (36) *Listen to the beginning of an interview. Check (✔) the best prediction of what the listening is about. There is only one right answer.*

_____ **A.** studies related to Dr. Rauscher's experiment

_____ **B.** experiments conducted by Dr. Kelly

_____ **C.** the basis of abstract reasoning

_____ **D.** Dr. Rauscher's future experiments

1.2 CD7 (37) *Now listen to the entire interview. Use the information to choose the correct answers. Check (✔) the answers.*

1. Dr. Kelly's current research _____.

   _____ **A.** examines the neurological basis of abstract thinking

   _____ **B.** shows that listening to music improves math skills

   _____ **C.** compares the results of experiments to Rauscher's study

   _____ **D.** investigates the need for art and music in curriculums

2. Both Dr. Kelly and Dr. Rauscher study _____.

   _____ **A.** the neurological basis of abstract reasoning

   _____ **B.** the pattern of neural activity in response to music

   _____ **C.** how children's brains react to musical stimuli

   _____ **D.** how music primes the brain for abstract reasoning

3. The subjects in Dr. Cuevas' study were _____.

   _____ **A.** researchers

   _____ **B.** music students

   _____ **C.** high school students

   _____ **D.** university students

4. Dr. Cuevas' study was conducted in _____.

   _____ **A.** 1993

   _____ **B.** 1995

   _____ **C.** 1998

   _____ **D.** 2000

(continued on next page)

5. What does Dr. Kelly most likely think about Dr. Shaw?

_____ **A.** He respects his work.

_____ **B.** He disapproves of him.

_____ **C.** He questions his intelligence.

_____ **D.** He doesn't trust him.

6. Dr. Kelly most likely thinks that _____.

_____ **A.** students should listen to music before taking math tests

_____ **B.** schools should have more music classes

_____ **C.** schools should play Mozart in math classes

_____ **D.** math scores would improve if students listened to music

1.3 CD ₁ *Listen to "Does Music Enhance Math Skills?" in* NorthStar: Listening and Speaking
⓷⓼ *5, Unit 9. Use the information from this listening and the listening from Part 1.2 to
complete the activity. Write the letters of the statements that tell about the studies.
You will not use all of the statements. The first one has been done for you.*

Control Groups

A. students who played Bach

B. students who took the standard curriculum

~~**C.** students who didn't listen to music~~

Results

D. The groups showed no significant difference on a math test.

E. The experimental group was significantly ahead in learning in math.

F. The control group performed significantly better on a math test.

	Dr. Cuevas' Study	**Martin Gardiner's Study**
Control Group	C	2.
Results	1.	3.

PART 2: VOCABULARY

2.1 *Read the paragraph. Use the words and phrases from the box to fill in the blanks. Not all of the words and phrases will be used.*

abstract reasoning	do more for	neurological
boost	hallmark	prime
curriculum	have nothing to do with	reaped benefits

Memorizing facts may involve a different kind of learning than

_____ does. However, there is a _____ basis for all
⎯ 1. ⎯   ⎯ 2. ⎯

learning. If we knew how to _____ the part of the brain specific to
                              ⎯ 3. ⎯

memorizing lists or applying spatial reasoning, perhaps we would be able to

perform these skills more easily. However, even without understanding how the

brain functions, a teacher can make an environment that helps learning. In fact, the

_____ of a good teacher is the ability to understand what helps her
⎯ 4. ⎯

students succeed. A good teacher can _____ a student than a well-
                                        ⎯ 5. ⎯

balanced _____ can.
          ⎯ 6. ⎯

2.2 *Check (✔) the best answer to complete each sentence.*

1. To *underscore* an idea means to _____ it.

_____ **A.** emphasize

_____ **B.** understand

_____ **C.** repeat

_____ **D.** learn

2. To put things in *sequential* order is to _____.

_____ **A.** rank them from best to worst

_____ **B.** lay them side by side

_____ **C.** arrange them one after another

_____ **D.** turn them inside out

(continued on next page)

   3. To do something *regardless* of the consequences is to do it _____

   them.

      _____ **A.** in place of

      _____ **B.** without

      _____ **C.** rather than

      _____ **D.** in spite of

   4. The *building blocks* of a theory are its _____.

      _____ **A.** fundamental parts

      _____ **B.** important roles

      _____ **C.** specific goals

      _____ **D.** recognized accomplishments

PART 3: SKILLS FOR SPEAKING

3.1 *Read the paragraph. Fill in the blank with the correct form of the passive voice. The first one has been done for you.*

The term *Mozart effect* originates from an experiment that ____was done____
                                                (do)

in 1993 by Dr. Francis Rauscher and Dr. Gordon L. Shaw. The results of their study

concerned patterns of neural activity in the brain. However, since this study, these

results _____ in a more general way. Today, it _____
      1. (apply)   2. (commonly, believe)

that listening to music can improve a person's abstract and spatial reasoning. The

curricula of many elementary schools now include more music classes than before

the Mozart effect became popular. Regardless of its popularity, the Mozart effect has

not yet _____ to enhance learning, and research _____.
       3. (prove)   4. (still, conduct)

3.2 CD 7 *Listen to the phrases. Write the letter of the rule that applies to the pronunciation*
    39 *of final consonants. If the phrases are pronounced incorrectly, write I on the line.*

Pronunciation rules:

- **A.** When the next word starts with a vowel, join the final consonant and vowel clearly.
- **B.** When the next word starts with the same consonant or sound, hold one long consonant. Do not say the consonant twice.
- **C.** When the next word starts with a different consonant, keep the final consonant short. Hold it, and then immediately say the next word.

___I___   scientific experiment

_____ **1.** building blocks

_____ **2.** neural language

_____ **3.** regardless of

3.3 *Read about the experiment. Then read the sentences. Use the words from the box to fill in the blanks. Not all of the words will be used. The first one has been done for you.*

Experiment:

1. The participants memorized a list of words.

2. The participants listened to five minutes of Beethoven, hip-hop music, or nothing.

3. The participants recalled the list of words.

Results: Both experimental groups remembered about 50% of the words on the list. The participants in the control group remembered 75% of the words on the list.

~~however~~	is different from	similarly
in contrast	is similar to	

The control group remembered 75% of the words; _____however_____, the experimental group remembered only 50% of the words.

1. Thirty participants were given a dictionary; _____, thirty other participants had access to an online dictionary.

2. Some groups memorized a list of words; _____, other groups were given a list of words to keep.

3. One researcher's experiment _____ Dr. Brown's in that they both tested the number of words retained after one week.

PART 4: SPEAKING

4.1 *Tell how the groups in Dr. Cuevas' experiment from Part 1.2 were different. You may listen again to Part 1.2.*

4.2 *Compare the group you talked about in Dr. Cuevas' experiment to the experimental group in Dr. Gardiner's experiment. Use a phrase that tells how the groups were similar or different.*

4.3 *Music and Learning*

Speak for 1 to 2 minutes on your opinion about whether or not music enhances learning.

- Before you speak, take notes about your ideas.
- Link ideas with expressions that compare and contrast.
- Join final consonants correctly.
- Use the vocabulary and grammar from Unit 9.

Unit 9 Vocabulary Words			
abstract reasoning	curriculum	primed	to do more for
advancing toward	hallmark	regardless	underscore
building blocks	interventions	sequential	well-rounded

Unit 9 Grammar: Passive Voice and Passive Causative
• Passive voice: The experiment *was conducted* in 1994.   • Passive causative: The psychologist *got* her study *published* in a well-respected journal.

Achievement Tests
Unit 10

Name: _____

Date: _____

PART 1: LISTENING

1.1 *CD7 40* *Listen to the beginning of an interview. Check (✔) the best prediction of what the listening is about. There is only one right answer.*

_____ **A.** when microfinancing is not helpful

_____ **B.** who does not think microfinancing is a solution

_____ **C.** how many people live below the poverty level

_____ **D.** how microfinancing helps people get out of poverty

1.2 *CD7 41* *Now listen to the entire interview. Use the information to choose the correct answers. Check (✔) the answers.*

1. This is a(n) _____.

_____ **A.** debate about how families can use microfinancing

_____ **B.** argument about the pros and cons of microfinancing

_____ **C.** interview about where microfinancing does and does not work

_____ **D.** lecture about why microfinacncing does not work in some areas

2. Based on this listening, which statement about microfinancing is true?

_____ **A.** Some people do not think it is a solution.

_____ **B.** People in some areas do not want to accept it.

_____ **C.** It helps only the poorest people in a village.

_____ **D.** It is the best solution for places with small economies.

3. Why is microfinancing called a Band-Aid solution?

_____ **A.** It doesn't address the root of the problem.

_____ **B.** Poverty can be treated as an illness.

_____ **C.** A solution to poverty does not exist.

_____ **D.** It covers up the pain of poverty.

(continued on next page)

4. Which of these factors was NOT mentioned as a necessary condition for microfinancing to work?

_____ **A.** a small business system

_____ **B.** a working infrastructure

_____ **C.** a healthy population

_____ **D.** a literate population

5. According to Dr. Lim, what is an alternative to microfinancing when it is not applicable?

_____ **A.** loans

_____ **B.** grants

_____ **C.** credit

_____ **D.** welfare

6. What does the host most likely think about microfinancing?

_____ **A.** He does not believe it will work.

_____ **B.** He does not believe in its principles.

_____ **C.** He is not convinced by the arguments against it.

_____ **D.** He is not convinced by Dr. Lim's defense of it.

1.3 CD7 42 *Listen to part of "Microfinance" in* NorthStar: Listening and Speaking 5, *Unit 10. Use the information from this listening and the listening from Part 1.2 to complete the activity. The first one has been done for you.*

Statements about Microfinance	Interview with Dr. Lim	"Microfinance"	Neither
It helps people with no safety net.		✓	
1. It can help illiterates learn to read.			
2. It can cause people to overextend themselves.			
3. It helps individuals, not villages.			

PART 2: VOCABULARY

2.1   *Read the sentences. Use the words and phrases from the box to fill in the blanks. Not all of the words and phrases will be used.*

compelling	malnourished	overnight	pitfalls
cottage industry	overextend	panacea	safety net

1. Don't be fooled by people who tell you they have a _____ for the world's problems. If such a thing existed, we would be living in a perfect world.

2. The pictures of the war-torn country were so _____ that I volunteered to join the relief organization.

3. Many of the people who were helped by microcredits were women who had no _____ to fall back on.

4. One of the _____ of the organization is that it cannot help people who are just above the poverty line.

5. The problems of poverty-stricken communities are not cured _____.

2.2   *Match the words in Column A with their definitions in Column B. Not all of the definitions will be used.*

Column A	Column B
_____ **1.** characterization	A. reach a limit
_____ **2.** sustainable	B. to speak in more detail
_____ **3.** elaborate	C. to describe a character
_____ **4.** diminish	D. able to continue without support
_____ **5.** hit a ceiling	E. the defining feature of something
	F. completely destroyed
	G. make less or smaller

PART 3: SKILLS FOR SPEAKING

3.1 *Read the sentences. Write a conditional structure with the word(s) in parentheses to complete each sentence. The first one has been done for you.*

Past unreal conditional

Some people think microfinancing is not a good solution to poverty. They believe that if people hadn't invested their money in banks like Grameen Bank, then larger, nationally-funded programs like CARE <u>would have received</u> (receive) more donations.

1. *Past result of a present condition*

   If microfinancing _____ (be) the solution to poverty, then poverty would have been wiped out long ago.

2. *Past unreal conditional*

   Thousands of families would not have received loans if Muhammad Yunus _____ (not, develop) the system of microfinancing.

3. *Present result of a past condition*

   Ma-Dong got a loan from a microfinance organization. Today, she has a small business that supports her extended family. If she _____ (not, get) the money, she would not be out of poverty.

4. *Present unreal conditional*

   Marie-Sainte lives in Haiti, the country with the highest poverty rate in the western world. She makes jewelry to sell at the market, but now she would like to double her income. If she got a loan, she _____ (increase) her income by at least one-third.

3.2 🔊 *Listen to the sentences. Check (✔) the underlined word that has heavier stress/higher pitch. The first one has been done for you.*

She did not have to pay any <u>income tax</u> on her new business.

   _✓_ **A.** income

   ____ **B.** tax

1. The <u>cottage industry</u> had windfall profits this year.

   ____ **A.** cottage

   ____ **B.** industry

2. As the population increased, there were too many <u>human beings</u> to care for.

    _____ **A.** human

    _____ **B.** beings

3. The <u>microloan</u> the woman received allowed her to develop a cottage industry.

    _____ **A.** micro

    _____ **B.** loan

3.3 *Read the paragraph. Write the phrases that introduce details and examples. The first one has been done for you.*

    The story of Haiti shows how decades of governmental strife have contributed to its nearly bankrupt economy. What we've witnessed time and time again is a democratic government being overthrown by a dictatorship. Today Haiti has the highest poverty rate in the western world. One figure that supports this is that today nearly two-thirds of the population do not have formal jobs. Another thing to keep in mind is that this country has the highest rates of AIDS and malnutrition in this hemisphere. Today Haiti hopes that microfinancing can help lift it out of such a severe state of poverty.

The story of Haiti shows _____

1. _____

2. _____

3. _____

PART 4: SPEAKING

4.1 *Say one of the pitfalls of microfinancing that Dr. Lim mentioned in Part 1.2. You may listen again to Part 1.2*

4.2 *Give a detail or an example that supports what you said in 4.1. Introduce it with an expression.*

4.3 *Microfinancing*

Speak for 1 to 2 minutes about microfinancing.

- Before you speak, take notes about your ideas.
- Give an illustration or tell a story about how someone might benefit from microfinancing.
- Use expressions to introduce ideas or examples.
- Use the vocabulary and grammar from Unit 10.

Unit 10 Vocabulary Words				
backlash	compelling	malnourished	overextend	sustainable
bear the brunt of	cottage industry	panacea	overnight	wiped out
characterization	diminished	pitfalls	safety net	

Unit 9 Grammar: Unreal Conditionals—Present, Past, and Mixed
• Past: If the system of microfinancing **had not been developed**, many people **would not have been able** to start up their businesses. • Present: Many women **would have** no means of escaping poverty if Grameen Bank **did not exist**. • Mixed: If Marie-Sainte **had not been** the recipient of microcredits, she **would probably still be** in poverty today.

Achievement Tests Audioscript

UNIT 1

1.1

Carlos Jimenez: This is Carlos Jimenez, your host on *The American Beat.* This afternoon I'm down in the subway to find out why people are driven to tune out from the world around them and tune in to their iPods®, cell phones, BlackBerry® devices, whatever the latest model is. These advances in information technology are overwhelming. No one really engages in face-to-face interaction; instead they're blogging, googling, IM-ing. It's as if people are always plugged into their own reality. So just what's going on in people's minds? Here's a young woman now, attached to a pair of headphones.

1.2

Carlos Jimenez: This is Carlos Jimenez, your host on *The American Beat.* This afternoon I'm down in the subway to find out why people are driven to tune out from the world around them and tune in to their iPods®, cell phones, BlackBerry® devices, whatever the latest model is. These advances in information technology are overwhelming. No one really engages in face-to-face interaction; instead they're blogging, googling, IM-ing. It's as if people are always plugged into their own reality. So just what's going on in people's minds? Here's a young woman now, attached to a pair of headphones.

Ah, excuse me, miss?

Young woman: Are you talking to me?

Carlos Jimenez: Yes, well I'm trying to. I'm doing a report on why people are always plugged in.

Young woman: You mean this iPod? I'm always listening to something.

Carlos Jimenez: Doesn't it interfere with your work?

Young woman: Are you kidding? I work much faster when I'm listening to music. I would be so bored if I had to just stare at my computer all day. Not only that, but I've heard that multitasking actually increases intelligence. How could that be a problem?

Carlos Jimenez: Well, how can I argue with that?

How about you, sir? I see you're one of the few people who aren't attached to a cell phone or BlackBerry or . . .

Male 1: If you ask me, the more of those gadgets people use, the stupider they get. I don't use them at all.

Carlos Jimenez: I know how you feel.

Excuse me. Ah, excuse me. Sir, uh, I'm interviewing people about what they're plugged into. And I have to admit, I've never seen earphones like that before.

Male 2: Oh these? These are ear plugs. Man, I just can't stand listening to everyone else's music and conversations invading my space. That's why I wear these.

1.2, Question 5

Young woman: I work much faster when I'm listening to music. I would be so bored if I had to just stare at my computer all day. Not only that, but I've heard that multitasking actually increases intelligence. How could that be a problem?

Carlos Jimenez: Well, how can I argue with that?

1.3

Warren Levinson: It's *Newsweek on Air.* I'm Warren Levinson of the Associated Press.

David Alpern: I'm David Alpern of *Newsweek.*

Warren Levinson: David Brooks, you argue that we already live in an over-communicated world that will only become more so in the next tech era. What exactly do you mean by that?

David Brooks: The problem is that we've developed technology that gets us so much information that we've got cell phones ringing every second, we've got computers and laptops, we've got personal organizers and it's just—we're just being bombarded with communication and every advance and technology seems to create more and more communications at us. I do believe at the end of the day it shapes our personality because we are sort of overwhelmed by the information flow.

David Alpern: Seriously though, just last week we reported on research suggesting that all the multitasking may actually make our brains work better and faster producing as it's been reported a world-wide increase in IQ up to 20 points and more in recent decades. Can you see any benefit in all these mental gymnastics we now have to go through?

David Brooks: Yeah I, I, I don't think we're becoming a race of global idiots. Uh, but I think certain skills are enhanced and certain are not. You know the ability to make fast decisions, to answer a dozen e-mails in five minutes, uh to fill out maybe big SAT-type tests. That's enhanced. But creativity is something that happens slowly. It happens when your brain is just noodling around, just playing. When it puts together ideas which you hadn't thought of or maybe you have time, say, to read a book. You are a businessperson but you have time to read a book about history or time to read a book about a philosopher and something that happened long ago or something or some idea somebody thought of long ago. Actually, you know, it occurs to you that you can think of your own business in that way, and so it's this mixture of unrelated ideas ah that feeds your productivity, feeds your creativity and if your mind is disciplined to answer every e-mail, then you don't have time for that playful noodling. You don't have time for those unexpected conjunctions so I think maybe we're getting smarter in some senses but I think it is a threat to our creativity and to our reflection.

David Alpern: So how wired or wireless are you tied into the new technology?

David Brooks: A total addict. When I'm out there with my kids playing in our little league or something like that, I've got my cell phone in my pocket. I'm always wondering, "Gee, did I get a voicemail"? uh and that's why I think I'm sort of driven to write about this because I do see the negative effects it's having on my own brain patterns.

David Alpern: Could be *Newsweek on Air* calling . . . David Brooks, thanks a lot.

David Brooks: Thank you.

UNIT 2

1.1

Dr. Smith: This is *Talk Therapy* with Dr. Smith. Call in today when we discuss lies: who tells them and why. You're on the air.

1.2

Dr. Smith: This is *Talk Therapy* with Dr. Smith. Call in today when we discuss lies: who tells them and why. You're on the air.

Caller 1: Hi. This is Arlette from Lawrence, Missouri. Last week my daughter, she's thirteen, told us she was going to her friend's house to study. An hour later we saw her at Starbucks with some kids from school. Then today I was looking in her drawers and I found a picture of her and a guy who must have been sixteen years old. We're wondering what else she might be concealing from us.

Dr. Smith: First, I have a question for you. Why were you looking in her drawers?

Caller 1: Well, she's at an age where kids need their parents' guidance, and I feel we have a right to know what they're doing.

Dr. Smith: True, but if she feels you are too intrusive, she might become more secretive. While the fact that she is lying is not trivial, try to see the reason for her behavior from her angle as well. Next we have a call from Los Angeles.

Caller 2: My problem is about a friend. See, a group of us who hang out together are all applying to college this year. Tim applied to all the Ivy League schools. So we're all talking about where we got accepted. Then Tim says he got into Harvard, but he had to turn them down because his parents said it's too far away. Yeah, right. Why would he try to put one over on us? He *couldn't have* thought we'd believe him.

Dr. Smith: It sounds like your friend must have some deep insecurities. He needs to feel that you admire him for getting into such a prestigious school. Someone his age who is trying to mislead people to boost his ego should probably seek help. Our next caller is from Baton Rouge, Louisiana.

Caller 3: Well, this guy in my math class has a crush on me. And, you know, I like him as a friend. But he got like the totally wrong idea. He asked me to go to the dance with him, so I told him I was going to New Orleans to visit my aunt. I feel bad that I wasn't up front with him.

Dr. Smith: We've all probably done something like that. The truth can be very painful in some situations, but be careful because one lie can lead to a slippery slope. Pretty soon you find yourself telling another fib to cover up the first one.

1.3

PART 3

Dr. Paul Ekman is professor of psychology at the University of California Medical School, San Francisco, and director of the Human Interaction Laboratory.

Welcome to *The Infinite Mind*, Dr. Ekman.

Dr. Ekman: Thank you.

Dr. Goodwin: Nice to have you. Now start out with basics. Why don't you tell our listeners how do you define a lie? What is a lie?

Dr. Ekman: Well, a lie is a very particular kind of deception that lies meet two criteria. First, it's a deliberate choice to mislead another person. That one's pretty obvious. But the second, a little less obvious, is that you don't give any notification of the fact that you're going to do that. And in many situations in life, we either notify someone, like a magician does. A magician lies to us, a magician fools us, but we're notified.

Dr. Goodwin: Is there more to the definition than that?

Dr. Ekman: That's all it requires. There are many different ways to tell a lie. You can conceal information. You can falsify information. You can even sometimes tell the truth in a mocking fashion. I call it telling the truth falsely.

PART 4

Dr. Goodwin: Have you cataloged sort of why people tell lies?

Dr. Ekman: Yes. And there are nine different reasons. The most common one for both children and adults is to avoid punishment for something that you've done. You know, you—you tell the traffic cop, "Gee, officer, I didn't think I was going over 55."

The second is to get a reward that you couldn't get otherwise or you couldn't get as easily, so you cheat on an exam 'cause you're more certain that you're going to get a high mark, or you don't want to put in all the time studying and preparing for it.

The third is to protect another person from being punished. That's an altruistic lie. And, in fact, we disapprove. If one—if a brother tells on a sister, we say that's tattling. We expect kids to protect each other.

A fourth is to protect yourself from the threat of physical harm.

Another is to win the admiration of others. You know, it's—it is the name droppers. The father who says, "Well, you know, the last time I saw George W., he said so-and-so and so-and-so." It's—it's—it's trying to get people to admire you.

A very common one is getting out of an awkward social situation, even a trivial one, like the telephone salesman.

Another is to avoid embarrassment. You see it particularly in kids who make mistakes. Kids who wet their pants will lie about it because they're so embarrassed.

Another is to maintain privacy. This particularly occurs in adolescents who have overly intrusive parents.

And the last is to get power over other people. It's—the greatest power and the most complete power in the world is to have somebody believe something that you've told them that you know is untrue. You've really got control over them. Most adolescents will do this once or twice or three times. They can now put it over the old man, or they can fool their mom now. But they won't continue to do it. But there are people who continue that as a lifelong pattern.

UNIT 3

1.1

Dr. Mendez: I'm Dr. Mendez, for those of you who don't know me already. You are here tonight because you suffer from various social problems, most of which are ultimately related to shyness. In this group setting you're among kindred souls. But rather than me lecturing, I want to start out with an exercise that you all know and probably fear: breaking the ice. We won't go any further than each of you introducing yourself to one other person and exchanging a few nonthreatening lines.

1.2

Dr. Mendez: I'm Dr. Mendez, for those of you who don't know me already. You are here tonight because you suffer from various social problems, most of which are ultimately related to shyness. In this group setting you're among kindred souls. But rather than me lecturing, I want to start out with an exercise that you all know and probably fear: breaking the ice. We won't go any further than each of you introducing yourself to one other person and exchanging a few nonthreatening lines.

So you survived, even though you may feel petrified when this happens at a party. For many of you, shyness is a handicap, but it doesn't have to be. How has it affected your lives? Gloria?

Gloria: Well, when I'm in a new situation, like a new job, I'm way too timid to talk to anyone. Sometimes a week can go by and I still won't have had the nerve to start a conversation. I know that everyone thinks I'm aloof or unfriendly.

Dr. Mendez: How about you, Hamid?

Hamid: That happens to me all the time. And because I'm not lively or laughing, people assume I'm unhappy.

Dr. Mendez: Unfortunately, people make these misattributions all the time. And these false assumptions can be pretty harsh. For example, in some studies people have said they think shy people are not interesting, they're dumb, they don't have many friends. All kinds of negative qualities. But let's think about the positive aspects of being shy.

Female speaker 2: Like what?

Dr. Mendez: Well, what are some of the qualities people look for in a good friend? In surveys a good percentage of people respond that having a friend who is a good listener is crucial. Another merit is that people who are reserved, sometimes even the wallflowers at a party, are exceptionally good observers of their surroundings. The extroverts, many of whom are absorbed in their own conversations, don't really have the vantage point of watching the world around them.

Female speaker 2: Yeah, that makes sense. I never thought about the advantages of being shy.

Dr. Mendez: It might be helpful for all of you to think of the positives rather than the negatives. That's your homework for next week. I'll see you all on Tuesday.

1.3

Alex Chadwick: Professor Zimbardo, when you say shy, when you say it's a problem, what kind of shyness do you mean? Many people feel some awkwardness in social situations, especially if they get attention from others, if they're the object of attention from others.

Philip Zimbardo: Virtually all the people that we have surveyed, certainly 75 percent of them, say shyness is undesirable, has adverse consequences. Shy people are less popular, they have fewer friends, they have lower self-esteem, they make less money, their life is more boring, they have less intimate . . . less intimacy, less sex, they have fewer leadership skills, less social support, they're more likely to be depressed and, as you get older, more likely to be lonely. That's a terrible syndrome of negative consequences.

Alex Chadwick: So this is not just a momentary shyness that . . . that . . . people feel; this is something that really marks their lives?

Philip Zimbardo: Yeah. The momentary shyness is something we call situational shyness. That is if . . . if you're on a blind date, if you're asked to perform in public, we are not really prepared. Or if your mother says, you know, "Play the piano for Aunt Tilly." Well, you have feelings of shyness, the . . . the arousal, the negative thoughts, the . . . the physical tension, but that is situational. So you say to yourself, "Well, that's not me; that's that external situation which I have to avoid." It's when it becomes chronic and dispositional. You begin to see shyness as Quasimodo's hump, the thing you carry around with you that's always there and even . . . even if . . . if people in the world don't notice it, you know it's there ready to emerge.

Alex Chadwick: When . . . when you're at a cocktail party, or just in conversation with someone anywhere and you recognize that they're shy, what do you do to draw them out or try to make them more comfortable?

Philip Zimbardo: Essentially what we say, for example, to shy people is, "If you begin with the knowledge that maybe half the people out there are also shy, then when you're in a situation, do your best to find those other people, those kindred souls." And a great way to break the ice is to talk about how uncomfortable these situations make you feel, and you presume the other. Admitting your shyness is really an important first step because if you don't, people make misattributions. That is, if you don't perform in a situation where people expect you to perform, to smile, to be outgoing, to start a conversation, people assume you're dumb, you're unmotivated, you're boring, or you're not interested in them. You're bored or boring, and those are terrible misattributions, especially if you're attractive as a man, or beautiful as a woman, and shy. Then it's a double handicap because people then assume you are aloof, you are condescending, you think you're too good for them.

UNIT 4

1.1

John Sorrel: I'm John Sorrel and tonight on *Talking Heads* we have three guests who have very different perspectives on crime in our city. First, Mr. Mitchell, could you explain to our listeners your theory about what triggers someone to commit a crime?

1.2

John Sorrel: I'm John Sorrel and tonight on *Talking Heads* we have three guests who have very different perspectives on crime in our city. First, Mr. Mitchell, could you explain to our listeners your theory about what triggers someone to commit a crime?

Mr. Mitchell: I must give credit to George Kelling for this theory. He believes that the environment plays a big role in criminal behavior, but not in the "nature vs. nurture" sense that we're accustomed to thinking. Certain environmental conditions attract crimes. If a place looks like no one cares about it, it can attract vandalism.

Ex-criminal: I've heard all about that and how it applies to the subways in New York. But I did time in the State Prison, and from a criminal's point of view, that theory just doesn't hold. Yeah, the subways were such a mess back in the '80s that robbing someone for a few bucks was like taking candy from a baby. Now the subways are supposedly crime free.

Mr. Mitchell: Yes and that's because we literally cleaned them up. We got rid of the graffiti, picked up the litter, and stopped people from jumping the turnstiles. We made the subways so clean that they no longer attracted criminals.

Ex-criminal: But how did you stop people from jumping the turnstiles? You put police all over, ready to catch anyone. But when there are police at every turnstile, what kind of idiot is going to pull a knife on someone?

John Sorrel: Ms. Sanchez, would you like to add something?

Ms. Sanchez: Mr. Mitchell, you don't win me over with that theory either. At the root of the problem is the criminal mind.

John Sorrel: I'm not sure I understand. How would you profile a person with a criminal mind?

Ms. Sanchez: It's a person with no moral conscience. Let's say someone wants to buy a car. Well, the normal person would work hard to get the money to buy it. But for the morally corrupt, they get a hold of an idea—the desire for a car—and they do whatever comes easy. If that means stealing the money, then that's what they'll do.

John Sorrel: What about a person's upbringing? Don't parents have any influence on a person's conscience?

Ms. Sanchez: Unfortunately, as much as they try, this kind of immorality comes from Mother Nature.

John Sorrel: Well I think we've all got food for thought now. We'll be here next week, same time, same channel.

1.3

Todd Mundt: Let's talk about a social condition that you wrote about then, there are a few that I want to touch on but the first one is the one I mentioned in the introduction, crime in New York City. Crime was a problem for a very long time in New York City and it was rising and rising and rising and then it started dropping and um, I suppose there could be a number of different reasons for it but I can't really find that anybody really knows exactly for sure what caused it.

Malcolm Gladwell: Crime is so—is such a fundamentally contagious thing that once we reached a kind of tipping point and once certain influential people in communities hard hit by crime stopped behaving in that way, it was contagious, and there was a kind of sea change that happens all at once.

Todd Mundt: Maybe we can go into those little triggers, because I find this really interesting because we're talking about such a big change that takes place uh, being triggered by very small things, uh, what do you think some of those were?

Malcolm: Well, I'm very impressed by this idea of "caught the broken windows theory" which is an idea George Kelling has put forth in New England. He's argued for some time that criminals and criminal behavior is acutely sensitive to environmental cues and he uses the example, the broken window—that if you—if there is a car sitting on the street with a broken window, it is an invitation to someone to vandalize the car. Why? Because a broken window on a car symbolizes the fact no one cares about the car. No one's in charge, no one's watching, no one's . . . and if you think about it, this is a fundamentally different idea about crime than the kind of ideas that we've been carrying for the past 25 years. We have been told by conservatives over and over again that crime is the result of moral failure, of something deep and intrinsic within the hearts and souls and brains of criminals, that a criminal is by definition in the sort of conservative topology, someone who is insensitive to their environment, right? They just go out and commit crimes because that's who they are, they're criminals. Well, Kelling came along and said well no, a criminal is like all of us, someone who is acutely sensitive to what's going on in the environment, and by making subtle changes in the environment, you can encourage and induce much more socially responsible behavior.

Well, in New York we had the perfect test case of that idea. It starts in the subway. You know, in the early '80s they decided to clean up the subway. Well, how did they do it? The subway was a complete mess, right? It was . . . crime rates were going through the roof. They bring in a man who is a big disciple of this idea, of "broken windows," and what does he do? Well, the first thing he does is he picks up all the litter. The second thing he does is he cleans up the graffiti, and the third thing he does is he says from now on, no one will ever jump a turnstile in a New York City subway station again. He puts cops by the turnstiles and if someone jumps, he arrests them. Everybody said he was crazy, but you've got a subway system where people are killing, and robbing, and assaulting and raping each other and what do you do? You go after the two kinds of criminality that, the only two kinds of criminality that in fact don't hurt anybody else, right? Turnstile jumping and graffiti, you know, littering and graffiti . . . but it turns out that those were tipping points. Once they put those three changes in place, the subway starts to come around really quite dramatically. It's because if you're on a subway that's clean and if you're walking into the subway and no one's allowed to jump the turnstile anymore, all of a sudden, everyone gets the message that someone's in charge, and somebody cares about this. It's not a space that permits this kind of criminal behavior.

UNIT 5

1.1

Therapist: I know the first session can be a little intimidating and I already see some skeptical looks. But every family goes through some rocky times and it's important to get help sooner rather than later. There's a quote from Margaret Meade, you know, the anthropologist. She said, "Nobody has ever before asked the nuclear family to live all by itself in a box the way we do." I think it's interesting that she uses the metaphor *box* for *house.* A box is usually shut tight. There's no air circulating through a box.

1.2

Therapist: I know the first session can be a little intimidating and I already see some skeptical looks. But every family goes through some rocky times and it's important to get help sooner rather than later. There's a quote from Margaret Meade, you know, the anthropologist. She said, "Nobody has ever before asked the nuclear family to live all by itself in a box the way we do." I think it's interesting that she uses the metaphor *box* for *house.* A box is usually shut tight. There's no air circulating through a box. Ms. Dubois, I see you're nodding your head.

Kimberly: Please call me Kimberly. Well, sometimes I get home from work and I can just sense the tension in the air. It's almost suffocating. We haven't really felt like a family in a long time. Everyone's off in their own corner of the house. Matthew is . . .

Matthew: But, Mom, you know I have to study for the entrance exams. I can't concentrate anywhere else. Nicole is always on the phone and . . .

Nicole: Don't worry. As soon as I can afford it, I'll be out of here. I just have to get enough money for my own apartment.

Kimberly: I think half the problem is our house. I wouldn't say we don't have family issues, but this house just makes them worse. No one feels comfortable here. And Matthew, you've seemed depressed lately.

Matthew: Yeah, I guess I have been, a little. I didn't think you noticed, Mom.

Therapist: Well, it's clear that you're having communication problems, but on top of that I think the house is working against you. Have you ever heard of feng shui?

Matthew: Yeah, we read about it last semester. It's something about the energy in a place—how things are aligned to keep harmony.

Therapist: That's right. Well, it's frowned upon in my profession to believe that basic human problems have a transcendent explanation. On the contrary, psychologists look for logical answers to our behavior. But I think we should look beyond the logical answers to your family's problems. We'll start by examining the energy in your house. Let's talk about this next session.

1.3

Steve Scher: Kirsten Lagatree is our guest. Her book is *Feng Shui: Arranging Your Home to Change Your Life—A Room by Room Guide to the Ancient Chinese Art of Placement.* OK, so, I would like to walk into our newsroom, if we can, and have you just quickly look at it and figure out what we can do for some of the people here who need a little help in their careers or their happiness. Any initial thoughts you have looking at this room?

Kirsten Lagatree: Umm . . . There are some very good things about this newsroom. For one thing, some of the writers are facing northeast. Northeast is the direction that governs mental ability, acuteness of thinking, scholarly success. So, those people in this newsroom, who are facing this, they not only get an extraordinarily peaceful and beautiful view out the window, they are facing in the direction that's going to make them sharp, and make their writing better.

Steve Scher: OK, so this is my desk, over here, scattered with a barrel of monkeys, and they're red, so that's good . . . I'm facing east here, right? I'm facing east, almost to the southeast. Am I blocked up a little bit?

Kirsten Lagatree: Yeah, well, facing east, actually . . . when you face east you are facing the direction of growth, vitality, the color green. Health, vitality, youth: Those are the things that come with the direction. So maybe that's what makes you so peppy, Steve, and so young at heart. I'd like to say something about the southeast wall right here. That is your money corner. Southeast is the direction that governs money. You haven't done anything with this direction. You've got lots of equipment there . . . what you should have is the color purple, the number 4.

Steve Scher: And a fish tank.

Kirsten Lagatree: Well, one thing at a time. The color purple and the number 4 go with that one direction, with the southeast. I'm glad you mentioned a fish tank . . . water flow symbolizes cash flow. There's a lot in feng shui that does word play, both in the Chinese language and in the English language, so, water flow equals cash flow. You walk in to some major corporate buildings nowadays, in New York or Los Angeles or Hong Kong, you are going to see fountains in the lobby. A lot of that. The fish that are in the tank . . . they symbolize abundance, as in "there are always more fish in the sea." What's your goal? You know . . . if your goal is to be a better writer, talk somebody into changing places with you here so that you can face northeast. If your goal is to become wealthy, do some enhancement there on your southeast wall, or do it at home. Say you want to get in a relationship in your life . . . at home, enhance a southwest wall with the color yellow and the number 2. The southwest corner governs marriage, partnerships, motherhood. You pay attention to what, umm you know what, you can do to make something happen, and then you work with these outward symbols.

UNIT 6

1.1

Host: If you're just joining us, I'm talking to John Everly, who has just returned from a four-week journey through the Himalayas. You mentioned before the break that you came home with a feeling of well-being. Tell me more about this.

John: Well, just getting away from the hectic pace of the city had the effect of replenishing my energy, and I think it had something to do with visiting the monasteries. It's amazing to see the ascetic life the monks lead. They have such little reliance on material things.

1.2

Host: If you're just joining us, I'm talking to John Everly, who has just returned from a four-week journey through the Himalayas. You mentioned before the break that you came home with a feeling of well-being. Tell me more about this.

John: Well, just getting away from the hectic pace of the city had the effect of replenishing my energy, and I think it had something to do with visiting the monasteries. It's amazing to see the ascetic life the monks lead. They have such little reliance on material things.

Host: How do they do it? What compensates for the hundreds of things we have that fill up our lives?

John: Definitely fasting plays a major role in their lives. To possess the will to refrain from eating or drinking anything for up to three days—this gives them both strength and serenity.

Host: How many monasteries did you visit?

John: Three.

Host: Well, we don't have much time left. Why don't you talk briefly about one of the monasteries you visited?

John: Definitely the best experience I had was in a small monastery in the Ladakh region. I just happened to arrive on the day of a full moon, which is when these monks begin to fast. So I actually fasted along with them.

Host: Fascinating. Can you tell us more about this experience?

John: Well, the first thing that hit me was how incredibly out of touch I had been with myself, both physically and spiritually.

Host: Do you think you experienced the same feelings a Buddhist monk does after a three-day fast?

John: I don't think it's really possible for someone from our lifestyle to reach the same level they do. They use the fast as a means of purification. And this allows the mind to be totally free. I think most of us have so much inner turmoil it would take years to free our minds to this point. Doing yoga in my regular life would probably help calm some of that turmoil.

Host: I'd love to have you back on the show to share more of your experiences.

John: Well, there's a lot left to talk about.

1.3

Duncan Moon: Fasting is an ancient tradition. The three Abrahamic religions, Judaism, Christianity, and Islam, all trace it back to the prophets of the Old Testament. For example, many people believe the prophet Mohammed's first fast was probably Yom Kippur. Many Eastern religions trace their roots of fasting to ancient yogic and ascetic traditions. But while there are differences in approach and style, those who fast are most often hoping to increase spirituality and come closer to the divine. Dr. Diana Eck, professor of comparative religion at Harvard Divinity School, says fasting accomplishes this in part by breaking an attachment to material things.

Dr. Diana Eck: And of course the most repetitive attachment to earthly things is that that we enact every day by our desire for food. So there is a way in which breaking that, even in a symbolic way, speaks against the consumption, the materialism that is so pervasive in our world.

Duncan Moon: Professor Barbara Patterson of Emory University is an Episcopal priest. She says fasting is similar to the discipline displayed by an athlete in a gym, although in the case of fasting, it's a spiritual gym.

Professor Barbara Patterson: There is a celebration itself in establishing a discipline for oneself and actually working, making decisions, forming the will, if you would say, intention to be able to move through a time where there's a certain amount of stress that's not undoing but that gives you a sense of your capacities. It's very much a way of sharpening the heart's capacities.

Duncan Moon: The Church of Jesus Christ of Latter Day Saints, the Mormons, fast the first Sunday of every month. They skip two meals and take the money they would have spent on those meals and give it to the poor. Mormon Bart Marcoy says fasting helps to foster humility and gratitude, allowing him to put aside his human competitiveness. In Islam during the holy month of Ramadan, Muslims fast from sunrise to sunset, refraining from food, water, smoking, and sex. Dr. Ahbar Ahmed, a professor of Islamic studies at American University, says in this time of rapid change and fear, fasting is vital to spiritual well-being.

Dr. Ahbar Ahmed: Because if you do not withdraw during the day, then the replenishment of the soul is not being affected, and when that does not happen, then over time the individual begins to become exhausted, spiritually exhausted.

Duncan Moon: Dr. Ahmed says the rhythm of life has become so hectic, so fast moving, that finding time to pull back from our daily lives, even temporarily, has become more difficult than ever. But he says that only means the need for it has never been greater, and that the ancient tradition of fasting is still necessary, even in the 21st century. Duncan Moon, NPR News, Washington.

UNIT 7

1.1

Host: At issue here is "privacy in the workplace." New technologies have drastically changed the way we conduct business. Many of us use computers, e-mail, and voicemail routinely at work. They certainly make our jobs easier; however, they also make it easier for employers to monitor how we use them. Is it legitimate for employers to use these technologies as surveillance systems in the work place? Let's hear your views on this issue. Hello?

1.2

Host: At issue here is "privacy in the workplace." New technologies have drastically changed the way we conduct business. Many of us use computers, e-mail, and voicemail routinely at work. They certainly make our jobs easier; however, they also make it easier for employers to monitor how we use them. Is it legitimate for employers to use these technologies as surveillance systems in the work place? Let's hear your views on this issue. Hello?

Jim Tate: Hi, this Jim Tate. I'm calling from Dayton, Ohio.

Host: Hi Jim. First, are you calling as an employer or employee?

Jim Tate: I'm calling to explain how Big Brother nearly cost me my job.

Host: Well, I guess we know which side you're taking.

Jim Tate: In my case, the company kept an eye on its employees by maintaining a log of our phone usage. This was all done electronically of course, so no one was actually eavesdropping on our conversations. There was just a record of the amount of time spent on the phone and the destination of each call. Obviously, this was meant to deter people from making non-work related calls on the company's dime. It just so happens that four calls to Ankara in one month were made on my phone. Well, our company doesn't have any clients in Turkey, so this was highly suspicious. And the burden was on me to explain these four calls. In the end, I could show that two of the calls were made on days when I was traveling. The company never did find out who made those calls, but the point I want to make is that it's easy for a case of mistaken identity to occur when the evidence is a record of phone calls or e-mails or computer use.

Host: Yes, well let's take the next call.

Anne Winslow: Hi, my name is Anne Winslow and I supervise 20 employees in the legal department of a large business. I don't like the idea of Big Brother watching over my employees and keeping track of everything they do. Well, one day a woman in the department came into my office extremely upset. She said she had been receiving e-mails that contained one racial slur after another. She tried to ignore them at first, but after a while she felt so demeaned that she had to take several days off work. I immediately contacted technical support and within hours they had located the source of the e-mails. So, I think you'd have to agree that while Big Brother can be sinister, he can benefit both employers and employees as well.

1.3

Speaker 1: I own a small data-processing company in which I employ about eight to ten workers. The point I want to make has to do with trust. Listen, I know it's possible to force people to be 100 percent efficient. But when you do that you lose morale, confidence, trust. I let my employees use our equipment, computers, make personal phone calls, whatever. They are more than welcome to decide what is right and wrong. You can't run a company by just issuing orders to robots and watching them like Big Brother. You have to trust people, respect them, and give them a little freedom. Also, as far as phone calls and all that go, I want my people to call home and check on their children, and know their children are OK, because then they can refocus on the job . . . and their work is better. As a result, I have dedicated employees who are willing to go that extra mile . . . to show up at work smiling. I get more satisfaction and rewards by trusting my employees than by suspecting them of doing something wrong.

Speaker 2: I'm an attorney in a large law firm in Seattle. In my firm, there's a capability, sure, of monitoring my performance. I input a lot of my work into computer systems with limited security. And you know what? I'm not bothered in the least. The real question is, if we're not doing anything wrong, what do we have to worry about? I think employers have the right to keep an eye on what goes on in their businesses, just like home owners have the right to use video and audio surveillance to protect their own homes. I mean, you would have to agree that when you're in the office, you're at work, you're not conducting your private life. You're conducting business. In some cases, such as lounge areas at work, there's a fine line; but mostly I believe it's OK for, you know, an employer to actually listen and watch while you're working. They're just looking out for their own investment. They're safeguarding their businesses.

UNIT 8

1.1

Professor: OK, so last class we looked at the evolution of war. Today we'll take up the issue of the legitimacy of war.

Student: How can people think there's any *good* reason for war?

Professor: Well . . . , that's a complicated question, and there's a lot of disagreement about it. In fact, this topic can be quite volatile.

1.2

Professor: OK, so last class we looked at the evolution of war. Today we'll take up the issue of the legitimacy of war.

Student: How can people think there's any *good* reason for war?

Professor: Well . . . , that's a complicated question, and there's a lot of disagreement about it. In fact, this topic can be quite volatile. Pacifists like me believe that the barbarism and savagery of war are cause enough to condemn it for *any* reason. But believe it or not, pacifists are a very minor part of the population. Another view is that war unleashes such extreme violence that it is a form of institutionalized mass murder. And then there are people who see that war has existed throughout history and believe that it is inevitable. They subscribe to the notion that war is a human universal.

Now, there's also a branch of philosophers and political scientists who specialize in the ethics of war. The theory that examines this is Just War Theory, and today the most eminent authority on it is a political philosopher named Michael Welzer. Just War Theory looks at the codes of war and asks three questions: 1) when is it justified to start a war, 2) what is justifiable conduct during war, and 3) what needs to happen after a war for a just transition from war to a stable peaceful state.

So what *is* a legitimate reason to start a war? Probably the prevailing view is given by Welzer. He believes that there is only one just reason for turning to war, and that is to resist aggression. Basically what aggression means is that one group uses armed force against another group, which violates that group's basic rights. I've just given you a very simplified explanation of a very complex concept, but come and see me after class if you're interested in learning more.

The second question concerns the conduct of people directly involved in a war. One issue deals with weapons—what can and cannot be used. Another very important issue is the conduct of the soldiers during war. For example, soldiers must be restrained from using their weapons against civilians. They must also follow the Geneva Conventions in the treatment of Prisoners of War.

Well it looks like we've run out of time, so tomorrow we'll look at the third question—how to make the transition from war to peace.

1.2, Question 6

Just War Theory looks at the codes of war and asks three questions: 1) when is it justified to start a war, 2) what is justifiable conduct during war, and 3) what needs to happen after a war for a just transition from war to a stable peaceful state.

So what *is* a legitimate reason to start a war? Probably the prevailing view is given by Welzer.

1.3

PART 2

Michael Ignatieff: And war in fact is a natural, necessary, and sometimes, dare I say it, even desirable way to solve certain social conflicts between ethnic groups. Oppressed groups sometimes can only use war to free themselves. Well, if that's the case, if we can't abolish war from human culture, then we'd better find some way to tame it.

PART 3

Michael Ignatieff: And that's the ethic that the Red Cross lives by, and I think the simple rules that the Red Cross tries to enforce, which is: You don't shoot prisoners, you don't make war on noncombatants, you try and stay away from civilian targets, you kill people, you don't torture or degrade their bodies.

PART 4

Michael Ignatieff: You know, just very, very simple rules of humanity are an important addition to civilization. And there is no necessary reason . . . I suppose that this is what I've learned . . . to equate war with barbarism. There's a distinction between war and barbarism. And we should keep to that distinction and struggle to ensure it, and that's what the Red Cross tries to do. And . . . I don't want to sound like a recruiting sergeant from the Red Cross; I'm critical of some of the things they do . . . but I did learn that from them. And I respect this morality.

UNIT 9

1.1

Interviewer: Dr. Kelly, you're a colleague of Dr. Rauscher's, aren't you?

Dr. Kelly: Yes, we both study the neurological basis of abstract reasoning. Dr. Rauscher's original studies were the building blocks for future work on learning and neural activity. Currently I'm doing a comparison of her results to those of similar studies.

Interviewer: Interesting. And what have you found?

1.2

Interviewer: Dr. Kelly, you're a colleague of Dr. Rauscher's, aren't you?

Dr. Kelly: Yes, we both study the neurological basis of abstract reasoning. Dr. Rauscher's original studies were the building blocks for future work on learning and neural activity. Currently I'm doing a comparison of her results to those of similar studies.

Interviewer: Interesting. And what have you found?

Dr. Kelly: Well, first let me say that Rauscher's study in 1993 initially examined neural responses to music. The results showed specifically that there is a pattern of neurons firing in a sequential order when a person listens to music, and these results underscored the fact that neurons may show this response to both abstract reasoning and musical processing. Her colleague, Dr. Shaw, influenced parents and teachers by applying the results more generally to learning. They were excited when Dr. Shaw said, "We have this common internal neural language that we're born with and so if you can exploit that with the right stimuli then you're going to help the brain develop to do the things like reason." Anyway, Dr. Shaw's interpretation became the hallmark of their work.

Interviewer: So did further experiments come out with similar results?

Dr. Kelly: There were a number of experiments in 1995 and later that looked at the effect of Mozart on mathematical performance. And I'm afraid that many of those experiments did not show that music primed the brain for math or other spatial reasoning tests. Let me tell you about one experiment conducted by Dr. Cuevas in 2000. The purpose of this experiment was to see the effect of listening to Mozart or Bach on the ability to take a 10-minute math test. The subjects were randomly chosen from a population of university students. They were divided into three groups: a control group, a Bach group, and a Mozart group. The experiment was similar to Rauscher's in that one group listened to ten minutes of a Mozart Sonata. The other experimental group listened to Bach, and the control group didn't listen to anything. The findings showed no significant difference among the performances of the three groups. But regardless of the results, I have to say that Rauscher's study has done more for our field than any experiment could by teaching the average guy a little bit about neurons and the brain.

Interviewer: It's certainly given me a lot to think about.

Dr. Kelly: And even better, it's gotten the government to put music and art back into the curriculum.

1.3

Michelle Trudeau: A class of six-year-olds getting a special music lesson, part of a special arts program that researcher Martin Gardiner and his colleagues at the music school in Rhode Island designed for several elementary schools in the state.

Martin Gardiner: We started out wanting to see the impact of arts training in some first- and second-grade kids.

Michelle Trudeau: So, some classrooms had an extra hour of this special arts curriculum incorporated into their normal school week.

Martin Gardiner: And other classrooms getting the standard curriculum in the arts, which was pretty standard for Rhode Island and rather representative of the country as whole.

Michelle Trudeau: The standard curriculum, say the researchers, gave students music lessons twice a month and art lessons twice a month. The typical music lesson tended to be somewhat passive, says Gardiner. Students listened to tapes and concerts and talked about music in class. In contrast, the special arts classes met twice weekly and got students actively involved as a way to teach them the basic building blocks.

Martin Gardiner: The kinds of skills that they are learning in these grades are . . . in music, they're learning to sing together properly, sing together on pitch, sing together in rhythm, sing together songs; and, in the visual arts, they're learning to draw shapes and deal with colors and forms, and so forth.

Michelle Trudeau: A very interactive, experiential approach that took advantage of children's natural inclination to master enjoyable tasks and build upon sequential skills.

Martin Gardiner: And at the end of seven months, all the kids in the school took standardized tests, and we looked not only at how these teachers rated the kids on attitude and so forth, but also how the kids scored on their tests.

Michelle Trudeau: And here's what the researchers found. First of all, those kids who'd entered the first grade toward the bottom of the class in reading and then received the special arts program for the year had now caught up to the average in reading.

Martin Gardiner: And that in itself is wonderful. But, in addition, they were now statistically ahead in learning math.

Michelle Trudeau: Dramatically ahead in math, compared to the kids who had not received the special arts classes throughout the year. The researchers found also that the kids who continued their special arts classes for a second year continued to improve in math.

UNIT 10

1.1

Host: Yesterday we talked about how the impact of microfinancing has helped some of the more than one billion people in poverty-stricken parts of the world. Dr. Lim, I'm curious, are there any pitfalls to microfinancing?

1.2

Host: Yesterday we talked about how the impact of microfinancing has helped some of the more than one billion people in poverty-stricken parts of the world. Dr. Lim, I'm curious, are there any pitfalls to microfinancing?

Dr. Lim: Well, there are people who find faults with it in principle and there are others, like me, who believe in it, but recognize that microfinancing is not a one-size-fits-all solution.

Host: Interesting, could you elaborate on that?

Dr. Lim: Some say it's just a Band-Aid solution. It may have a small effect on one family, but that's where it hits the ceiling. It does nothing to bring an entire village out of poverty. Another problem is that it helps only families that already have resources to draw on. The poorest people can't get microcredit because they have no means of paying it back.

Host: Those are some pretty convincing arguments.

Dr. Lim: Well there is no panacea, but what we've seen time and time again is women whose lives have changed when they've gotten loans through microfinancing. For example, there's Maria, from a small village in Brazil. She's a talented weaver. If she hadn't gotten her loan, she wouldn't have been able to set up a stall in the market and sell coats. She now has a sustainable income and a safety net to fall back on.

Host: So that's a case where microfinancing has helped diminish poverty. Are there cases where it doesn't apply?

Dr. Lim: Unfortunately, yes. There are places where people are nomadic—this population doesn't stay in one area long enough to benefit from small loans. And though some of the most compelling cases are in countries with a high rate of disease or poor nutrition, microfinancing is not going to be the ideal economic solution for these people either.

Host: So, do we just give up in those cases?

Dr. Lim: Thankfully, systems that were in place before microfinancing are still viable. Grants are necessary to help a country develop an infrastructure so systems of transportation, communication, and healthcare can be built.

Another thing to keep in mind is without a literate population, an economic system cannot be developed. Literacy and employment programs must come before microfinancing.

Host: This is fascinating. But I'm afraid we'll have to end here. Thank you so much for being with us, Dr. Lim.

1.3

Ross Reynolds: There are obvious benefits to credit, but there are also pitfalls. You can get overextended, you don't own anything, the bank ends up owning it. It some ways, paying as you go might be a better idea. Is credit always a good thing, particularly for poor people?

Alex Counts: Well, see for poor people who don't have access to jobs and don't have a safety net, the only alternatives are to starve or to work for yourself. For most of the poor, they have so little money that their businesses are highly undercapitalized. So the option of doing the same things they're doing but having them at a more reasonable capital level, that's an option that people should have. They shouldn't, obviously, be forced to take it, but many of them are extremely happy to be able to take $60 or $70 which triples the capital of their simple, rural business doing trading or a cottage industry of some kind, and that becomes then a pathway to break the poverty cycle.

Ross Reynolds: Tell us how $60 or $70 can make a big difference.

Alex Counts: Well, again, just to take a very simple example that I saw many times when I was living in Bangladesh was a woman who knew how to raise chickens and she would sell the eggs and that was how she would meet her daily needs. But she never had enough capital to have more than 3 chickens at any given time and every so often they would be wiped out by disease. By taking $60 she would be able to have 12 or 13 chickens and do it on a larger scale and generate enough income to send her child to school, to treat illness with modern medicine. And, again, this is a very small amount. Some of the women who do that ultimately end up four years later having a poultry farm of 500 chickens.

Achievement Tests Answer Key

UNIT 1

1.1
B

1.2
1. D   2. A   3. C   4. D   5. C   6. B

1.3
1. David Brooks
2. Young woman
3. David Brooks

2.1
1. what's going on
2. engaged in
3. blog
4. IM-ing
5. compulsiveness
6. addict
7. driven to
8. overwhelming
9. google
10. multitasking

3.1
1. A   2. G   3. D   4. B

3.2
1. calling   2. still   3. home

3.3
1. Another thing I'd like to add
2. Not only that,
3. And to add to Dr. Green's point,

4.1
Answers will vary. Suggested answer:
Carlos Jimenez found out that the woman works faster when listening to music.

4.2
Answers will vary. Suggested answer:
Not only that, but I would also say that listening to music while working makes people focus better.

4.3
Answers will vary. See the scoring rubric on page T-77.

UNIT 2

1.1
A

1.2
1. A   2. A   3. C   4. B   5. C   6. D

1.3
1. C   2. B   3. A

2.1
1. up front
2. tattle
3. trivial
4. slippery slope
5. intrusive
6. pull the wool over his eyes
7. concealing
8. mislead
9. put one over on
10. inflated

3.1
1. B   2. C   3. C   4. A

3.2
1. A   2. A   3. B

3.3
1. it depends on
2. if you look at it from the angle of
3. And another point might be

4.1
Answers will vary. Suggested answer:
Dr. Smith told one listener that lying can lead to a slippery slope.

4.2
Answers will vary. Suggested answer:
On the other hand, the truth can be very painful in some situations.

4.3
Answers will vary. See the scoring rubric on page T-77.

UNIT 3

1.1
C

1.2
1. B   2. B   3. D   4. A   5. A   6. C

1.3
1. Both
2. Dr. Mendez
3. Both

2.1
1. handicap
2. standoffish
3. misattributions
4. merits
5. petrified

2.2

1. E   2. F   3. A   4. B   5. D

3.1

1. N   2. I   3. l   4. Q

3.2

1. A   2. B   3. A

3.3

1. D   2. E   3. A

4.1

Answers will vary. Suggested answer:
Gloria said that when she is too shy to start a conversation at work, people think she is aloof or unfriendly.

4.2

Answers will vary. Suggested answer:
What kind of work do you do?

4.3

Answers will vary. See the scoring rubric on page T-77.

UNIT 4

1.1

C

1.2

1. A   2. B   3. B   4. D   5. B   6. B

1.3

1. B   2. F   3. A

2.1

1. epidemic
2. word of mouth
3. hold
4. tide turned
5. get a hold of
6. root
7. profiled
8. vandalism
9. mess
10. generate

3.1

1. so quickly that
2. such a powerful speaker that
3. so clever that
4. so much vandalism that

3.2

1. ca   2. po   3. lar

3.3

1. infected
2. epidemic
3. turn the tide

4.1

Answers will vary. Suggested answer:
Mr. Mitchell said that dirty places attract crimes.

4.2

Answers will vary.

4.3

Answers will vary. See the scoring rubric on page T-77.

UNIT 5

1.1

A

1.2

1. A   2. A   3. C   4. C   5. B   6. A

1.3

1. Southwest   2. Southeast   3. Northeast

2.1

1. aligned
2. quote
3. circulating
4. skeptical
5. hard-bitten
6. transcendent
7. frowned upon
8. sense
9. caught off guard
10. anecdotes

3.1

1. on top of that
2. However
3. Plus
4. so

3.2

1. no comma
2. no comma
3. Anyway, I think you should take my advice.

3.3

1. D   2. B   3. C

4.1

Answers will vary. Suggested answer:
A feng shui master might tell Nicole to put a purple painting or a fish tank in the southeast corner of her bedroom.

4.2

Answers will vary. Suggested answer:
Boy, was that feng shui master right! I'd have to say that I started to make more money soon after I decorated the southeast corner of my office!

4.3

Answers will vary. See the scoring rubric on page T-77.

UNIT 6

1.1

C

1.2

1. A   2. D   3. B   4. D   5. A   6. B

1.3

1. F   2. E   3. B

2.1

1. fasting
2. refrain from
3. replenish
4. hectic
5. out of touch
6. well-being

2.2

1. E   2. F   3. D   4. B

3.1

1. B   2. B   3. A   4. B

3.2

1. B   2. A   3. C

3.3

1. C   2. B   3. D

4.1

The best part of John's trip was his time in a small monastery in the Ladakh region.

4.2

Answers will vary. Suggested answer:
Why don't you talk briefly about this experience?

4.3

Answers will vary. See the scoring rubric on page T-77.

UNIT 7

1.1

A

1.2

1. D   2. B   3. C   4. B   5. C   6. D

1.3

1. C   2. B   3. E

2.1

1. deter
2. employers
3. Big Brother
4. keeping an eye on
5. surveillance
6. eavesdrop
7. a log
8. demeaning
9. safeguarding
10. legitimate

3.1.

1. getting
2. turning in
3. to take
4. accepting

3.2

1. A   2. A   3. D

3.3

1. C   2. C   3. A

4.1

Answers will vary. Suggested answer:
Tracking e-mails can benefit an employees who is receiving inappropriate e-mails by identifying the person sending the e-mails.

4.2

Answers will vary. Suggested answer:
The point I want to make is that if employees are doing their jobs, they have nothing to worry about.

4.3

Answers will vary. See the scoring rubric on page T-77.

UNIT 8

1.1

C

1.2

1. A   2. B   3. A   4. C   5. D   6. B

1.3

1. D   2. C   3. E

2.1

1. subscribe
2. legitimate
3. barbarism and savagery
4. codes
5. restrained

2.2

1. G   2. D   3. F   4. E   5. A

3.1

1. A   2. B   3. A

3.2

1. A   2. C   3. B

3.3

1. B   2. A   3. C

4.1

Answers will vary. Suggested answer:
What is justifiable conduct during war?

4.2

Answers will vary. Suggested answer:
Well, that's a complicated issue. One issue deals with weapons—what can and cannot be used.

4.3

Answers will vary. See the scoring rubric on page T-77.

UNIT 9

1.1

A

1.2

1. C   2. A   3. D   4. D   5. A   6. B

1.3

1. D   2. B   3. E

2.1

1. abstract reasoning   4. hallmark
2. neurological   5. do more for
3. prime   6. curriculum

2.2

1. A   2. C   3. D   4. A

3.1

1. have been applied   3. been proven
2. is commonly believed   4. is still being conducted

3.2

1. C   2. I   3. A

3.3

1. similarly
2. in contrast
3. is similar to

4.1

One experimental group listened to Bach and the other experimental group listened to Mozart. The control group didn't listen to anything.

4.2

Answers will vary. Suggested answer:
Dr. Cuevas' experimental group did not perform differently from the control group. However, Dr. Gardiner's experimental group improved in math.

4.3

Answers will vary. See the scoring rubric on page T-77.

UNIT 10

1.1

A

1.2

1. C   2. A   3. A   4. C   5. B   6. C

1.3

1. Neither
2. "Microfinance"
3. Interview

2.1

1. panacea   4. pitfalls
2. compelling   5. overnight
3. safety net

2.2

1. E   2. D   3. B   4. G   5. A

3.1

1. were   3. had not gotten
2. had not developed   4. could increase

3.2

1. A   2. B   3. A

3.3

1. What we've witnessed time and time again is
2. One figure that supports this is
3. Another thing to keep in mind is

4.1

Answers will vary. Suggested answer:
Microfinancing helps only families that already have resources to draw on.

4.2

Answers will vary. Suggested answer:
To illustrate this point, the poorest people can't get microcredit because they have no means of paying it back.

4.3

Answers will vary. See the scoring rubric on page T-77.

NorthStar 5 Achievement Test Scoring Rubric: Speaking

Score	Description
4	A response at this level demonstrates exceptionally clear and automatic speech, with no awkward pauses and hesitations, and pronunciation is such that the listener has no difficulty with the message; a response at this level is also marked by: • accurate information with very relevant and logical connections to listening • consistent use of complex grammatical features (relative clauses, infinitives, and compound sentences), and discourse features (transitions and connectors) • use of variety of vocabulary words relevant to unit • few noticeable mistakes with grammar and vocabulary use
3	A response at this level demonstrates clear and automatic speech, with no awkward pauses and hesitations, and pronunciation is such that the listener has no difficulty with the message; a response at this level is also marked by: • accurate information with logical connections to listening • consistent use of complex grammatical features such as relative clauses, infinitives, and compound sentences • use of variety of vocabulary words related to unit • minor mistakes with grammar and vocabulary use
2	A response at this level demonstrates generally clear and automatic speech, with one or two short pauses and hesitations, and typically correct pronunciation of words; a response at this level is also marked by: • mostly accurate information with logical connections to listening • consistent use of complex grammatical features such as relative clauses, adverb phrases, and longer formulaic expressions • use of multiple vocabulary words from and related to unit • mostly accurate grammar and vocabulary use
1	A response at this level demonstrates somewhat clear and automatic speech, with some short pauses and hesitations, and generally correct pronunciation of words; a response at this level is also marked by: • generally accurate information with somewhat logical connection to listening • consistent use of grammatical features such as prepositional phrases, modals, simple verb tenses, and direct objects • use of some vocabulary words from unit • generally accurate grammar and vocabulary use
0	A response at this level attempts to address the prompt in English and has multiple long pauses, very slow speech, and limited correct pronunciation of words; a response at this level is also marked by: • general information that needs to be more accurate and more connected to listening • use of few basic formulaic expressions • reliance on one or two vocabulary words from prompt; language often recycled • frequent errors in grammar and vocabulary use A response at this level could also include no attempt to respond.

Notes

Notes

CD Tracking Guide
Achievement Tests